Judith Butler. Courtesy of Judith Butler

BUTLER MATTERS

For our students

Butler Matters
Judith Butler's Impact on Feminist and Queer Studies

Edited by

MARGARET SÖNSER BREEN
University of Connecticut, USA

WARREN J. BLUMENFELD
Iowa State University, USA

ASHGATE

Published by
Ashgate Publishing Limited
Gower House
Croft Road
Aldershot
Hampshire GU11 3HR
England

Ashgate Publishing Company
Suite 420
101 Cherry Street
Burlington, VT 05401-4405
USA

Ashgate website: http://www.ashgate.com

British Library Cataloguing in Publication Data
Butler matters : Judith Butler's impact on feminist and
    queer studies
    1. Butler, Judith P. 2. Feminist theory 3. Sex role
    I. Breen, Margaret Sönser II. Blumenfeld, Warren J.
    305.4'2

Library of Congress Cataloging-in-Publication Data
Breen, Margaret Sönser.
    Butler matters : Judith Butler's impact on feminist and queer studies / Margaret
Sönser Breen, Warren J. Blumenfeld.
        p. cm.
    Includes index.
    ISBN 0-7546-3885-5 (alk. paper)
    1. Butler, Judith. 2. Feminist theory. 3. Sex role. 4. Gender identity. 5.
Language and sex. I. Blumenfeld, Warren J., 1947– II. Title.

HQ1190.B75 2004
305.42'01—dc22
                                                                2004003235
Reprinted 2005

ISBN 0 7546 3885 5

Printed and bound in Great Britain by MPG Books Ltd, Bodmin, Cornwall

Contents

List of Figures   *vii*
List of Contributors   *viii*
Foreword   *xi*
Acknowledgements   *xii*

PART I: INTRODUCTION

1   Introduction to the Collection
    Margaret Sönser Breen   3

2   'There is a Person Here': An Interview with Judith Butler
    Compiled by Warren J. Blumenfeld and Margaret Sönser Breen,
    with Susanne Baer, Robert Alan Brookey, Lynda Hall, Vicki Kirby,
    Robert Shail, and Natalie Wilson   9

3   Becoming Butlerian: On the Discursive Limits (and Potentials) of
    Gender Trouble
    Frederick S. Roden   27

PART II: LANGUAGE, MELANCHOLIA, AND SUBJECTIVITY

4   When All That is Solid Melts into Language
    Vicki Kirby   41

5   Judith Butler and the Images of Theory
    Mena Mitrano   57

6   The Plague of the Subject: Subjects, Politics, and the Power of Psychic
    Life
    Kirsten Campbell   81

7   Excitable Speech: Judith Butler, Mae West, and Sexual Innuendo
    Angela Failler   95

PART III: BODY MATTERS: ARCHAEOLOGY, LITERATURE, AND PEDAGOGY

8 Past Performance: The Archaeology of Gender as Influenced by
   the Work of Judith Butler
   Elizabeth M. Perry and Rosemary A. Joyce   113

9 Renaissance Body Matters: Judith Butler and the Sex That is One
   Belinda Johnston   127

10 *Gender Trouble* in the Literature Classroom: Unintelligible
   Genders in *The Metamorphosis* and *The Well of Loneliness*
   Margaret Sönser Breen   147

11 Butler's Corporeal Politics: Matters of Politicized Abjection
   Natalie Wilson   161

PART IV: AGENCY, POSTSTRUCTURALISM, AND PRAGMATISM

12 Strange Tempest: Agency, Poststructuralism, and the Shape of
   Feminist Politics to Come
   Edwina Barvosa-Carter   175

13 Changing Signs: The Political Pragmatism of Poststructuralism
   Robert Alan Brookey and Diane Helene Miller   191

Index   *207*

List of Figures

Frontispiece   *Judith Butler.* Courtesy of Judith Butler.

Figure 1   De Kooning, Willem, *Woman II* (1952). Oil on
                    canvas, 149.9 x 109.3 cm. The Museum of
                    Modern Art, New York.   60

Figure 2   De Chirico, Giorgio, *La Statue Silencieuse (Ariane).*
                    (1913). Oil on canvas, 99.5 x 125.5 cm. The
                    Kunsstammlung Nordrhein-Westfalen, Düsseldorf,
                    Germany.   77

List of Contributors

Susanne Baer is a professor of Law and Gender Studies at Humboldt University, Berlin, Germany.

Edwina Barvosa-Carter is an assistant professor of Chicano Studies at the University of California, Santa Barbara. Her work has appeared in the journals *Black American Literature Forum*, *Contemporary Justice Review*, and *PS: Political Science and Politics*, and in the collection *Chicano Renaissance: Contemporary Cultural Trends*.

Warren J. Blumenfeld is an assistant professor of Multicultural Education and International Curriculum Studies at Iowa State University. He is the founding editor of the *International Journal of Gender and Sexuality Studies*. Co-author with Diane Raymond of *Looking at Gay and Lesbian Life*, published by Beacon, he has also edited *Homophobia: How We All Pay the Price*, also published by Beacon, and co-edited *Readings for Diversity and Social Justice: An Anthology on Racism, Anti-Semitism, Sexism, Heterosexism, Ableism, and Classism*, published by Routledge. He is also co-producer of the documentary *Pink Triangles*.

Margaret Sönser Breen is an associate professor of English and Women's Studies at the University of Connecticut. She has served as associate editor of the *International Journal of Sexuality and Gender Studies*, and she has edited the collections *Understanding Evil: An Interdisciplinary Approach* and *Truth, Reconciliation, and Evil*, both published by Rodopi. She specializes in the British novel and gender studies and has published a range of articles in these areas.

Robert Alan Brookey is an associate professor of Communication at Northern Illinois University. His research examines how sexual minorities are represented in scientific discourse and popular culture. He is the author of the book *Reinventing the Male Homosexual: The Rhetoric and Power of the Gay Gene*. His work has also appeared in *Critical Studies in Media Communication* and *Communication Studies*.

Kirsten Campbell is a lecturer in the Department of Sociology at Goldsmiths College, University of London, where she teaches social theory and socio-legal studies. Her forthcoming book, *Jacques Lacan and Feminist Epistemology*, published by Routledge, explores the relationship between feminist politics and psychoanalytic social theory. Campbell's current research takes up her interest in the formation of social subjectivity in the field of contemporary international humanitarian law, including most recently her paper 'Legal Memories: Sexual

Assault, Memory, and International Humanitarian Law', which appeared in *Signs* in 2002.

Angela Failler is a PhD candidate in Women's Studies at York University in Toronto, Canada, where she is writing a dissertation on psychoanalytic and feminist narratives of anorexia nervosa. Her work has appeared in *Atlantis: A Women's Studies Journal, Journal of Psychoanalysis of Culture and Society*, and *A Reader's Guide to Lesbian and Gay Studies*.

Lynda Hall teaches in the Department of English at the University of Calgary, Canada. Her research focuses on lesbian autobiographical writings, the female body, racism, and gender as performance. Her articles have appeared in numerous journals, including *Callaloo: A Journal of African-American and African Arts and Letters, Canadian Literature, International Journal of Sexuality and Gender Studies*, and *Journal of Lesbian Studies*. She has also edited *Lesbian Self-Writing: The Embodiment of Experience*, published by Haworth Press in 2000.

Belinda Johnston lectured in English and Cultural Studies at the University of Melbourne and completed her PhD there. Her doctoral thesis examined Jacobean stagings of witchcraft and her research interests are in Shakespeare studies and feminist theory. She currently works in higher education policy with the Victorian State Government.

Rosemary A. Joyce is a professor of Anthropology at the University of California, Berkeley. She has authored, co-authored, and co-edited numerous books, including *Gender and Power in Prehispanic Mesoamerica, Sister Stories, Beyond Kinship: Social and Material Reproduction in House Societies, Social Patterns in Pre-Classic Mesoamerica*, and *Women in Prehistory: North American and Mesoamerica*.

Vicki Kirby is a senior lecturer in the School of Sociology at the University of New South Wales in Sydney. She has an enduring fascination with questions about language and system, and finds Derrida's work on 'textuality' especially provocative. She is author of *Telling Flesh: The Subject of the Corporeal*, published by Routledge in 1997, and *Judith Butler: Live Theory*, forthcoming from Continuum. Her more recent work explores post-human concerns. She is currently working on a manuscript, *Quantum Anthropologies*.

Diane Helene Miller is Director of International and Multicultural Services at Brenau University in Georgia. She is the author of *Freedom to Differ: The Shaping of the Gay and Lesbian Struggle for Civil Rights*, published by New York University Press. Her articles have appeared in *Women and* Therapy, *Women's Studies in* Communication, and *Affilia: Journal of Women and Social Work*.

Mena Mitrano holds PhD's in American literature from Rutgers University and the University of Rome. She specializes in Gertrude Stein and critical theory. She is currently completing a study of theory within the context of twentieth-century avant-gardes, which is sponsored by the Università degli Studi di Roma 'La sapienza', Facoltà di Lettere e Filosofia. Her book on Gertrude Stein, *Gertrude Stein: Woman Without Qualities*, is under contract with Ashgate.

Elizabeth M. Perry is an archaeologist and doctoral candidate at the University of Arizona, where she specializes in the archaeology of the pre-Hispanic American Southwest. She has written articles on the topics of power, gender oppression, and feminism in the practices of modern archaeology.

Frederick S. Roden is an assistant professor of English at the University of Connecticut, where he specializes in Victorian literature and gender studies. He is author of *Same-Sex Desire in Victorian Religious Culture*, published by Palgrave and editor of *Palgrave Advances in Oscar Wilde Studies*.

Robert Shail is a graduate student in the Department of English at the University of Exeter. His article 'Masculinity and Visual Representation: A Butlerian Approach to Dirk Bogarde' was published by the *International Journal of Sexuality and Gender Studies* in 2001.

Natalie Wilson completed her doctorate, entitled 'Bodily Subversions: Grotesque Corporeality in American Fiction and Culture', at Birkbeck College, University of London in May 2003. Her areas of expertise include twentieth-century American fiction, cultural studies, and corporeal theory. She has published essays on Flannery O'Connor and contemporary American fiction, and she writes frequent film reviews for the online journal *Scope*. Her essay 'Got Milk?: Advertising Homogeneity in American Culture' will be included in the forthcoming anthology *Ingestation*.

Foreword

Butler Matters: Judith Butler's Impact on Feminist and Queer Studies is the result of four years of collaboration. When we began this project in 1999, we were aware of Judith Butler's profound influence on our own work on gender and sexuality within our respective disciplines of English and Education. Even so, we were surprised by the disciplinary range of the essay proposals that we received in response to the initial Call for Papers. The contributors to *Butler Matters* are scholars from a range of academic fields, including Anthropology, Archaeology, Chicano Studies, Cultural Studies, Communications, Education, English, Sociology, and Women's Studies. Taken together, their examinations of Butler's work from the vantage points of their particular disciplines yield, we believe, a rich collection, useful to students and professors across the academic curriculum who are interested in critical discussions of gender, sexuality, and theory.

Margaret Sönser Breen and Warren J. Blumenfeld
August 2003

Acknowledgements

The editors wish to thank Colgate University and the University of Connecticut's Research Foundation and English Department for research grants for this project. At the University of Connecticut, Doreen Bell, John Gatta, Margaret Higonnet, and Bob Tilton were especially supportive and resourceful.

This project also depended on many careful readers who reviewed article submissions, among them Jonathan Alexander, Harriette Andreadis, Marian Eide, Paul S. Franklin, Lynda Hall, David Hansen-Miller, Clare Hemmings, Catherine Mills, and Robert Mitchell.

We also wish to acknowledge the various groups and individuals that have facilitated our reproduction of images in this collection. Getty Images provided us with the cover image; many thanks to Anthony Sullivan for his work on this transaction. Similarly, Andrea Begel and John Benicewicz of Art Resource helped us obtain an image of de Kooning's *Woman II*. Jutta Bock and Diana Hunnewinkel of The Kunstsammlung Nordrhein-Westfalen in Düsseldorf supplied us with photographer Walter Klein's photo of de Chirico's *La Statue Silencieuse (Ariane)*. Fernanda Meza of the Artists Rights Society facilitated and coordinated the permissions for reproducing this image as well as the image of *Woman II*. In this regard, as well, many thanks to the de Kooning Foundation.

We also wish to acknowledge Kluwer Academic for permission to reprint pieces that originally appeared in the *International Journal of Sexuality and Gender Studies*.

Judith Butler has been gracious throughout this project; we thank her especially for her willingness to respond to interview questions and to supply us with the photo that serves as the collection's frontispiece.

Finally, we are indebted to our editors at Ashgate, Sarah Charters, Ann Donahue, and Erika Gaffney, for their support, guidance, and advice, and to the collection's contributors for their enthusiasm and commitment. They have all been crucial to the realization of this project.

PART I
INTRODUCTION

Chapter 1

Introduction to the Collection

Margaret Sönser Breen[1]

Butler Matters: Judith Butler's Impact on Feminist and Queer Studies began as a journal project. In 1999, Warren Blumenfeld issued a Call for Papers for a special issue of the *International Journal of Sexuality and Gender Studies*, which would mark both the tenth anniversary of the publication of *Gender Trouble: Feminism and the Subversion of Identity* (1990), and the release of the book's anniversary edition. The result was an April 2001 issue that we co-edited. Versions of many of its essays, together with its interview of Butler, appear in this collection.

The eleven essays included in *Butler Matters* consider, in addition to various essays and interviews, four of Judith Butler's major works published between 1990 and 1999: *Gender Trouble: Feminism and the Subversion of Identity* (1990, 1999), *Bodies That Matter: On the Discursive Limits of 'Sex'* (1993), *Excitable Speech: A Politics of the Performative* (1997a), and *The Psychic Life of Power: Theories in Subjection* (1997b). The essays themselves range from analyses of Butlerian theory, to articles on archaeology, pedagogy, and Renaissance representations of the body, to politicized examinations of bodily abjection, performativity, and poststructuralism.

The rationale behind our project is clear enough. Since *Gender Trouble*'s publication, Judith Butler has affected (and effectively shaped) many different fields of inquiry, including Gender and Sexuality Studies, Feminist and Queer Theory, and Cultural Studies. Both within and outside the academy, her work has had a profound influence on people's understandings of gender and sexuality, corporeal politics, and political action.

We have divided *Butler Matters* into four parts: Introduction; Language, Melancholia, and Subjectivity; Body Matters: Archaeology, Literature, and Pedagogy; and Agency, Poststructuralism, and Pragmatism.

Part 1, Introduction, consists of three chapters. Chapter 1 is, of course, this introduction to the collection. Chapter 2, '"There is a Person Here": An Interview with Judith Butler', was compiled by Warren J. Blumenfeld and myself. The interview offers the transcripts of email exchanges wherein Judith Butler responds to questions that we solicited from an international group of scholars specializing

---

[1] A version of this essay appeared as the introduction to the special issue on Judith Butler in the *International Journal of Sexuality and Gender Studies*, vol. 6, nos. 1-2 (April 2001). Reprinted with permission of Kluwer Academic.

in feminist and gender studies. The interview covers a lot of ground. Butler offers her views on the post-9/11 climate in the United States and on the performativity of race. She responds as well to questions regarding theoretical dis/connections between her work and that of other lesbian, gay, bisexual, transgender, and queer writers; to concerns with queer theory's representations of bodily abjection and race and class positioning; to queries regarding the accessibility and political impact of her work.

Like the interview that it follows, Frederick S. Roden's essay 'Becoming Butlerian: On the Discursive Limits (and Potentials) of *Gender Trouble*', Chapter 3, demonstrates the wide-ranging relevance of Butler's work to scholars and activists alike. Focusing on the terms 'performativity' and 'materiality', Roden considers how Butler's discussions of these terms have been misunderstood and how the political import of her work has, in turn, gone unrecognized or been discounted. The key example that he cites is Martha Nussbaum's 1999 *New Republic* article, 'The Professor of Parody: The Hip Defeatism of Judith Butler'. Roden argues that Nussbaum's critique, which also may be understood as a more general indictment of poststructuralism, fails to recognize how destabilized identities can themselves attest to individual agency and resistance to social oppression. Feminist struggle does not, in other words, simply depend on essentialist notions of gender identity. As Roden concludes, '…just as feminism can contain a Catharine MacKinnon and a Pat Califia, it can also benefit from both Butlerian destabilizations of identity and pragmatic calls to activism for the improvement of the material conditions of women around the world'.

Part 2 includes, in turn, four articles. The first of these is Vicki Kirby's 'When All That is Solid Melts into Language', Chapter 4. This article draws on Butler's work in *Bodies That Matter* in order to extend and complicate the 'conflation of "writing" with culture'. Kirby considers 'writing' vis-à-vis biology and argues that Nature is itself literate.

Chapter 5, Mena Mitrano's 'Judith Butler and the Images of Theory', examines Butler's concepts of performativity and gender melancholia in *Gender Trouble* and *The Psychic Life of Power*, respectively. For Mitrano, Butler follows in the footsteps of American visual responses to European thought and the latter's attachment to subjection. Responding to both European thought and feminism, Butler's notion of performativity suggests an exhilarating definitive exit from oppressive scenarios. Her later notion of melancholy is, in turn, less iconoclastic. The American grief that Butler writes inside the theoretical subject is simultaneously an American grief that Theory writes outside, projecting it, that is, on an outside that continues to foreclose such grief with an imaginary America congealed in the cliché of a body without a mind.

Following Mitrano's article is Kirsten Campbell's 'The Plague of the Subject: Subjects, Politics, and the Power of Psychic Life', Chapter 6. In this article, Campbell examines *The Psychic Life of Power*. Campbell argues that, while *The Psychic Life of Power* is an important political and theoretical project, the crucial connection that Butler's book makes between Foucauldian and psychoanalytic theories is in need of further development. For Campbell, Butler's theory of the psychic life of power needs to be extended to include a theory of the power of psychic life. Campbell concludes that Butler must continue to examine 'the problematic relationship between the political subject of Foucault and the unconscious subject of Freud'.

Rounding off Part 2 is Angela Failler's 'Excitable Speech: Judith Butler, Mae West, and Sexual Innuendo', Chapter 7. Simultaneously drawing on Butler's *Excitable Speech: A Politics of the Performative* and paying homage to Mae West, film star of the 1930s, Failler examines sexual innuendo as a speech act. Together, Butler's theory and West's sexual suggestiveness provoke Failler to consider the linguistic agency that performative speech acts engender.

Part 3 begins with 'Past Performance: The Archaeology of Gender as Influenced by the Work of Judith Butler', Chapter 8, by Elizabeth M. Perry and Rosemary A. Joyce. This essay offers an overview of recent archaeological writing that focuses on gender difference, especially as discussed in *Gender Trouble* and *Bodies That Matter*. Specifically, the essay examines how archaeologists employing Butler's concepts of abjection and gender performance in order to understand the production and regulation of gender in prehistoric cultures have extended Butler's work, especially with regard to 'the material dimensions of gender performance'.

Following Perry and Joyce, Belinda Johnston, in 'Renaissance Body Matters: Judith Butler and the Sex That is One', Chapter 9, applies Butler's work on performativity to her examination of the construction of gender in Renaissance England. Johnston holds that 'If *Gender Trouble*...offers a framework for thinking about Renaissance practices of theatricality, then it is *Bodies That Matter*...that offers a framework for questioning those notions and for negotiating one of the most vexed issues in Renaissance studies, the sexed body'. Johnston addresses these concerns with theatricality and gendering in her analysis of the staging of female witchcraft. Arguing against the 'one-sex' model of the body that dominates Renaissance studies, she focuses on how witchcraft in Early Modern England proved 'a key site in the struggle to *materialize* gender, to split the one-sex body in two, inaugurating binary sexual difference'.

The next essay, '*Gender Trouble* in the Literature Classroom: Unintelligible Genders in *The Metamorphosis* and *The Well of Loneliness*', Chapter 10, is my own. This essay examines the importance of Butler's works for students and teachers alike. In doing so, it offers readings of gender and sexual transgression in late nineteenth- and early twentieth-century fiction.

The final essay of this section is Natalie Wilson's 'Butler's Corporeal Politics: Matters of Politicized Abjection', Chapter 11. This essay considers Butler's concept of politicized abjection as presented in *Bodies That Matter*. Through readings of two novels, Katherine Dunn's *Geek Love* (1989) and Barbara Gowdy's *Mister Sandman* (1996), Wilson discusses the abject body's potential to function as an active agent capable of subverting corporeal and gender norms. In so doing, Wilson demonstrates the centrality of politicized abjection to Butler's concept of performativity.

Part 4 consists of two essays. The first of these is Edwina Barvosa-Carter's 'Strange Tempest: Agency, Poststructuralism, and the Shape of Feminist Politics to Come', Chapter 12. Barvosa-Carter examines how the concepts of agency and performativity have affected feminism, particularly feminist political practice. She then suggests how scholarship that combines 'Butler-informed political visions with traditional accounts of feminist political practice' anticipates feminist politics of the future.

Finally, 'Changing Signs: The Political Pragmatism of Poststructuralism', Chapter 13, returns to the concerns raised by Martha Nussbaum's 1999 critique, discussed by Frederick Roden in Chapter 3. In 'Changing Signs' Robert Alan Brookey and Diane Helene Miller refute the attack on Butler in specific and poststructuralism in general, and insist on the political value of her work. For Brookey and Miller, Butlerian theory informs a political pragmatism wherein homophobic discrimination rather than sexual identity proves to be the primary issue in the struggle for sexual rights.

To our knowledge, *Butler Matters* is the only collection to date that focuses on Butler's work and its application to various fields across the humanities and social sciences. Judith Butler's work has been widely anthologized. Yet, it is only recently that volumes devoted solely to her work have begun appearing. Sara Salih is responsible for two such projects: *The Judith Butler Reader*, which she edited with Judith Butler, was published by Blackwell in 2004; *Judith Butler*, a guide to Butler's texts, was published by Routledge in 2002. Finally, Vicki Kirby, one of the contributors to our own volume, critically engages Butler's work in *Judith Butler: Live Theory*, forthcoming with Continuum. Within the context of these important collections, the particular strength of *Butler Matters* is, we believe, its ability to engage a wide-ranging academic audience.

References

Butler, Judith (1990, 1999), *Gender Trouble: Feminism and the Subversion of Identity*, Routledge, New York.
——— (1993), *Bodies That Matter: On the Discursive Limits of 'Sex'*, Routledge, New York.
——— (1997a), *Excitable Speech: A Politics of the Performative*, Routledge, New York.
——— (1997b), *The Psychic Life of Power: Theories in Subjection*, Stanford University Press, Stanford.
Dunn, Katherine (1989), *Geek Love*, Abacus, London.
Gowdy, Barbara (1996), *Mister Sandman*, Steerforth Press, South Royalton, Vermont.
Hall, Radclyffe ([1928]1981), *The Well of Loneliness*, Doubleday and Co., New York.
Kafka, Franz ([1915] 1972), *The Metamorphosis*, S. Corngold (trans. and ed.), Bantam, New York.
Kirby, Vicki (forthcoming), *Judith Butler: Live Theory*, Continuum, New York and London.
Nussbaum, Martha (1999), 'The Professor of Parody: The Hip Defeatism of Judith Butler', *The New Republic*, vol. 220, 22 February, pp.37-45.

Salih, Sara with Butler, Judith (eds) (2002), *Judith Butler*, Routledge, New York.
———— (2004), *The Judith Butler Reader*, Blackwell, Oxford.

Chapter 2

'There is a Person Here':[1]
An Interview with Judith Butler

Compiled by Warren J. Blumenfeld and Margaret Sönser Breen,
with Susanne Baer, Robert Alan Brookey, Lynda Hall,
Vicki Kirby, Robert Shail, and Natalie Wilson[2]

This interview was compiled between 2000 and 2003. The process began in early 2000, when we contacted Judith Butler and asked her if she would be interested in responding to contributor questions for a special double issue of the *International Journal of Sexuality and Gender Studies*. Butler agreed and answered the questions submitted through an email format. More recently, in the summer of 2003, we posed two additional questions.

We have divided the interview into two sections. The first consists of the most recent questions and responses; the second section offers several questions and responses from the earlier interview.

Interview with Judith Butler, Summer 2003

1. **Margaret Sönser Breen:** Since September 11, 2001 and particularly since the war on Iraq, there has been in the U.S. a rise in the authority of various nationalistic bodies (where 'body' may be understood in terms of individual people and in terms of various cultural, social, and political organizations and institutions) and a decrease in the authority, even condemnation of various dissenting bodies. What are the implications of such a conformist political climate, especially for socially marginal groups?

Judith Butler: My sense is that directly after September 11, 2001 there was a general resistance to asking questions about why these bombings had occurred. One editorial writer in *The New York Times* said he did not want to hear any 'explanations' since they would be taken as 'exonerations'. I thought at the time

---

[1] See Judith Butler, 1999, p.xvi.
[2] A version of the second part of this interview (Winter 2000) appeared under the same title in *International Journal of Sexuality and Gender Studies*, vol. 6, nos. 1-2 (April 2001). Reprinted with permission of Kluwer Academic.

that this sentiment, which turned out to be widely shared, was not only confused but quite dangerous. After all, one can and does condemn the horrible murders that took place that day, and one endeavors to do something about the world to make sure that such events don't get repeated. But in order to know what to know, we need to know what happened and why. My sense is that sometimes people believe, even intellectuals believe, that moral condemnation requires paralyzing one's capacity to think, to analyze, to consider all the contributing factors to a situation. And yet, it is only when we operate critically with regard to political phenomena such as 9/11 that we stand a chance of thinking through what reconfigurations of global power must take place to avert repetitions of this kind.

In addition to the anti-intellectualism that emerged, there were, and remain, numerous instances of xenophobic and racist public discourse and public practice. It was amazing to see how little U.S. citizens knew not only about Islam, but about the internal composition of the Arab-American community. Panic and racism were explicitly authorized by the state in the name of 'security' and 'self-defense'. And if one objected to the racial profiling procedures or, indeed, if one objected, or objects, to the treatment of Islamic prisoners in Guantanamo, one is often accused of not taking the threat to security seriously enough. Or if one opposed the wars against Afghanistan and Iraq, which I did publicly, then one is accused not only of a lack of patriotism (a relatively banal accusation), but with complicity, collaboration, even terrorist-sympathy. These accusations are not only ways of patrolling critical speech and quelling dissent, but they also actively circumscribe a public sphere in which only certain kinds of views may be heard, only certain kinds of images may be seen, and only certain interpretations of reality are authorized.

Although I do see more critical discourse emerging after the war on Iraq and its dubious consequences, it remains true that there is a struggle going on about how the public sphere, the sphere of the speakable and visible, will be circumscribed. Certain lines are drawn which, if transgressed, put the transgressor at risk of a damning accusation. I have also experienced this in my work as a progressive Jew to advocate for peace in Israel/Palestine and against the Israeli occupation. If one puts the position into public, one risks the accusation of anti-Semitism. And though there is clearly anti-Semitism in abundance, it is a tactic of censorship to claim that any and all criticisms of Israel during this time are anti-Semitic. It's simply not true, and it produces a situation in which one must brave a terrible and intolerable slur in order to pursue critical public debate.

2. **Warren J. Blumenfeld:** Critical race theorists remind us that the historical emergence of the concept of 'race' arose concurrently with the advent of European exploration as a justification and rationale for conquest and domination of the globe beginning in the fifteenth century C.E. and reaching its apex in the early twentieth century. Geneticists tell us that there is often more variability within a given so-called 'race' than between 'races'. 'Race', they assert is, therefore, discursively constructed. In many Western societies, non-European-heritage bodies are constructed as abject bodies—bodies that do not matter (to borrow your language), or at least do not matter as much as 'white' bodies. In *Bodies That*

Matter (1993), you state that '"race" might be construed as performative' (Butler, 1993, p.275, n.4). Could you elaborate on your overarching understanding of the performativity of 'race'?

Judith Butler: I think that early on in my academic career I was influenced by Anthony Appiah's reading of race in W.B. DuBois as well as Collette Guillaumin's essays in *Feminist Questions*.[3] They both took the view, in different ways, that race was produced as a category in the service of racism. Sandra Harding has made a similar argument, and I believe that Paul Gilroy's *Against Race* gives the argument new force within a political context of overdetermined identity politics. If one accepts, as Appiah and Guillaumin have argued, that racial phenotypes, for instance, are arbitrarily constructed, that they tend to divide into 'units' what is actually a continuum, then one can surely trace the way in which geneticists, for instance, have decided when and where the line ought to be drawn. The drawing of the line that distinguishes races even when there are no good biological grounds for the distinction and even when the cultural fact of mixed race heritage is more prevalent than can be fully accounted for, is one way of understanding how race, as a concept, is produced. I suppose that one could call this drawing of the line performative insofar as it brings into being what it names.

My sense, however, is that this kind of argument needs to be supplemented equally and forcefully by another, one which locates scientific practices of demarcation within the context of institutional racisms. Then one could ask how racism produces race not only in the scientific domain, but in various other institutions: social welfare organization, educational institutions, census bureaus, and medical research, to name a few. At this point, one can see that the terms of race designate populations in the service of control, but also that they govern the terms by which subject formation can and will take place. Someone who is of mixed or indeterminate race will not quite function in a public sphere in which racial demarcations are mandated in clear and unequivocal ways. Fears of miscegenation seem to rest upon the insight that racial categories can and do break down; and laws and norms meant to separate races physically are tactical and forcible efforts to keep racial demarcations distinct. In this sense, we can see that institutional exercises repeatedly construct race within a set of differentials that seek to maintain and control racial separateness. This could also be described as part of the performativity of race.

But whether we are talking about how racial categories are produced and maintained in discourse or in power, it seems crucial to recognize that one cannot simply decide upon a strategy that acts as if 'race' is unreal or fabricated and, therefore, ought not to come into play in political discourse. That decision would misrecognize the power that the category wields, but also the possibilities of resignification that it has and does carry. Although I would always be skeptical of rigidly indentitarian uses of race, I would insist that racial identifications and identities have to be mobilized against the racism by which they were spawned. To refuse the name as if it were merely or only the property of a racist strategy would

---

[3] *Feminist Questions* is the French journal *Questions Féministes*.

be to miss the opportunity to subject the name to a counter-racist strategy. It seems crucial to follow Stuart Hall in these matters and to recognize that Blackness, for instance, has its historicity, and its future. It also seems crucial to theorize whiteness as a racial category, to attend to its internal specificities, and to account for, and expose the ways in which whiteness poses as the race that is not one.

Interview with Judith Butler, Winter 2000[4]

1. **Margaret Sönser Breen:** One might say that there are sharp divisions between queer critics or between writers of earlier times and those of the present. Yet, one might also speak of intergenerational indebtedness. Could you comment on the value of reading your work along side that of earlier, 'essentialist' or 'experiential' discussions of gender and sexuality?

Judith Butler: It is difficult for me to know whether, in relation to your question, I exist in the present or the past, since I think of myself now, ten years after *Gender Trouble* (1990), as already part of the earlier generation of queer writing. I do recognize, though, in what you say a tension between writers associated with gay and lesbian history, for instance, for whom the *lives* of gay people form the focus of analysis and certain strains within queer theory, where conceptual and textual analysis are more prominent. I'm not sure I would call the former 'the past', however, since there are now historians doing such work and writers who write of their own lives, or the lives of others, such as Kate Bornstein or Leslie Feinberg or Dorothy Allison who are, in fiction and prose, having a profound transformative effect on the cultures of gender. I am certainly not opposed to such writing, nor do I understand what I do to have surpassed that writing in some way that might be tracked generationally. My sense is that theory is certainly borne of lives and passions in various ways, but it offers a refracted view on its origins, and its origins are perhaps not as salient as its effects. It would be an impoverished world if all we had were queer theory without biography or autobiography. Samuel Delaney represents, I believe, a form of experience-based narrative that is at once pervasively theoretical. So your question catches me off guard.

As for essentialism, I think that there have been strong arguments in favor of its reemergence in feminism, which Naomi Schor, Rosi Braidotti, and Diana Fuss have made perhaps most eloquently. I gather that what is interesting there is the way that claims to essentialism can be separated from claims of biological determinism. Since those feminists, at least, have no desire to return to the biology is destiny argument. But even if they seek to protect their views against an

---

[4] The list of participants (in order of their questions) includes Margaret Sönser Breen (University of Connecticut); Warren J. Blumenfeld (Colgate University); Vicki Kirby (University of New South Wales, Sydney, Australia); Lynda Hall (University of Calgary, Canada); Natalie Wilson (Birbeck College, University of London); Susanna Baer (Humboldt University, Berlin, Germany); Robert Alan Brookey (Northern Illinois University); and Robert Shail (University of Exeter, United Kingdom).

assimilation to that disdained argument, I am not sure that they can keep their view from acquiring the same kind of function in political discourse.

The notion that sexual difference is fundamental to culture, for instance, which became something like a structuralist truth that survives in Lacanian discourse today, has a way of making sure we consider as unintelligible forms of sexual differentiation that do not conform to the 'sexual difference' at hand. Thus, I wonder whether we can even begin to think transgender and intersex within such a restrictive framework. The point is not to argue that there are more than two sexes, but that we do not know what cultural variations differences may take. There are not only important overlaps between the sexes, but people don't always stay with the sex to which they have been assigned. Moreover, if we take sexual difference to be a foundation of culture, we cannot ask how the assignment of sex—which is such a volatile political issue—takes place as a cultural practice. My view is that it is crucial to understand sex as assigned rather than assumed, and to recognize that there are a variety of ways through which 'assignment' works culturally, and that these are systematically obscured by the presumption that sexual difference is a condition of every and all culture.

I understand that the main way that essentialism has emerged within the gay and queer movements recently is through the gay gene debate. I've learned a lot from Ed Stein on this matter. I think that the assertion of such ostensibly 'hard-wired' differences almost always takes place through metaphors, which belie a misunderstanding about what kinds of genes there are—and can be—and how genes function non-causally in relation to behavior. I'm much more interested in why people find it necessary to find the cause of their desire in their machinery. It is another moment in which cultural variability—and its anxieties—are eclipsed in favor of a false universality.

I have seen how arguments in favor of gay essentialism, however, are used politically for gay rights advocacy. Since if you can say that you cannot help your condition, then homosexuality becomes ostensibly more like race and sex, and its chances are increased for gaining protection under the precedents currently forming anti-discrimination law. But I would be skeptical of a cynical use of essentialism for advancing rights, if only because the very essentialism can be used against lesbian, gay, bi-, and trans people when it turns out that they do not conform to the definitions of their identity that the law, under other circumstances, came to accept.

2. **Margaret Sönser Breen** and **Warren J. Blumenfeld:** One might say that the pre-Stonewall era 'butch' came out of a working-class context, a context that does not necessarily direct the performance of butch identity today. We are interested in how issues of class may be understood in terms of your discussion of performativity.

Judith Butler: This is a good question. There is surely a class background to the emergence of butch identity, as we've seen from recent studies, but I would be a bit hesitant to say that it emerges exclusively from working-class backgrounds. I think we would have to think carefully about butch identities in elite classes, and certainly that would be necessary in the European context. What is salient, though, is that certain risks of social violence are no doubt enhanced for those who lack class protection, and that we can also find many narratives in which upper-class status is 'lost' by virtue of the performance of butch identity.

But perhaps your question seeks to get at another dimension of the matter, namely, how butch becomes legible, and in what social spaces butch becomes performed. There is no doubt the bar, for instance, has been and continues to be often a working-class space in which certain performances become readable as 'butch' within an evolving set of perceptual conventions. And it seems also to be the case that we would need to think in the U.S. context about certain forms of high culture heterosexual femininity, and how 'butch' has signified an alternative to heterosexuality, femininity, and class. There is no doubt important work to be done in thinking about how class and butchness cross, but also about class and femininity.

3. **Vicki Kirby:** Your sustained attention to the nature/culture division acknowledges that the politics of identity and how we think intercourse, relationality, abjection, and so on, are already rehearsed there. In view of this, when you elide 'matter' with a fairly conventional notion of cultural production, namely 'signification', 'meaning', and 'sign', haven't you reinstantiated the division and assumed that nature (albeit under erasure) is inarticulate?

Judith Butler: Your question suggests that I have elided matter, but I'm not sure that I agree. My view in *Bodies That Matter* was that there is an insistent materiality of the body, but that it never makes itself known or legible outside of the cultural articulation in which it appears. This does not mean that culture produces the materiality of the body. It only means that the body is always given to us, and to others, *in some way*. I believe that I wrote there that it is important to affirm the materiality of the body, but added the caveat that the very form that that affirmation takes will be cultural, and that that cultural affirmation will contribute to the very matter that it names. So it seems to me much more like a conundrum than a strict 'divide'.

But your question turns to the question of 'nature' and here I can only plead guilty. I have not written on this topic, although I have written on the 'naturalization' of genders, which is something different. 'Naturalization' is the process by which genders come to appear as natural, and I became concerned to argue against it in the context where certain gender ideals were treated as natural features of any gender. The consequence, of course, is that genders that don't manifest those features by which 'natural' gender is defined are then treated as pathological, aberrant, or unnatural.

It would make sense to ask, then, whether there is room for thinking about nature apart from the process of 'naturalization'. I think there are many people who have done interesting work on this question: Bruno Latour, Donna Haraway, Anne Fausto-Sterling. I would venture to say that in each of those writers there is no denial of nature, but there is a serious and rigorous inquiry into the ways in which it is framed, saturated with social meaning, brought forward for study, made to function as a sign of itself or other matters. So I do believe that it is very worthwhile for critical cultural theorists to examine the problem of nature, acknowledging the ways in which it has shifted historically, figuring out the ways in which nature also 'frames' us in various ways. I don't think it will do to say that nature is only a sign or that it is really always culture. But neither do I think that it will do to act as if we know with epistemological certainty where and how the line between nature and culture ought to be drawn. The drawing of that line belongs to a certain practice, and the distinction is made differently, even if invariably, by virtue of that practice. The interesting question for me is to find out for what purposes that line is drawn when it is.

I do have some arguments in my forthcoming book on Antigone against the Levi-Straussian way of handling the nature/culture distinction.[5] But I don't know whether you want to pursue this kind of question, or whether you have particular difficulties with my way of handling the problem of cultural production. Can you elaborate?

4. **Vicki Kirby:** In the face of contemporary medical research on the body in genetics, the cognitive sciences (I'm thinking of the similarity between neural-net behavior and Saussurean linguistics), immunology, and so on, there is a serious suggestion that 'life itself' is creative encryption. Does your understanding of language and discourse extend to the workings of biological codes and their apparent intelligence?

Judith Butler: I take it that [you] want to know from this question and the earlier one what my engagement with science is. And here the question seems to be: does my view of discourse include 'biological codes'. I confess to not knowing the literature to which [you] refer. [You] may need to take me through the theory that interests [you] here so that I might more intelligently respond.

From my recent exposure to the work of Evelyn Fox-Keller, I would, however, say the following, reiterating what I take [your] view to be. There are models according to which we might try to understand biology, and models by which we might try to understand how genes function. And in some cases the models are taken to be inherent to the phenomena that [are] being explained. Thus, Fox-Keller has argued that certain computer models used to explain gene sequencing in the fruit fly have recently come to be accepted as intrinsic to the gene itself. I worry that a notion like 'biological code', on the face of it, runs the risk of that sort of conflation. I am sure that encryption can be used as a metaphor or model by which to understand biological processes, especially cell reproduction, but do we then make the move to render what is useful as an explanatory model into the ontology of biology itself? This worries me, especially when it is mechanistic models which lay discursive claims on biological life. What of life exceeds the model? When does the discourse claim to become the very life it purports to explain? I am not sure it is possible to say 'life itself' is creative encryption unless we make the mistake of thinking that the model is the ontology of life. Indeed, we might need to think first about the relation of any definition of life to life itself, and whether it must, by virtue of its very task, fail.

---

[5] Butler's *Antigone's Claim: Kinship Between Life and Death* was published in 2000.

5. Vicki Kirby:[6] As I understand your position, interpretation/language defines what is properly human against an outside that is actually a misrecognized inside; in other words, the world will always appear uncannily human because our reflections are anthropomorphic projections. There is an obvious resonance here with Derrida's 'there is no outside of text'. But I prefer to read his refraction of language as something that opens the question of communication and intercourse, as well as the question of 'the human', in a more unsettling way. Why should we equate the technology of language/writing with 'the human' (culture/meaning/intention/modeling), as if human species-being is an enclosed identity defined against a 'pre-scriptive' (radical) outside? How did this inarticulate non- and/or pre-human, figure forth the complex algorithms of cultural representation? Why couldn't the world, as Derrida suggests, be 'algorithmic through and through', such that Man is displaced as its author/reader and instead becomes a particular instantiation of an errant complexity (textuality)? These questions are surely alive, albeit in a different guise, in much of your own work, for you have rigorously questioned the sexual politics wherein a dumb or abjected 'other' must wait to receive its sentence.

Judith Butler: I can see why you might be drawn to the conclusion that I believe that 'interpretation/language defines what is properly human', but I would like to hesitate for a moment before this attribution, since I think that, in the end, it cannot be right. I am not sure that interpretation and language can be brought together so easily, since there are many aspects of language, including its gaps and silences, that are profoundly constitutive of what we are, and might be said to operate as part of what interpolates both the human and the inhuman. Indeed, the line that variably demarcates the human from the non-human will be part of the very language in question, although it may be the moment of that language's opacity. I do not think that the world is composed of our projections, since some horizon will always both exceed and condition whatever projections we make and, in the end, give the lie to projection itself. Anthropomorphism is secured through humanist norms that regularly undo themselves, since the distinction between human and animal, between human and inhuman, between organic and inorganic, both participates in both sides of the opposition and is exhausted by neither. It is here that I prefer to think with Merleau-Ponty on the 'chiasmus' that structures that set of binaries. But it will not do to rehabilitate the human at the center of such a world, for that would be not only to subscribe to the norms which require abjection, but to deny the constitutive complicity of the human with its (own) alterity, a complicity which will have to decenter the human itself in favor of a dynamic and chiastic set of relations. I don't want those relations to be reduced to a mechanism or, indeed, to a formalism, so I'm not sure what to do with the notion of the algorithm. I would take the 'rhythm' part of that suggestion as long as the governing metrics remained open-ended, improvisational.

---

[6] After responding to question three, posed by Vicki Kirby, Judith Butler suggested that Kirby might wish to ask a follow-up question, which she did. Number five is the additional question, which we subsequently inserted into the original order of interview questions.

6. **Lynda Hall:** The current apparent rise in the number of transsexual surgeries being performed again brings into play the significance of your 1990 *Gender Trouble*. You state:

> 'becoming' a gender is a laborious process of becoming *naturalized*, which requires a differentiation of bodily pleasures and parts on the basis of gendered meanings.
>
> …Very often what is wanted in terms of pleasure requires an imaginary participation in body parts, either appendages or orifices, that one might not actually possess, or, similarly, pleasure may require imagining an exaggerated or diminished set of parts (Butler, 1990, pp.70-71; emphasis in original).

How do you see the contemporary demand for transsexual surgery in terms of your suggestion that 'the phantasmatic nature of desire reveals the body not as its ground or cause, but as its *occasion* and its *object*' (Butler, 1990, p.71; emphasis in original)?

Judith Butler: I think that there are important resonances between what I wrote in *Gender Trouble* and what has emerged in recent years as transsexuality has become a more public discourse. I am very pleased that we are starting to hear new voices on this topic and am quite sure that it will continue to be an important area for academic and popular writing for the next years.

The point I made over ten years ago was simply that it is not possible to derive the kind of sexuality that one has from the kind of body that one has, since bodies come into play in sexuality in a variety of ways. And what comes into play is not the body in some positivist sense, but the body as it is lived and imagined. My interest in the bodily ego in Freud derived from this perspective as well, for there it turns out that the given body is not the same as the bodily ego, the sense of a body's bearing and possibility, the sense of its morphology and contour. My view is that it is in reference to this bodily ego or, in Merleau-Ponty's terms, bodily schema, that sexuality emerges.

Of course, the question of the relation between anatomy and the bodily schema is an important one, but let us not forget that the scientific practices which, in relation to the question of sexuality, determine for us what will and will not be our relevant 'anatomy' labor under their own interpretive schemas. Thus, the 'anatomy' that is said to be positively given, which is said to be incontestable, is described by a theory that has its own vested interests in deciding where erotogeneity will and will not take place. This is not to say that there is no anatomy, but only to insist that when and where descriptions of anatomy come into play in the determination of the sexual field, we need to be careful not to be imposing an erotic scheme on bodies who carry conflicting erotic schemas.

I think some of the older models of transsexuality derived from John Money and his associates were very problematic because they sought at every instance to 'correct' aberrant genders and establish them in grids of normality. But some of the more recent writings on this topic suggest that transsexuality can be very complicated. It is not always about 'becoming heterosexual', and it is not always about becoming another gender. Kate Bornstein says it is about 'becoming itself', which coincides with my own views on what gender 'is'. Moreover, it seems to me that many transsexuals live with a complicated sense of morphology, since surgery marks only a transition from one version of one's body to another, but it does not found a new being altogether. One lives with the traces of the earlier version and with the marks and consequences of the surgery, if one chooses to undergo that. It is a difficult, and often very brave transformation in which something profound about a person's psychic and bodily sense of self is at stake. And it is also important to remember that the decision emerges both out of suffering and desire.

Although the passage you offer from my earlier work implies that the erotogenic body is refigured by its place and meaning within sexual exchange, it is important to remember that for many transsexuals, the transition is not about altering one's sexuality, but only one's gender. The distinction is important to many, and it remains important to remember that not all gender transformation is done in the name of sexuality.

7. **Natalie Wilson:** In *Bodies That Matter*, you refer to 'the politicization of abjection', and assert that the political aspects of abjection could assist in 'a radical resignification of the symbolic domain, deviating the citational chain toward a more possible future to expand the very meaning of what counts as a valued and valuable body in the world'. You refer to abjection as 'an enabling disruption' that could offer 'the occasion for a radical rearticulation of the symbolic horizon in which bodies come to matter at all'. Here, you seem to place the material body in a political domain, endorsing materiality as potentially disruptive to the symbolic domain of viable bodies. However, contemporary U.S. culture seems ever more intent on normalizing bodies. Given the 'human genome project', which is involved in coding DNA so as to eradicate various bodily 'abnormalities', as well as other regulatory phenomenon such as surgically altering people with Down's Syndrome to 'normalize' their appearance, would you agree that there is a current cultural abhorrence of bodily difference? How can this politics of the normal be resisted through a reaffirmation of abject material bodily difference?

Judith Butler: This is a serious and large question. I think that the growing field of disability studies is very important in this way, drawing public attention to the ways in which ideal morphologies and mobilities seem to circumscribe what counts as an intelligible body. I believe that our very profound assumptions about what it takes to be a 'person' are structured by ideal bodily morphologies which produce fear and anxiety in the face of individuals whose bodies challenge the norm. I also agree that we are witnessing an intensification of normalization at this time, which involves a focus on the body and its perfectibility. This is not unlike certain fascist tendencies in Europe in the middle of the last century.

This also seems linked to a question that Foucault tried to pursue, namely, why has the regulation of bodies become an increasing focus of power in the last century? On the one hand, there is the need to control populations, something that will be facilitated by the human genome project and the loss of privacy that it threatens as well as the new norms for 'health' and 'perfectible humanness' that it promises. This is a knowledge/power regime in Foucault's sense, since it is a form of knowledge that constitutes the field in which new norms for the very intelligibility of the human are being created. To the extent that these projects extend the power of science, they also extend the power of the state, to the extent that the state maintains such research as part of its own purview, either through funding or sponsorship. Accordingly, there are forms of subjectification that correspond to this power/knowledge regime, ones that seek to approximate the new norms for humanity. But this is also the occasion for those very norms to be brought into crisis. I think this is done, for instance, by the visual arts in the work of Cindy Sherman, Anna Mendietta, and even Chris Ofili. And it is one reason that 'abject art' in particular is under close state scrutiny, even censorship. What might be important is to develop a political analysis, and a corresponding form of activism, in which 'the human' in its profound variegation, might be articulated over and against the calculable and perfectible versions of the human that are being produced through these processes of normalization. I also think that politicization on the meaning and use of the human genome project is extremely important. There are so many people who are understandably pleased by the apparent promise that the project has for the curing of diseases that they fail to see what implicit notions a uniform and calculable notion of the person are being produced and naturalized by the process.

Cheryl Chase and the ISA (Intersex Society of America) have made it very clear the physical and psychic costs to intersexed people that ideal gender norms and the very presumption of ideal gender dimorphism have had. Surgical correction very often turns out in these instances to be no more than violence perpetrated on very young children which turns out to have profound effects on their ability to survive—psychically and physically—as adults. Activism in this domain is currently changing the way the psychological profession counsels on this issue. So we can only hope for greater successes of this kind.

8. **Natalie Wilson:** In *Gender Trouble*, you write that 'as a strategy of survival within compulsory systems, gender is a performance with clearly punitive consequences. Discrete genders are part of what "humanizes" individuals within contemporary culture; indeed, we regularly punish those who fail to do their gender right' (Butler, 1990, pp.139-140). How can this concept be extended to those who fail to do their body right? What are the punitive consequences for having a materially abject body within contemporary culture—for having a disabled body, a deformed body, an obese body, a racially marked body? Do you see the punitive consequences allied to these types of bodily differences as analogous to 'those who fail to do their gender right'? If so, how do you account for the foregrounding of gender as the bodily difference within your work? Do you consider other bodily differences and the attempt to normalize these differences within culture as politically analogous to the policing of gender difference?

Judith Butler: I hadn't read this question before I answered the last, so I risk some overlap here. I do not think that punishments leveled against those who 'do not do their gender right' are the only punishments leveled against marked bodies. You ask, though, why I foreground gender in my work. It is clear that I have done that, although I have written on some of the other topics you mention as well. I did not seek to write a book, or set of books, on bodies that are socially punished for their differences. If I had, I would certainly be under an obligation to make sure I included in such a book the range of bodies that suffer in this way. There was, however, something specific to gender anxieties that drew me to the topics I have discussed, and though I am in complete agreement with you that there are a myriad of anxieties and fears and aggressions turned against marked bodies of various kinds, I do not believe that they are all the same. Indeed, a butch lesbian of color is going to receive several different kinds of social messages about how she appears in the world, and they are going to be, to a certain extent, distinct from those that a white woman undergoes. In the case of gender, I think that people who fear those who are gender dissonant fear something about losing their own sense of normativity, fear knowing that gender is labile, that norms are contingent, that they *could*, if they wanted to, do their gender differently than how it is being done, fear knowing that gender is a matter of doing and its effects rather than an inherent attribute, an intrinsic feature.

Disability brings up different kinds of fears: the contingency of birth, the fact of finitude, the privilege of mobility, but also the privilege that the ability to stand and move autonomously, all of which underwrite our notions of what it is to be a viable human. In liberal culture, this becomes exacerbated, since no liberal wants to avow the belief that a physically challenged child or one who lives with a chronic and disabling disease is 'not human'. And yet every liberal who fails to examine the cultural presumptions that work to support the very notion of the human will invariably fail to offer the kinds of recognition, respect, and resources that disabled persons deserve. Such bodies take us up against the very limit of liberalism's unexamined assumptions. Michael Berube's recent work has brought this into the fore. And the field of disability studies, especially its journal, has brought the critical study of ideal morphology into focus for many of us.

Similarly, I think that some accounts of racism have focused on the 'stigma' that people of color assume in society. But I wonder whether the stigma theory of racism is really sufficient. Isn't it rather the case, as Fanon made clear, that there is an epidermal presumption about the human, such that racism gives voice to the ways in which people whom we know to be people nevertheless do not get seen or recognized within the purview of the culturally elaborated notion of 'the people'. The kinds of erasures that happen when, for instance, Black people are not included in certain representations of 'america' (sic) or, indeed, in political theoretical discussions of 'citizenship' can take place precisely because the exclusion has happened at the level of presumption, as an epistemological condition of political judgment.

Performativity takes on a new meaning against such a backdrop, since what happens when the less than human nevertheless assumes its place within the human, producing a paradox and a tension for the norm? It exposes the norm as exclusionary and its ideality as normative. But it also produces an aberration with the power to redefine the norm. What is important, of course, is to keep the 'redefining of the norm' from being 'an assimilation to the norm' (which is what gay marriage is doing). The redefinition has to take aim at normativity itself, establishing the progressive and irreversible dissonance of human life, its radical non-unity, as the only viable definition.

9. **Susanne Baer:** In your texts, law, laws, and Law figure prominently. What is, according to your theoretical perspective, the relationship between them? What are the differences and what do they imply for the options of legal-political action? If we are to avoid law and Law, can we make use of laws? Or would you agree with Audre Lorde's famous 'the Masters tools can never dismantle the Master's house' here?

Judith Butler: One thing I have learned from my friends who teach in law school is that when the academic discourse turns to the question of 'the Law', the lawyers tend to tune out. I think this happens because there are so many different kinds of laws, and in present legal systems, laws do not always work in tandem with one another, and often present conflicting aims and agendas. I think that I use 'Law' mainly in relation to the notion of the Symbolic, which is not the same as the legal sense of law and laws. The symbolic Law has always made me angry, since it is the one that not only is said to mandate the exchange of women and to found sexual difference as primary to culture as such, but it is impervious to efforts at redefinition.

In *Excitable Speech* (1997), I sought to understand something about how the laws which decide the questions of what is speech and what is action are in the service of wider political agenda. I noted that in the case of pornography, some jurists were willing to accept the notion that the expressive and performative function of pornographic imagery were the same. I also noted with dismay that in cases in which racist speech was at issue, the distinction between what is merely expressive (and thus protected constitutionally) and what is conduct (not protected) tended to be upheld. The conclusion of this analysis was simply that it may not always work to hand over to the courts the question of what should be regarded as speech, and what should be regarded as action.

I have some skepticism about turning to the courts and to the state for all political solutions. I am interested in the Gramscian tradition in which civil society becomes the site for important political innovation, and I also worry about the opportunities we give to the state to augment its own regulatory control. These last concerns are very much allied with Foucault's. But I do not think I am for these reasons a libertarian. I am strongly in favor of welfare, of anti-discrimination law, and of a stronger state role in guaranteeing national health care privileges to everyone (regardless of marital status). And I don't even think that I am a First Amendment absolutist. That I am skeptical about the differential ways that the courts decide the speech/conduct distinction does not mean that I believe that the First Amendment represents the most important freedom or that hate speech legislation is never warranted. In fact, I do think that hate speech legislation is important, but it needs to be clearly defined so that minority communities are not played off one another with the consequence that some are deprived of protection against violence (*RAV v. Saint Paul*), and others are held to be engaging in injurious conduct by speaking their desires (Department of Defense regulations on gays).

10. **Rob Alan Brookey:** The direction of the contemporary gay, lesbian, bisexual, and transgender (GLBT) movement is currently dominated by national organizations that have focused these issues of same-sex marriage and partner benefits. Given the influence of such organizations, what are the benefits and the risks of allowing national organizations to represent GLBT interests? Do you believe these organizations can be molded in such a way so as to better assist the cause of sexual rights, or should we redirect our energies and resources to build coalitions of sexual minorities on more localized levels?

Judith Butler: This is a good question, and a difficult one. I am dismayed by the fact that so many national gay organizations have taken the right to marriage to be the most important item for the gay political agenda. Of course, I am opposed to the homophobic discourses that oppose gay marriage, but I am equally opposed to ceding the national political agenda to the marriage issue. In the first instance, the pro-marriage agenda prescribes long-term monogamous pairs when many people in the lesbian, gay, bi- community have sought to establish other forms of sexual intimacy and alliance. Second, it breaks alliance with single people, with straight people outside of marriage, with single mothers or fathers, and with alternative forms of kinship which have their own dignity and importance. Third, it seems to me to be a move away from a focus on AIDS, and so a move by which we seek to produce a public picture of ourselves as a religious or state-sanctioned set of upstanding couples rather than as a community still afflicted by an epidemic for which adequate research and medical resources are rarely available, especially to those who are poor or without adequate means. Fourth, I object to the notion that having marital status is important for health benefits, since what we are saying with this argument is that those who are outside the traditional couple form are not worthy of health benefits. This seems to me, once again, to demonize individuals who engage in multiple partners or who live in non-traditional alliances. I believe we would not be so quick as a community to engage in this demonization if the spectre of the de-coupled individual with multiple partners were not unconsciously or consciously held to be the 'cause' of AIDS. In other words, we leave the most vulnerable people behind in this current effort to make ourselves over as married couples.

I think the strategy has to be two-fold. On the one hand, it is important to lobby to get progressive people on the boards of NGLTF [National Gay and Lesbian Task Force], LAMBDA [Lambda Legal Defense Fund], and especially the Human Rights Campaign, whose donor basis and political connections should not be underestimated. I think that we have begun to hear some public criticisms of their agenda by Michael Warner and John D'Emilio, among others, but I do wonder whether those voices will ever have the kind of circulation and popularity that Andrew Sullivan has. I can only hope that they will. Local organizing is also very important, not only because that is the beginning of coalitions among local groups (which can ultimately pose a productive crisis for the national groups), but because that is the way in which political participation and activism is most clearly fostered.

11. **Margaret Sönser Breen** and **Warren J. Blumenfeld:** In your 1999 Preface to *Gender Trouble*, you write of the 'productive political dimensions' of 'a coalition of sexual minorities' (Butler, 1999, xxvi). Yet, doesn't 'coalition' presume the necessity of identity-based politics, which your groundbreaking work on gender and sexuality deconstructs? Can you explain this apparent contradiction?

Judith Butler: I don't know whether a coalition of sexual minorities necessarily assumes a coalition of established identities. Indeed, sometimes coalitions find a broad rubric under which to function. I think 'queer' operates in that way (and not as an identity) as does 'sexual minority' (a term that Gayle Rubin offered some time ago). I think it is quite possible to enter into coalition without first declaring one's identity, and it may also be the case that a new collective identity forms in the context of coalitional work. The recent protests against the World Bank, for instance, drew from many communities, but the people who showed up very often allied with a specific agenda, the dismantling of international structures that promote the wealth differentials of globalization. I haven't yet heard of identity squabbles there.

I would also say that the deconstruction of gender and sexuality does not mean that identity categories are no longer available. One can still organize as a lesbian, but one has to be open to the notion that we don't yet know who else will ally with that sign, or when that sign will have to be relinquished in order to promote another political goal, i.e. gay, lesbian, bi-, trans, solidarity, for instance. To enter into that solidarity is already to undergo a certain deconstruction, for that identity is neither the reason for one's being there nor the end-goal of politicization itself. It marks something about my position in my travels, but it is not my ground, my epistemology, or indeed my final stand.

12. **Robert Shail:** In recent years in both Britain and the U.S.A., there has been a noticeable movement amongst some feminist writers towards a reassertion of traditional and restrictive definitions of gender. The development of the so-called 'men's movement' has added to this impression. Can the type of liberalization and hybridity of gender identity that you have suggested encompass the reassertion of these more traditional identities, or is there a legitimate political boundary beyond which a conception of a hybrid gender identity could not go without risking subjugation within a repressive ideology?

Judith Butler: I think that there is a certain return of the repressed in certain feminist writing lately, and I agree that it tends to uphold certain traditional gender roles. I wonder whether it is itself a reaction against a perceived 'postmodernism' in gender studies, but also a re-heterosexualization of feminism. I think that the most useful way to respond to it might be to establish a critical form of heterosexuality studies, one that does not take its norms to be established or beyond criticism, one which asks how sexuality and gender interrelated within heterosexuality, and how heterosexual definition is, as Sedgwick has taught us, bound up with homo definition. If the reason for the reaction is that heterosexual women want their 'place' back, then it probably makes sense to seize the occasion to rethink heterosexuality itself. My own sense is that it is usually more queer than it is willing to know.

As for the part of your question which asks whether there are limits beyond which gender hybridization cannot go, I am tempted to take a step back. For the purpose of my work is not to say: let's all become more hybrid! I think that the hybridity of dissonance you refer to is already here, already structuring the gendered lives of many people. It is surely there among those who have experienced gender 'dysphoria' in myriad ways, but it is also experienced as the lived anxiety of those who live most closely tied to the gender norm. Indeed, I do not think there is a normative gendered life that does not know—at some level—its own radical contingency, the possibility of its being otherwise. And even if we accept the descriptive viability of terms such as 'masculine' and 'feminine', who among us has identifications with just one? And is it even possible to identify with one without at the same time establishing an identificatory relation to the other? Gender trouble is not new. It's already arrived. It's not a utopian vision, but a way to lend a language of description to what has been foreclosed from normative discourse for too long.

As for the arguments that transgender 'goes too far', that it wars with nature or with the symbolic—I would suggest only that that war has also been going on for a long time, and that people have been living, suffering, and desiring outside the symbolic and outside of that 'nature' for a long time. The only question is whether we will become capacious enough as a community to find a language in which such lives might live in the open.

13. **Margaret Sönser Breen:** One might say that your writing style assumes an academic readership or a readership that welcomes very demanding prose. In *Gender Trouble*'s 1999 Preface, you address this issue of 'language and accessibility'. You ask whether there is 'a value to be derived from…experiences of linguistic difficulty' (Butler, 1999, p.xix). Please comment on this value; what is its relation to readers whose experience of educational disenfranchisement is marked by 'linguistic difficulty'?

Judith Butler: I actually teach in a voice that is for the most part very different from the written voice in *Gender Trouble*. I have also probably written in ways that are not quite as difficult as that voice was. You make an apt point, though, since when I wrote that book, I had no idea that there might be an audience for it. Indeed, I was surprised by the audience that it has assumed.

I think it is important for pedagogical reasons, especially for a theorist, to know how to shift registers. But I also think it is important not to underestimate the intelligence of lay readers, readers from various backgrounds and educational privilege. I certainly did write that book for an academic audience, but what is strange is that, despite its obvious difficulty, it was read rather widely outside of the academy. I take it that there was something there that people wanted to read, and though I did hear from people who found it difficult, I heard from those who also felt that something was at stake in that theoretical work that made the reading worthwhile.

I don't know exactly how this can be taught. But I think it is important that critical teaching and critical writing not only seek to be communicable, and reach people where they live, but also pose a challenge, and offer a chance for readers to become something different from what they already are. It is not just that some readers want the chance to understand something new and difficult, but that the received meanings that we have about gender are so entrenched in our everyday way of talking that it won't make sense to try to change the meaning of gender without critically assessing everyday language. If one were to offer that critical assessment within everyday language, then we would, to some extent, be reaffirming the very language that we seek to subject to critical scrutiny. This doesn't mean that one should strive to become obscure. In fact, I think intellectuals are under a double obligation to both speak to people where they live, in the language in which understanding is possible, but also to give them the critical point of departure by which they might risk a certain destabilization of that familiar language, become exposed to the new, and begin to imagine the world otherwise.

References

Butler, Judith (1990, 1999), *Gender Trouble: Feminism and the Subversion of Identity*, Routledge, New York.

———— (1993), *Bodies That Matter: On the Discursive Limits of 'Sex'*, Routledge, New York.

———— (1997), *Excitable Speech: A Politics of the Performative*, Routledge, New York.

———— (2000), *Antigone's Claim: Kinship Between Life and Death*, Columbia University Press, New York.

Gilroy, Paul (2000), *Against Race: Imagining Political Culture Beyond the Color Line*, Harvard University Press, Cambridge.

Chapter 3

Becoming Butlerian:
On the Discursive Limits (and Potentials)
of *Gender Trouble*

Frederick S. Roden[1]

Judith Butler's *Gender Trouble: Feminism and the Subversion of Identity* (1990)
has defined a field. Indeed, it has defined several fields, several interrelated but
only recently articulated areas of inquiry. First and foremost, *Gender Trouble* is a
work of feminist theory. In the case of Eve Kosofsky Sedgwick's equally
iconoclastic *Between Men: English Literature and Male Homosocial Desire*
(1985), feminist theory and literary criticism have gone forth and multiplied,
birthing gender studies and queer theory. The question remains whether this
transformation has diversified and enriched or diluted feminist concerns in favor of
a male-centered hegemony.

'What is queer theory?' This question was posed more than ten years ago.
Butler herself asked it, as she recounts in a 1993 interview printed in *Radical
Philosophy* in 1994 (Butler, 1994, p.32). How did feminist theorists become, for
better or worse, queer theorists?

Butler and Sedgwick have a lot in common. Perhaps the most striking aspect of
their shared claim to fame in shaping these disciplines is that both radically
redefined their positions in books that appeared a short time after they published
definitive works in the field. Sedgwick dramatically reshaped her feminist analysis
of the continuum of male homosociality in her 1990 *Epistemology of the Closet*.
The work placed the literary critic's concentration on male homosexuality rather
than on the marginalization of women. Similarly, while Butler's *Gender Trouble*
caused both rave and rage, her *Bodies That Matter: On the Discursive Limits of
'Sex'* (1993a) allowed her to revise the performance-related terms she used in
Gender Trouble. There she also explained the strained categories of materiality and
corporeality. Critics of *Gender Trouble* were waiting for such clarification.

The theoretical models of both Sedgwick and Butler are highly dependent on

---

[1] A version of Roden's essay appeared under the same title in *International Journal of
Sexuality and Gender Studies*, vol. 6, nos. 1-2 (April 2001). Reprinted with permission of
Kluwer Academic.

other theorists. While this may seem to be a moot point, it is an important observation to make because both Sedgwick and Butler have been canonized as founders of gender studies/queer theory. This detail is not intended to denigrate their fame. One could hardly challenge the groundbreaking roles that the two theorists have played in sculpting the scholarly terrain of gender, not to mention their influence in reshaping the humanities academy as a whole. This essay, then, is concerned with Butler's popularity.

Theorists are often liberally cited without taking into account the full measure of their arguments. At the time of this writing, the Modern Language Association Bibliography showed 206 hits for works bearing the keywords 'Judith Butler'; however, 'performative' brought 261 and 'performativity' 126. In this study, I wish to explore, interrogate, and contextualize the Butler phenomenon: the dissemination of *Gender Trouble*, whether diluted or distilled, in the years since its first publication.

In tracing a history of ideas, Sedgwick's *Between Men*, while influenced by Michel Foucault and many other thinkers, owes a particular debt to Gayle Rubin on the question of exchanges of women between men, and simply for setting up a model of triangulation. Butler's *Gender Trouble* made words such as 'performative', 'performativity', and even 'performance' central terms in the examination not only of gender, but of any notion of identity. It was not until 1993, however, that Butler offered a full treatment of past inquiry utilizing her vocabulary: specifically with regard to J.L. Austin's *How to Do Things with Words* (1962), published some thirty years earlier. I do not fault Butler for failing to discuss Austin at length in 1990. Rather, I think that we can observe the degree to which she had changed focus by 1993, a crucially important year for her. The annual English Institute's topic produced a volume of essays entitled *Performativity and Performance*, edited by Sedgwick and Andrew Parker (1995). These essays are inquiries into the broader history of 'performance' prior to Butler. She includes a piece there that discusses Austin, as do other contributors to that collection.

It is evident, therefore, that within a short period of time, the key terminology of Butler's *Gender Trouble* had to be redefined and made particular. Butler was truly timely—witness the proliferation of departments of performance studies—but she also raised critical awareness on the usefulness of a certain kind of engagement in the subject of identity and discourse. The year 1993 also marked the publication of the first issue of *GLQ: A Journal of Lesbian and Gay Studies*. Two articles stand out in that issue: Sedgwick's on 'Queer Performativity' and Butler's 'Critically Queer', where she notes:

> The following is indebted to Eve Sedgwick's 'Queer Performativity', published in this issue of *GLQ*. I thank her for the excellent essay and for the provocations, lodged in her text and perhaps most poignantly in earlier drafts, which have inspired this essay in important ways (Butler, 1993b, p.29, n.1).

A version of 'Critically Queer' also appears in Butler's *Bodies That Matter* (1993a).

Butler's theories of gender had been under some attack for neglecting the body and for overreaching with her term 'performative', which she claims (and continues to charge in the 1999 edition of *Gender Trouble*) readers have misinterpreted. She writes in 'Critically Queer':

> Gender is performative insofar as it is the *effect* of a regulatory regime of gender differences in which genders are divided and hierarchized *under constraint*. Social constraints, taboos, prohibitions, threats of punishment operate in the ritualized repetition of norms, and this repetition constitutes the temporalized scene of gender construction and destabilization. There is no subject who precedes or enacts this repetition of norms (Butler, 1993b, p.21, emphasis in original).

She further teases out 'performativity' there:

> Performativity is a matter of reiterating or repeating the norms by which one is constituted: it is not a radical fabrication of a gendered self. It is a compulsory repetition of prior and subjectivating norms, ones which cannot be thrown off at will, but which work, animate, and constrain the gendered subject, and which are also the resources from which resistance, subversion, displacement are to be forged (Butler, 1993b, p.22).

Finally, on 'performance':

> *In no sense can it be concluded that the part of gender that it performed is the truth of gender; performance as bounded 'act' is distinguished from performativity insofar as the latter consists in a reiteration of norms which precede, constrain, and exceed the performer and in that sense cannot be taken as the fabrication of the performer's 'will' or 'choice'... The reduction of performativity to performance would be a mistake* (Butler, 1993b, p. 24, emphasis in original).

These points do not just show the ways in which a writer may be read out of context in moving from theory to praxis. They also indicate the abundance of Butlerian practical criticism that developed following *Gender Trouble*'s publication. The active aftershock sought to label any kind of performance as the Butlerian performative, whether the intention to gender-bend is present or not. Butler warns in 1993: 'Performativity, then, is to be read not as self-expression or self-presentation, but as the unanticipated resignifiability of highly invested terms' (Butler, 1993b, p.28).

This theme is taken up in Butler's 1993 visit to the London Institute of Contemporary Arts, where she was interviewed by Peter Osborne and Lynne Segal. There she stated: 'I don't think that drag is a paradigm for the subversion of gender' (Butler, 1994, p.33). What could be made of this observation at a cultural moment when Butler had been claimed as theoretical support for an array of modes—material and immaterial—of gender inversion and subversion? As Butler was swift to state, drag was an example, not a prototype; gender play may politically be celebrated, but it is not the model: This issue has been the crisis in applying Butler's work since the publication of *Gender Trouble*. The text is a highly sophisticated theoretical evaluation of what shapes and constitutes gender identity. *Gender Trouble*, however, is of course highly politically-invested as well. The book has been allied more with queer—lesbian, gay, bisexual, and transgendered—popular liberation than with feminism *per se*, in part because of Butler's critique of the heteronormativity inherent in feminist theory. Yet to take the theory out of the ivory tower problematizes its implications. Some would ask: How can a theory that denigrates the centrality of anything so fixed as materiality be used in political activism concerned with the lives of 'real people'? Perhaps the better question might be: how can resonances of a theoretical work that depends on a university-level education in a variety of continental philosophers be effectively and accurately put to use outside of the academy?

The relationship between theory and praxis is often strained, and perhaps nowhere more so than in liberation politics. What does it mean that the very individuals who exist in privileged spaces of the academy also have an investment in—and attachment to—marginalized cultural groups, or identify as members of those subcultures? The most noteworthy aspect of *Gender Trouble*'s reader-reception is that it has been taken seriously by a conservative, traditional intellectual community in a way that other works on gender and sexuality have not. This is a testament not only to Butler's brilliance and the elegance of her ideas but also to the particular kind of education and canon she is drawing on—as well as a long western European tradition of writing in a certain philosophical prose style. This very style and intellectual foundation makes Butler queer within queer culture, because her work has the danger of placing her in opposition to a popular politics that might reject the hegemony of the academy. Instead, she became vulnerable to misinterpretation and misuse.

In the 1999 preface to a new edition of *Gender Trouble*, Butler acknowledges her personal place in the queer cultures of the late twentieth century. As in the title of her 1993 book, bodies *do* matter. She states in the 1993 interview: 'I think that I overrode the category of sex too quickly in *Gender Trouble*', versus 'how a norm actually materializes a body' (Butler, 1994, pp.32-33). In that interview, Butler also observes: 'I would say that I'm a feminist theorist before I'm a queer theorist or a gay and lesbian theorist' (1994, p.32). It is this contested place of the body, however, that puts Butler in conflict with many contemporary feminists. In the 22 February 1999 issue of *The New Republic*, Martha Nussbaum—perhaps more 'humanist' than 'feminist'—published a scathing attack on Butler and the kind of feminist scholarship Nussbaum sees her to represent. The Ernst Freund Professor of Law and Ethics at the University of Chicago Law School, Nussbaum is a distinguished scholar who has worked with the United Nations and other public and private organizations outside of the academy. As philosopher and classicist, she has written on human rights, sexuality, and sexual orientation. According to Nussbaum, those feminists who have chosen to stay in the traditional academy should keep their 'eyes always on the material conditions of real women, writing always in a way that acknowledges those real bodies and those real struggles' (Nussbaum, 1999b, p.37). Instead, American academic feminism has moved to what she calls 'quietism and retreat': 'the virtually complete turning from the material side of life toward a type of verbal and symbolic politics that makes only the flimsiest of connections with the real situation of real women' (Nussbaum, 1999b, p.38).

Does Nussbaum mourn the victory of postmodern theory over *engagé* activism, or does she—like the 'performance' Butlerians—fail to understand the relationship between theory and praxis? Butler represents the triumph of the old Deconstruction, of Derrida: even gender identity collapses into wordplay, yet it is never 'mere' wordplay. The equally-powerful Nussbaum attacks the privilege of the Butlers of the academy: that the 'uninitiated' (i.e., those unfamiliar with various theorists) will not understand her kind of writing. Is Nussbaum simply lamenting the death of the 'general reader'? She writes: 'It is also obvious that Butler's work is not directed at a non-academic audience eager to grapple with actual injustices. Such an audience would simply be baffled by the thick soup of Butler's prose, by its air of in-group knowingness' (Nussbaum, 1999b, p.38). Nussbaum's critique, while at times seeming to be more a personal attack on a variety of theoretical projects, highlights many of the real problems in reading Butler both inside and outside of the academy. One could easily make the same argument about any number of dead, straight, white male thinkers in the canon, which makes Butler oddly assimilationist in her rhetoric. As Nussbaum is eager to observe, Butler was awarded first prize in the annual Bad Writing Contest sponsored by *Philosophy and Literature* for one especially contorted sentence. Yet Nussbaum critiques not only Butler's style and argument, but also her originality, pointing out that gender has been denaturalized from Plato on, citing the Victorian J.S. Mill and mentioning Nancy Chodorow's theory on gender replication (1999b, p.40). David Leverenz, in an article on feminist and gender studies in *Amerikastudien*, notes that 'performativity' has a recent history not only of Austin, but also Barbara Johnson, Shoshana Felman, Lyotard, and Teresa de Lauretis (Leverenz, 1996, p.223).

The 19 April 1999 issue of *The New Republic* published responses to Nussbaum's '*ad feminam* attack on Judith Butler', as Drucilla Cornell and Sara Murphy label her piece (Nussbaum, 1999a). The collection is a veritable star-studded array of prominent feminist theorists. Gayatri Spivak maintains that Butler's performative theory is not the same as Austin's or social construction theories. She also critiques Nussbaum's assertion that Butler's work is in contrast to more 'practical' Third World feminists' projects, argues that Nussbaum is as privileged as Butler, and even accuses the critic of being 'matronizing': speaking in a pseudo-'civilizing' colonial voice that claims to know the wants and needs of Third World women. Columbia University Professor Spivak comes to Butler's defense on these grounds, suggesting that the 'gender practice of the rural poor is quite often in the performative mode' (Nussbaum, 1999a). Nancy Fraser and Linda Nicholson maintain that Butler's proper place is as a philosopher, while Joan Scott is troubled by Nussbaum's dichotomization of the 'good' versus 'bad' feminists. Cornell and Murphy agree, in that the former is the activist, according to Nussbaum's rhetoric, while the latter is language-oriented. They insist that Butler, as feminist, does not believe that political goals can be achieved solely as Nussbaum caricatures her thought. Rather, for Butler, 'feminist work is grounded in an insistence upon the material force of representations', including the linguistic (Nussbaum, 1999a). Rather than contrasting Butler's views with those of anti-pornography feminist Catharine MacKinnon (as Nussbaum had done), Cornell and Murphy compare the two. Both focus upon 'the ways in which representations have constitutive force' (Nussbaum, 1999a). Nussbaum refutes the critiques in a rebuttal that concludes: 'Butler may well have admirable practical commitments, but this does not change the fact that what she writes as a theorist offers no helpful direction for practice' (Nussbaum, 1999a). Thus even the anti-postmodernist Nussbaum finds that language (or at least Butler's language) fails to create meaning.

This debate did not end in *The New Republic* circa 1999. Robyn Wiegman and others have continued to write on Nussbaum versus Butler (1999-2000). The impact of *Gender Trouble*, however, goes beyond American critiques, for as Sabine Hark (2001) has shown, Butler remains extremely controversial among German feminists. The book was first published in German as *Das Unbehagen der Gerschlechter, 'Gender and Its Discontents'*—alluding to Freud's *Das Unbehagen der Kultur*, that is, *Civilization and Its Discontents*. As Hark observes, '[b]y omitting the English subtitle ['Feminism and the Subversion of Identity'], the editors of the Gender Studies Series at Suhrkamp Verlag disconnected Butler's work from feminist theory and practice' (Hark, 2001, p.95). Hark (2001) notes that *Gender Trouble* was available in German before any works of American queer theorists had been translated—naming the canon to include Michael Warner, Eve Sedgwick, Lauren Berlant, Robyn Wiegman, and Sue-Ellen Case. 'Hence, instead of critically engaging with the role sexuality plays in the construction of all sociosymbolic forms, especially in the construction of gender, Feminist Studies continued to neglect the inherent heterosexism of its theories' (Hark, 2001, p.89). The absence of queer theory from the German academy points to larger questions of the relationship between 'old-style' feminist historiography/activism and 'new-wave' theory. These issues are similar to the concerns found within the Anglo-American history of gender studies' emergence, even given the more visible queer theoretical presence.

Ultimately, Nussbaum argued against postmodern theory. Ironically, Lisa Duggan anticipated such a critique in an 1998 article subtitled 'Who's Afraid of Judith Butler?' Duggan wrote: '[a]n undercurrent of hostility and suspicion of queer theories emerges from the writing of a number of leftist feminists who attack

Theory as pretentious nonsense' (1998, pp.12-13). These critics:

> aim their attacks at a very amorphous target called 'postmodernism', 'deconstruction', or 'cultural studies' – all very different intellectual practices, and not all guilty as charged – or just designated as Theory, or personified as Judith Butler – whom many see as having an almost magical power to destroy progressive activism (Duggan, 1998, p.13).

Nussbaum criticizes Butler's position that 'there is no agent behind or prior to the social forces that produce the self' (Nussbaum, 1999b, p.41). For her, Butler's minimization of corporeal reality fails to give feminism what it needs: an awareness of and an agenda for the improvement of the material conditions and physical health of 'real' women. This is a practical argument. It is also a particularly essentialist one that is no longer fashionable in the humanities academy. In popular feminism, however, Nussbaum certainly spoke for a vast majority. It is not only outside the theory academy that Nussbaum's opinions may be taken seriously. Many gay and lesbian liberation groups consistently value the importance of essentialist identities in campaigning for increased social rights. Regulations against openly-gay boy scouts, sodomy laws, and same-sex partner benefits do not depend on theoretical arguments on the fluidity of identity. Rather, such legislation is based on assimilationist claims that 'we are just like you'.

Molly Anne Rothenberg and Joseph Valente have pointed out how visible displays of gender-bending, instead of liberating, have at times resulted in a backlash of homophobic response. Again, here is the question of theory versus practice. What happens when right-wing journalists want to highlight the most gender-bending or sexually-explicit individuals as representative of the 'modern homosexual'? Those examples may be the very persons that some lesbians and gays *do not* want shown to Middle America, lest their visibility distort perceptions of the diversity (or idealized white-bread homogeneity?) of the lesbian and gay population and thus 'reinforce stereotypes'. The publicness of gender in praxis, rather than theory, raises the question of audience, what Rothenberg and Valente name as the 'ultimate undecidability of the import, the irreducibly *social* import, of parodic gender citation' (Rothenberg and Valente, 1997, p.302, emphasis in original).

Gender performance in praxis rather than theory—as Marjorie Garber's *Vested Interests* (1992) demonstrates with crossdressing—is an absolutely public gesture. The culture of the 1990s offered many sites for willful play with gender identity in the capacity to make and re-make performances. If the most obvious is in the area of clothing—the waxing and waning in popularity of dressing 'like a boy' or 'like a girl'—the public space with the least amount of disclosure is cyberlife. To be in a chatroom, to instant-message, or to e-mail reveals nothing but words. So the human agency involved allows for the continued practice of self-presentation at its most basic form. If the cultural production of the 1990s emphasized the destabilization of categories of gender identity—from novels like Sarah Waters's 1999 *Tipping the Velvet*, about a crossdresser on the *fin-de-siècle* British stage to a 1994 film of Virginia Woolf's *Orlando* and depictions of what the *Diagnostic and Statistical Manual* might label 'gender identity disorder' in *Ma Vie en Rose* (1997) and *Boys Don't Cry* (1999)—identity as a fixed category in the popular mind still mattered.

Butler's theories of gender have implications for the personal, individual process of naming one's identity. If some youth have embraced the liberating possibilities of being queer, others who come out may prefer a more grounded definition of self. Julia Creet (1995) discusses the problem of coming out when the existence of lesbian/gay identity has been destabilized. She writes:

> Loss of an/other (which in Lacan's formulation of the 'mirror stage' is an idealized part of the self) allows for the differentiation of the self. But these are processes of an early age, of infancy and early childhood and though they may be good descriptions of the beginnings of the idea of a self, they do not get at the formulation of adolescent and adult sexual identities that are necessarily *political* and historical as well as psychic (Creet, 1995, p.188, emphasis in original).

Creet is concerned with the particular psychological event of one person's coming out. She concludes that identity is '"psychically entrenched play", as Butler points out, but, one must insist, physically and historically entrenched play also' (Creet, 1995, p.196).

How 'historically entrenched' is gender, and *Gender Trouble*? How do Butler's theories address the question of historical, cultural moments—as well as the issues of destabilized 'personal' identity that Creet raises? There has been much attention given to the visible presence of activism in the 1980s and 1990s in relation to AIDS and gay/lesbian rights, such as public performances by groups like ACT-UP and Queer Nation. In the spring of 2000, a play entitled *The Laramie Project* opened in New York. Moisés Kaufman's work concerns the gay hate-crime murder of Matthew Shepard. The national attention given to Shepard's death demonstrates an awareness in American culture of the dangerous power of public (re)presentations of gender identity—performativities. The popularity of this play, like the film *Boys Don't Cry*, whose star Hilary Swank won an Oscar for her performance as a gender-bending murder victim, indicates a commitment to human rights, or at least the prevention of violence.

Butler's work is intimately connected with these public events. The community implications of her theory are real, contrary to Nussbaum's critique. In the 1999 preface to *Gender Trouble*, Butler writes:

> [T]he face of theory has changed precisely through its cultural appropriations. There is a new venue for theory, necessarily impure, where it emerges in and as the very event of cultural translation. This is not the displacement of theory by historicism, nor a simple historicization of theory that exposes the contingent limits of its more generalizable claims. It is, rather, the emergence of theory at the site where cultural horizons meet,

where the demand for translation is acute and its promise of success, uncertain (Butler, 1999, p.ix).

This introduction is as much about writing history as reflecting on historicism. If *Gender Trouble* was intended 'to criticize a pervasive heterosexual assumption in feminist literary theory' (Butler, 1999, p. vii), Butler observes that it also:

> was produced not merely from the academy, but from convergent social movements of which I have been a part, and within the context of a lesbian and gay community on the east coast of the United States in which I lived for fourteen years prior to the writing of this book. Despite the dislocation of the subject that the text performs, there is a person here: I went to many meetings, bars, and marches and saw many kinds of genders, understood myself to be at the crossroads of some of them, and encountered sexuality at several of its cultural edges...At the same time that I was ensconced in the academy, I was also living a life outside those walls, and though *Gender Trouble* is an academic book, it began, for me, with a crossing-over, sitting on Rehoboth Beach, wondering whether I could link the different sides of my life (Butler, 1999, pp. xvi-xvii).

Hence there is a person behind the book; a subject self behind the words; an identity represented in the pictures of Judith Butler on the www.theory.org.uk website that glamorizes her next to (<click>) Foucault or at the Southern Oregon University website; a Judith Butler in relation to the *Judy!* fanzine of 1993 *Lingua Franca*.

The 1999 preface articulates Butler's political commitments with respect to her purely theoretical engagements: 'What continues to concern me most is...what will and will not constitute an intelligible life, and how do presumptions about normative gender and sexuality determine in advance what will qualify as the "human" and the "livable"' (Butler, 1999, p.xxii). She continues: 'If there is a positive normative task in *Gender Trouble*, it is to insist upon the extension of this legitimacy to bodies that have been regarded as false, unreal, and unintelligible' (Butler, 1999, p.xxiii). In a September 1998 *Lingua Franca* article on Butler's 1997 *The Psychic Life of Power* and *Excitable Speech*, Michael Levenson asks, 'Will the philosophy and the politics converge?' (Levenson, 1998, p.61). The answer here is yes. 'Her power has no neighborhood, no nation, no epoch. Subjects have no names, no particularity, no histories. There are no people here' (Levenson 1998, p.64). Again, in the 1999 preface, they are—and she is—present.

Hence history, both in theory and practice, surrounds Butler. If the 1990s contained Andrew Sullivans and Bruce Bawers, the decade also was shaped by Urvashi Vaids and Michael Warners. Lesbian/gay studies has seen not only the emergence of queer theory in the past quarter-century, but has also promoted more essentialist voices, such as Rictor Norton and the late John Boswell. In social activism, a hard-wired, fixed subject self remains most palatable—perhaps because it is most comprehensible—to a lay American culture. This does not mean that the slippage of identities exemplified by the performativity of gender should be neglected or that a heteronormative homosexuality need be advanced as the ideal. Indeed, it is evident that less-fixed articulations of gender are gaining understanding and appreciation in popular culture. Limits of disciplines seem crucial in this question as well, for the data-driven practice of certain historians versus the conceptualizations by theorists of language inevitably create different paradigms of identity. Do gender studies and queer theory reenact the marginalization of women that feminism has sought to address? At times they do. Nevertheless, as Beatrice Hanssen asserts in her essay on 'Whatever Happened To Feminist Theory':

> [W]e need to see the different feminisms as standing side-by-side, ready to acknowledge a minimal division of labor, with limited objectives and tasks, so that a so-called cultural feminism that demands the recognition of identity claims can cohabit with other branches – for example, those concerned more specifically with economic redistribution (Hanssen, 2001, p. 82).

Just as feminism can contain a Catharine MacKinnon and a Pat Califia, it can also benefit from both Butlerian destabilizations of identity and pragmatic calls to activism for the improvement of the material conditions of women around the world. *Gender Trouble* remains a disturbing, provocative, challenging, and radical book. In the text, Butler repeatedly cites Simone de Beauvoir (1973): that one is not born, but rather *becomes*, a woman. Likewise, one is not born but becomes Butlerian. Judith Butler's contribution to the fields of gender and sexuality studies, queer and contemporary feminist theories is nothing short of foundational.

References

Austin, J.L. (1962), *How to Do Things with Words*, Harvard University Press, Cambridge.

Berliner, A. (1997), *Ma Vie en Rose*, Columbia/Tristar.

Butler, Judith (1990, 1999), *Gender Trouble: Feminism and the Subversion of Identity*, Routledge, New York.

——— (1993a), *Bodies That Matter: On the Discursive Limits of 'Sex'*, Routledge, New York.

——— (1993b), 'Critically Queer', *GLQ*, vol. 1, no. 1, pp.17-32.

——— (1994), 'Gender as Performance: An interview with Judith Butler', in Peter Osborne and Lynne Segal, *Radical Philosophy*, vol. 67, pp.32-39.

Creet, Julia (1995), 'Anxieties of Identity: Coming Out and Coming Undone', in M. Dorenkamp and R. Henke (eds), *Negotiating Lesbian and Gay Subjects*, Routledge, New York, pp.179-199.

De Beauvoir, Simone (1973), *The Second Sex*, H. M. Parshley (trans.), Vintage, New York.

Duggan, Lisa (1998), 'Theory in Practice: The Theory Wars, or, Who's Afraid of Judith Butler', *Journal of Women's History*, vol. 10, no. 1, pp.9-19.

Garber, Marjorie (1992), *Vested Interests: Cross-Dressing and Cultural Anxiety*, Routledge,

New York.

Hanssen, B. (2001), 'Whatever Happened to Feminist Theory', in E. Bronfen and M. Kavka (eds), *Feminist Consequences: Theory for the New Century*, Columbia University Press, New York, pp.58-98.

Hark, Sabine (2001), 'Disputed Territory: Feminist Studies in Germany and Its Queer Discontents', *Amerikastudien/American Studies*, vol. 46, no. 1, pp.87-103.

Levenson, Michael (1998), 'Speaking to Power: The Performances of Judith Butler', *Lingua Franca* 8(6), 61-67.

Leverenz, David (1996), 'Tensions between Feminist and Gender Studies: The Capitalist Subtext', *Amerikastudien/American Studies*, vol. 41, no. 2, pp.217-237.

Nussbaum, Martha (1999a), 'Martha C. Nussbaum and Her Critics: An Exchange', *The New Republic*, 19 April, retrieved 1 February 2003 from http://www.tnr.com/archive/0499/041999/nussbaum041999.html

——— (1999b), 'The Professor of Parody: The Hip Defeatism of Judith Butler', *The New Republic*, vol. 220, 22 February, pp.37-45.

Peirce, K. (1999), *Boys Don't Cry*, Twentieth-Century Fox.

Rothenberg, Molly Anne and Valente, Joseph (1997), 'Performative Chic: The Fantasy of a Performative Politics', *College Literature*, vol. 24, no. 1, pp.295-304.

Sedgwick, Eve (1985), *Between Men: English Literature and Male Homosocial Desire*, Columbia University Press, New York.

——— (1990), *Epistemology of the Closet*, University of California Press, Berkeley.

——— (1993), 'Queer Performativity', *GLQ*, vol. 1, no. 1, pp.1-16.

Sedgwick, Eve and Parker, Andrew (eds) (1995), *Performativity and Performance*, Routledge, New York.

Waters, Sarah (1999), *Tipping the Velvet*, Riverhead, New York.

Wiegman, Robyn (1999-2000), 'Feminism, Institutionalism and the Idiom of Failure', *Differences*, vol. 11, no. 3, pp.107-136.

PART II
LANGUAGE, MELANCHOLIA, AND SUBJECTIVITY

Chapter 4

When All That is Solid Melts into Language

Vicki Kirby[1]

Cultural Constructionism and the Foreclosure of Matter

Judith Butler's contribution to contemporary criticism is remarkable for its insightful provocations across a broad range of subjects. This ability to intelligently engage so many different issues is enabled by Butler's appreciation that apparently unrelated intellectual endeavors may be bound and committed to the same conceptual foundations. The value of Butler's style of criticism then comes in her tenacious interrogation of the very ideas whose taken-for-granted necessity may tend to exempt them from inquiry. In the following discussion I want to explore what I take to be one of the most important examples of this foundational excavation in Butler's work, namely, her investigation of the ontology of language/discourse and related debates about cultural constructionism.[2]

In *Bodies That Matter: On the Discursive Limits of 'Sex'* (1993) Butler offers her most detailed explanation of why the language question carries such political importance.[3] She begins her introduction to a corporeal politics by foregrounding the contamination that surrounds and inevitably undermines the integrity of a pure referent, arguing that there can be no access to a pure materiality outside or before signification, and, by extension, no access to a pure materiality of bodily life that is separate from language.

---

[1] A version of this essay appeared as 'When All That is Solid Melts into Language: Judith Butler and the Question of Matter' in *International Journal of Sexuality and Gender Studies*, vol. 7, no. 4 (October 2002). Reprinted with permission of Kluwer Academic.

[2] For a more elaborated discussion, see 'Substance Abuse: Judith Butler', in V. Kirby, (1997), *Telling Flesh: The Substance of the Corporeal.*

[3] Judith Butler's reputation as a significant contemporary scholar in theoretical and political debate derives from an impressive body of work whose span of address includes philosophical argument, feminist and queer theory, and the broader reach of art and political commentary. She is perhaps best known as the author of *Gender Trouble: Feminism and the Subversion of Identity* (1990); *Bodies That Matter: On The Discursive Limits of 'Sex'* (1993); *Excitable Speech: A Politics of the Performative* (1997a); and *The Psychic Life of Power: Theories in Subjection* (1997b).

Materiality cannot be opposed to language nor simply reduced to it, because, although there is a necessary connection between these domains, they remain radically different nevertheless. By figuring an overlap between ideality and matter, or language and the body, Butler can deny that 'the body is simply linguistic stuff', while at the same time insisting that '[the body] bears on language all the time' (Butler, 1993, p.68). Butler recognizes the insidious agenda that accompanies the assumption that matter is the stuff of exteriority, because if it is positioned outside analysis, then its nature is beyond question. She therefore strives to infuse matter with a constitutive energy and efficacy that will disrupt the inevitability of this logic, for if matter can be rescued from its location as both prior and passive with regard to the notion of production, then conventional understandings of corporeality and matter are significantly problematized. Accordingly, the need to reconfigure materiality becomes the pivot of Butler's argument with the discourse of construction, a need made evident in the following passage:

> In an effort to displace the terms of this debate, I want to ask how and why 'materiality' has become a sign of irreducibility, that is, how is it that the materiality of sex is understood as that which only bears cultural constructions and, therefore, cannot be a construction?...Is materiality a site or surface that is excluded from the process of construction, as that through which and on which construction works? Is this perhaps an enabling or constitutive exclusion, one without which construction cannot operate? What occupies this site of unconstructed materiality? And what kinds of constructions are foreclosed through the figuring of this site as outside or beneath construction itself? (Butler, 1993, p.28).

The difficulty in Butler's project is considerable, for she has to juggle a critique of the discourse of construction while still defending its most basic tenets. Wanting to secure a hearing from those whose patience with constructionist arguments is close to exhaustion, she begins by offering some basic reassurances about her own approach. As the discourse of construction is routinely perceived as linguistic idealism, Butler willingly acknowledges the insistent reality of bodies. She grants what she calls 'the alleged facts of birth, aging, illness and death' and agrees that some minimal existence must be allowed 'sexually differentiated parts, activities, capacities, hormonal and chromosomal differences' and so on (Butler, 1993, p.10). The complication, however, is that to concede the existence of certain bodily facts is also to concede a certain interpretation of those facts. Butler conveys the conundrum by asking, '[i]s the discourse in and through which that concession occurs...not itself formative of the very phenomenon that it concedes?' (Butler, 1993, p.10).

Butler's critique is unavoidably convoluted because it targets two quite different expressions of the same argument, an argument that uncritically chooses sides in the materiality/ideality split. If we situate this debate within feminism, then those who claim to represent real women without recourse to inverted commas will assume they have access to the truth of (the) matter, as if the compelling facts of women's lives simply present themselves. According to this view, signifying practices are the mere vehicles of such truths, having no formative input of their own. And although they may well be regarded as inadequate, it is assumed nevertheless that they can be corrected. The other side of this debate stresses the constitutive force of signifying practices, concluding that we have no access to an extra-linguistic reality because the truth of its apparent facticity is produced in language. Butler is in obvious sympathy with this latter position but disagrees with the conclusion which often accompanies it, namely, that the question of matter has been disposed of. The insight that there is no outside of discourse can be styled as a moral injunction if the intricacies of this statement go unacknowledged. Although Butler agrees that we cannot access an 'outside language' that is unmediated by language, she does not take this to mean that we can, or should, try to censor any mention of this outside. Indeed, her thesis tries to emphasize that the received grammar of the debate will necessarily produce an exteriority, an outside discourse that is nevertheless internal to discourse. Given this, the task is not to deny or presume to exclude this materiality but to analyze the '*process of materialization that stabilizes over time to produce the effect of boundary, fixity, and surface we call matter*' (Butler, 1993, p.9, emphasis in original).

Butler's analysis of corporeality focuses on the repudiation of matter because its rejection is a key ingredient in subject formation and in the determination of the subject's perceived value. When difference from a valued norm is made synonymous with deficiency, any deviation can be moralized and pathologized as a flaw or fault. More importantly, the implicated nature and history of this valuation or 'othering' is then difficult to articulate and acknowledge. Butler explores the political aspects of this denigrating process, arguing that the mark of deficiency that attaches to certain bodies is made a convenient explanation for their abject status. The existence of these abject bodies is then considered beyond cultural intelligibility, beyond representation, and therefore outside the concerns of the democratic process. Refused entry into the domain of the fully human, these outcasts are then aligned with the unruly dangers of the natural, the brutish, and the animal; in other words, with the threat that is perceived to emanate from matter itself. Butler's goal is to disrupt the economy of this logic by asking, '[w]hat challenge does that excluded and abjected realm produce to a symbolic hegemony that might force a radical rearticulation of what qualifies as Bodies That Matter...?' (Butler, 1993, p.16).

Butler's argument is clearly complex in both aim and execution, and I am in agreement with the passion and commitment of its overall direction. Yet if we are persuaded by Butler that the foreclosure of matter must be contested, then evidence of this same gesture in her own work deserves attention. In order to explore those parts of Butler's analysis where she retreats from her own insights, much of my argument will need to resemble hers, and to even endorse the same theoretical commitments. This sense of mimicry that discovers my own argument inside Butler's is reminiscent of the way that Butler, in her turn, engages the discourse of construction. She is also committed to the very terms whose meaning she disputes. There is a reason why this mode of argumentation is parasitic, a re-animation of the host argument. If we concede that oppositional logic persists in the very act of its rejection (crudely put, 'I am opposed to oppositional logic'), then its terms are more effectively destabilized and reinscribed if we do not pretend to abandon them.

The 'Outside' of Language

Butler's discussion of the discourse of construction acknowledged the necessity of foreclosure, the inevitability of producing an 'outside' or 'beneath', a 'before' or 'beyond' language and discourse. In other words, Butler would not exempt herself from this same necessity. Her point, however, is that spatial and temporal separations between the ideal and matter are in fact internal to discourse, and the political assumptions that inform them are therefore open to contestation. If language and discourse are constitutive of lived reality, then the possibility of change is discovered in the internal and interminable movement *within* language. Thus, inasmuch as Butler's position is predicated upon the delimitation of this movement in language, it does not preclude the existence of an outside language that truly does exceed our perceptions and representations. Butler's aim is to remind us that the perception and representation of this outside, despite its convincing transparency, is always/already a language effect—a cultural production. Indeed, Butler's reliance on the overarching term 'culture' as an explanatory category that both locates and frames this shifting production makes the point.

Unfortunately, however, by privileging the term 'culture' in this way the identity and sexualized hierarchy between ideality and matter, culture and nature, and mind and body are surreptitiously reinstalled. Although Butler's strategy might be described as placing the second term under erasure so that the actual meat of the matter is rendered unknown, the effect is to actually expand the identity of the first term. In other words, if what we thought was nature is really culture in disguise, then culture usurps the explanatory role of nature as causal origin. Thus, instead of opening *both* terms to a different reading, Butler has drawn a separating line of clarification between them. Interestingly, her critique of separability *within* language is founded upon this grounding separation. According to Butler the unavoidable confusion between matter and its representation can be explained if we remember that, '[t]o return to matter requires that we return to matter as a *sign*...' (Butler, 1993, p.49, emphasis in original).

As the title *Bodies That Matter* makes clear, Butler's aim is to contest and expand 'the very meaning of what counts as a valued and valuable body in the world' (Butler, 1993, p.22). The argument that the body's substance is a sign rather than a fixed and prescriptive referent is furthered in the happy coincidence between the words 'matter' and 'materialize'. While these words evoke a *notion* of physical substance, these signs are also synonyms for 'meaning' and the larger semantic process of meaning making. As Butler describes it:

To speak within these classical contexts of *Bodies That Matter* is not an idle pun, for to be material means to materialize, where the principle of that materialization is precisely what 'matters' about that body, its very intelligibility. In this sense, to know the significance of something is to know how and why it matters, where 'to matter' means at once 'to materialize' and 'to mean' (Butler, 1993, p.32, emphasis in original).

Butler's reworking of the terms through which corporeality is conventionally comprehended certainly challenges their received meanings. However, it should now be apparent that the in-itself of matter, the substantive something that Butler's minimal, if qualified concession to hormonal and chromosomal differences acknowledges is not at all the object of her analysis.[4] Ironically perhaps, its absence is required in order for her thesis to have some purchase. Our sense of the materiality of matter, its palpability and physical insistence, is rendered unspeakable and unthinkable in Butler's account, for the only thing that can be known about it is that it exceeds representation. Beyond cultural intelligibility, the existence of this external stuff ensures that our understanding of an outside, inasmuch as it is discourse dependent, can only be the dissimulation of an outside that *appears* as matter.

Butler on Slavoj Zizek: How an 'Outside of Theory' Can Endorse an Exclusionary Politics

At this point it might prove helpful to follow Butler's engagement with the political theorist and cultural analyst Slavoj Zizek, because her assessment of his work's usefulness is also an assessment of his conceptualization of language. What we will see is that Butler's critique of Zizek, a critique with which I am largely in agreement, inadvertently endorses the very aspect of his work that she most vehemently disputes. An explanation of how this instance of unacknowledged yet inevitable repetition has come about will serve to illustrate why the notion 'sign' has actually sabotaged the most important insights in Butler's intervention.

In the chapter 'Arguing with the Real', Butler explores the uses and limits of psychoanalysis in Zizek's work with the aim of developing a more inclusive 'theory of political performatives and democratic contestation' (Butler, 1993,

---

[4] I do not have the space here to explicate a possible and productive connection between debates about the nature of the sign among cultural analysts and argument about the peculiar identity of the atom in quantum physics. On both sides of what convention might regard as this disciplinary nature/culture divide, the 'unit' of analysis is peculiarly comprehensive and ubiquitous, and inclusive of its 'other'. For an accessible introduction to some of the implications of this work in the sciences, see Paul Davies and John Gribbin (1991), *The Matter Myth: Beyond Chaos and Complexity*; David Bohm (1980), *Wholeness and the Implicate Order*; and Renée Weber with David Bohm (1982), 'The Enfolding-Unfolding Universe: A Conversation with David Bohm' in K. Wilbur (ed.), *The Holographic Paradigm*.

p.20). Butler challenges the reasoning whereby certain subjects are exiled outside the pale of humanity proper, as though they do not matter, by interrogating the way in which limits are determined and meanings asoribed. Taking the structure of the sign as an indication of how such limits and exclusions are produced, Butler investigates how the limit falls short of itself, that is, how it ultimately fails to secure its integrity or identity. As Butler argues that our world is a world of representation/language, her argument concentrates on the way that language 'materializes' its own limit and exteriority. According to Butler, a true separation from this 'constitutive outside' cannot be achieved because 'identity always requires precisely that which it cannot abide' (Butler, 1993, p.188). Butler's question is, '[h]ow might those ostensibly constitutive exclusions be rendered less permanent, more dynamic?' (Butler, 1993, p.189).

In Zizek's use of psychoanalysis Butler perceives a foundational commitment to a notion of the limit as prohibition and injunction. Although she agrees with Zizek that the subject emerges through a set of repudiations and foreclosures, she disputes the need to mark foreclosure as the real. For if the real is truly outside symbolization as Zizek, following Lacan, suggests, then we are left with the following dilemma: 'Consider the rhetorical difficulty of circumscribing within symbolic discourse the limits of what is and is not symbolizable' (Butler, 1993, p.190). The Lacanian notion of the real is the lack of lack, the plenitude before the mark or cut of difference that is language. This account of originary integrity, or fullness, is appropriated by the symbolic order (The Law of the Father). As a consequence, the cultural domain of language and re-presentation is perceived to be full and self-sufficient, whereas the corporeal or natural ground of existence that precedes language is understood in terms of deficiency; a lack or loss deemed feminine in its very essence. The effect of misrecognizing this difference as absence (I am what I am by dint of *not* being that), means that the limit of the symbolic order is figured as the threat of castration or loss. Given the labor of feminist critics over the years to explain and disrupt the inherent phallocentrism of Lacan's schema, it is not surprising that Butler is critical of Zizek's approving adoption of it. Butler comments on the implications of Zizek's commitment:

> Zizek argues that 'the Real is [language's] inherent limit, the unfathomable fold which prevents it from achieving its identity with itself. Therein consists the fundamental paradox of the relation between the Symbolic and the Real: the bar which separates them is *strictly internal to the Symbolic*'. In the explication of this 'bar', he continues, 'this is what Lacan means when he says that "Woman doesn't exist": Woman qua object is nothing but the materialization of a certain bar in the Symbolic universe...' (Butler, 1993, p.279, emphasis in original).

This conflation of woman with what is barred from existence, that is, with what falls short of full inclusion into the symbolic order, equates woman with evacuation, with the black hole of the unrepresentable and ineffable space of the real. As the political agenda endorsed by this reading is disastrous, Butler argues that the limit of the real cannot be exempted from interrogation. In the presumptive given-ness of the real's purported ahistorical endurance and universal application, a symbolic normativity of sexed subjectivity and sexuality is sanctioned. Butler uncovers pernicious implications in this commitment:

> That there are always constitutive exclusions that condition the possibility of provisionally fixing a name does not entail a necessary collapse of that constitutive outside with a notion of a lost referent, that 'bar' which is the law of castration, emblematized by the woman who does not exist. Such a view not only reifies women as the lost referent, that which cannot exist; and feminism, as the vain effort to resist that particular proclamation of the law...To call into question women as the privileged figure for 'the lost referent', however, is precisely to recast that description as a possible signification, and to open the term as a site for a more expansive rearticulation. (Butler, 1993, p.218).

Butler must rupture the bar that cuts presence from absence (lack), and language from what is considered prior to, or not language, in order to open the possibility of a revaluation of different subjects. In other words, she must engage the mode of production of these determinations, the hidden indebtedness to 'the feminine' whose disavowal has rendered it bankrupt. Butler explores the metaphysics of presence that opposes identity to difference as presence to absence, with the aim of refiguring difference as a generative force within whose transformational energies the sense of a fixed identity (as presence to self) is radically destabilized.

In order to achieve this, and despite her criticisms of Zizek's use of psychoanalysis, Butler finds his discussion of 'political signifiers' particularly useful to this project. Zizek argues that political signifiers such as 'woman' should not be regarded as descriptive designations of subject positions because they do not represent pre-given constituencies. Butler explains why Zizek's qualification is an important one:

> No signifier can be radically representative, for every signifier is the site of a perpetual *méconnaisance*; it produces the expectation of a unity, a full and final recognition that can never be achieved. Paradoxically, the failure of such signifiers...fully to describe the constituency they name is precisely what constitutes these signifiers as sites of phantasmatic investment and discursive rearticulation. It is what opens the signifier to new meanings and new possibilities for political resignification. It is this open ended and performative function of the signifier that seems to me to be crucial to a radical democratic notion of futurity. (Butler, 1993, p.191).

Butler is taken by the suggestion that political signifiers can be sites of mobilization and contestation, identificatory anchors whose constitutive force is transformational. Via Zizek, then, Butler is able to rupture the fixed identity of the signifier and to insist that it is constantly mutating and therefore constitutionally incapable of erecting a secure barrier against exteriority. If women and other socially abjected subjects are themselves subjected to/through these same significatory transformations, then their existence and its significance must be determined *within* the symbolic order. Unfortunately, Zizek's reading of the bar as an absolute prohibition, as if the cut of castration is a definitive fact, reaffirms an 'outside discourse' in derelict terms of trauma and castration. By appropriating Lacan's notion of the real to explain this foreclosure, Zizek actually endorses the inevitability of this violent inheritance of abject subject formation. In view of this, Butler's intervention is important because it illustrates that the bar is not an absolute barrier but an *attempt* to bar or draw a line. The installation of the bar as an absolute frame achieves *the effect* of both discovering and repudiating that outside as inherently deficient and *naturally* base.

By interrogating the foundation, or what is supposedly 'given' as the indifferent ground of valuation, and by discovering that it is forged from the same political determinations as other significatory practices, Butler is able to dispense with the foreclosure of the real entirely. This strategy is surely reasonable enough when considered against Zizek's equation of difference with absence. However, inasmuch as Butler's theoretical approach continues to rely upon a notion of absence in other places in her argument, it is not surprising that the very same political problems in Zizek's work inevitably reappear in Butler's. For example, we see this in Butler's elaboration of how the significatory energy of transformation and desire is received by 'empty signs which come to bear phantasmatic investments of various kinds' (Butler, 1993, p.191). We are left to wonder about the nature of this significatory support in the body of the sign. It bears phantasmatic projections that form the constantly changing ground of meaning and legibility. Yet the sign's existence is surely compromised by an internal emptiness that nevertheless possesses the functional capacity to receive. What can it mean to describe phantasmatic projections in terms of emptiness, as if the body of the sign bears nothing? If these projections are also significations, as Butler suggests, then why is the differential of giving and receiving understood through presence and absence, value and lack, that mirrors a phallocentric logic? How is the difference of phantasmatic projections translated into anything given their apparent lack of identity, their non-existence?

Butler's Own Prohibition: The Commitment to the Sign

Despite Butler's explicit attempt to avoid Zizek's conflation of woman with absence, her reliance upon the sign dooms her to repeat this logic in a different form. If we return to the Saussurean sign and to the orthodoxies of its psychoanalytic interpretation in much cultural criticism, we see that the bar of prohibition remains foundational to this re-articulation.[5] Quite simply, the bar marks off the cultural order (glossed as 'language') as an identifiable and

---

[5] Although Butler is aware of the following work, describing it as 'a reading of Lacan which argues that prohibition or, more precisely, the bar is foundational' (Butler, 1993, p.268), she does not explore its implications for her own position. See Jean-Luc Nancy and Philippe Lacoue-Labarthe (1992), *The Title of the Letter: A Reading of Lacan*.

delimitable object of study. I will try to be as precise as I can about what is at stake in the maintenance of this reading. I am not suggesting that the bar of difference can simply be overcome or put aside. If this could be done it would reinforce the notion of difference as something superfluous; an extraneous supplement whose absence would not be missed. The problem with the Lacanian understanding of the sign is that the identity of the bar itself is completely barred from scrutiny (and here I am making a similar point to Butler's when she questions the exemption of the real from analysis). Unified, undifferentiated, and therefore utterly impermeable, the bar represents pure prohibition. Castration is absolute. Thus the bar or limit becomes a guarantee of property that encloses the concept sign within the domain of language. By extension, it also contains the intent of the sign, however wayward, within the domain of signification or meaning.

Butler's faith in the conceptual topography of the sign and its expression through presence and absence must inevitably hit up against a difference deemed to be *absolutely exterior* to culture/language. In sum, then, Butler's interrogation of the bar and its abjecting results, merely relocates the cut of prohibition rather than calling foreclosure and absence itself into question. In the assumption that the integrity of the bar is itself barred from scrutiny the bar's identity is reified as pure negativity. The bar of prohibition *internal* to the sign is therefore banished only to re-emerge as the sign's defining *outer limit*, the separating barrier between language and what is not language. The bar now surrounds the sign and protects its internal content, the domain of culture (language), from the threat of nature unveiled. It is important to appreciate that the bar that is internal to the sign represents the threat of castration, that is, the threat to the wholeness and autonomy of man's identity. However, the exterior limit of the sign in its enlarged identity as the language system (culture) represents the threat to the identity of humanity itself once its abjected exiles have been properly recognized as meaningfully human. On the other side of this line of defense lies an unspeakable threat—the body of nature, the substance of radical alterity.

If we use this reading of the bar or prohibition as an insight into how we might think of the law, we see that by unifying the law in this way we render resistance as a reactive and fairly futile response to the instrumental force of power as negation. Butler makes this very same point in her criticism of the Lacanian, or perhaps more accurately here, the Kristevan scheme that separates the Imaginary from the Symbolic registers. Butler queries:

...[D]oes this view of resistance fail to consider the status of the symbolic as immutable law? And would the mutation of that law call into question not only the compulsory heterosexuality attributed to the symbolic, but also the stability and discreteness of the distinction between symbolic and imaginary registers within the Lacanian scheme? It seems crucial to question whether resistance to an immutable law is *sufficient* as a political contestation of compulsory heterosexuality, where this restriction is safely restricted to the imaginary and therefore restrained from entering into the structure of the symbolic itself...feminine resistance is [thereby] both valorized in its specificity and reassuringly disempowered...By accepting the radical divide between symbolic and imaginary, the terms of feminist resistance reconstitute sexually differentiated and hierarchized 'separate spheres'....[R]esistance...cannot enter into the dynamic by which the symbolic reiterates its power and thereby alters the structural sexism and homophobia of its sexual demands (Butler, 1993, p.106, emphasis in original).

My argument with Butler draws upon her own insight here in the hope of extending its implications. By contesting the nature of the division between the domain of language as the law of the symbolic, and the domain of the imaginary as the pre- or proto-linguistic, Butler successfully undermines several assumptions, namely, the straightforward identity and integrity of the symbolic order; the integrity of the self-present male subject; and the marginalization and even erasure of women and other denigrated subjects in this system of identity formation. However, Butler conceives the power of the law as the power to name, to assign and to delimit, so that the very act of naming is considered a violence of sorts. As a consequence, the law itself appears as a unified force, just as the name is rendered coherent. Yet this notion of violence ignores an interesting ambiguity that resides at the heart of the word 'violence', for the force of rupturing and breaching involves both destruction and creation.

By reading power's purpose in terms of negation, prevention, constraint, and prohibition, Butler is unable to consider the possibility, indeed the inevitability, that a political rearticulation happens *within* the law or *within* the name itself. Unable to consider such an outcome, Butler is forced to locate hope for change in the signifer's historicity, that is, in the necessary repetition of a name. Butler reminds us that hegemonic norms require maintenance: the law must be laid down again and again. And this constant reinvocation of the law is likened to a form of speech act, suggesting that '[d]iscursive performativity appears to produce that which it names, to enact its own referent, to name and to do, to name and to make' (Butler, 1993, p.107). Butler takes the apparent closure in this tautological reflex as proof that the legitimacy of discursive authority is a fiction. It cannot ground itself in an original authority because the act of citation, the repetitive difference that is language, is a practice of perpetual deferral to a source now lost or absent:

> ...it is precisely through the infinite deferral of authority to an irrecoverable past that authority itself is constituted. That deferral is the repeated act by which legitimation occurs. The pointing to a ground which is never recovered becomes authority's groundless ground. (Butler, 1993, p.108).

Acknowledging Derrida's complication of the notion of repetition, however, Butler explains that a deconstructive *iterability* disrupts the sense of repetition that assumes a series of separate moments in time, and she goes on to explain why a Foucauldian sense of discourse and power will not sit comfortably with Derridean *iterability*. As Butler herself has noted, a deconstructive reading would suggest that repetition inheres even within an apparently isolated act or event. And further to this, Derridean 'textuality' cannot be subsumed to the Foucauldian understanding of 'the discursive', with its presumptions about social regulation and social possibilities. What emerges from a Derridean reading then is that there is never a simple failure, or absence, of production. Any and every 'act' is, in a sense, utterly efficacious: there is no outside of text, no absence of writing, and no lack of differentiating.

Although this may seem like a finicky point, the implications are considerable. Butler's reading assumes that there once was a definitive origin, a discrete entity quite separate from its re-presentation in language/discourse. It follows from this that language, inasmuch as it is perceived as a second order *construct* or *substitute* for something now lost, founds its very identity on the difference of this separating interval. Put simply, Butler's argument must assume that a now inaccessible reality precedes its re-presentation, a re-presentation whose status is that of fantasy and fiction, the phantasmatic field of *cultural* interpolation. Butler's insistence that these fictions are nevertheless powerful because they 'real-ize' effects reverses the logic of causality but does not contest its linear discriminatons of difference as separability. It is this linear sense of temporality and its corollary concepts of causality (efficacy here) that are quite confounded within the space/time complexity of Derridean *iterability*. As Butler herself concedes, a 'moment' is an emergence *within* differentiation that can have no exteriority.

The Political Implications of Founding an Explanatory Model on Absence

The relevance of this for re-reading power becomes clear if we return to Zizek's notion of 'political signifiers'. Zizek argued that signification should not be given the status of description for there is a permanent recalcitrance, or failure of fit, between the referent and symbolization. This gap, which implicitly identifies and contains difference, explains why Zizek might determine that the descriptive fact of the referent is more accurately understood as a phantasmatic construct, the desired product of hegemonic structures that are open to contestation. Endorsing this view, Butler emphasizes that political possibility is actually generated from the discrepancy between language and the actuality of the referent. As she explains here with specific reference to the signifier 'woman', '[t]hat the category ["women"] can never be descriptive is the very condition of its political efficacy' (Butler, 1993, p.221).

Butler eschews description because it is a gloss for what is purportedly timeless, essential, and outside the performative iteration, or alteration, of language. However, this founding exemption ties Butler once again to a notion of difference as substitution, wherein difference is read as the sign of something else, of some originary loss or absence. Loss and absence are therefore essential to Butler's reading, for she locates the problematic nature of identity in the constitutive *failure* to recuperate this loss. Because of the inevitable *incompleteness* of identity in this assumption, both Butler and Zizek understand any appeal to integrity in terms of *phantasmatic illusion*. However, against this psychoanalytic reading, the emergence and transformation of identity within Derridean iterability is not explained by an originary absence whose result is an inevitable impairment.

Butler is fully aware of the unfortunate consequences of an oedipal logic that aligns and fixes sexual positionalities. As her discussion of Zizek reveals, if the pre-discursive is read through the logic of lack, then a sexualized and racialized battery of incontestable prescriptions seems to be endorsed by nature itself. Butler is adamant on this point, and her argument is most persuasive when she maintains its importance. For example, in her discussion of Chantal Mouffe and Ernesto Laclau's theorization of radical democracy and its relevance to Zizek's thesis, Butler makes another assault on the insidious equation of difference with lack. She questions the compatibility between the Derridean logic of the supplement and the Lacanian notion of lack that these theorists assume. Mouffe and Laclau find the promise of an open-ended political futurity in the constitutive antagonisms and contingencies of identity formation. Making a similar point to Zizek's, they explain the possibility of renegotiating identity in terms of an inevitable failure of ideological structures to fix themselves as fact. Butler interprets Laclau to locate these contingencies and antagonisms within social relations which he ambiguously describes as being '"outside" of posited identity' (Butler, 1993, p.194). Given this, Butler's question concerns the status of Laclau's statements about 'the antagonizing force [that] *denies* my identity in the strictest sense' (Butler, 1993, p.194, emphasis in original). Butler asks:

> The question, then, is whether the contingency or negativity enacted by such antagonizing forces is part of social relations or whether it belongs to the real, the foreclosure of which constitutes the very possibility of the social and the symbolic. In the above, it seems, Laclau links the notions of antagonism and contingency to that *within* the social field which exceeds any positive or objectivist determination or prediction, a supplement within the social but 'outside' of posited identity (Butler, 1993, p.194, emphasis in original).

As we have seen, Butler criticizes Zizek for locating this constitutive antagonism and contingency outside the social as such, in the Lacanian real, and we can see why she might prefer Laclau's account. However, as Laclau also explains the production of identifications in terms of 'lack' while at the same time drawing on the Derridean notion of supplementarity, Butler inquires, '[i]f the "outside" is, as Laclau insists, linked to the Derridean logic of the supplement... then it is unclear what moves must be taken to make it compatible with the Lacanian notion of the "lack"...' (Butler, 1993, p.194). Butler's quandary is explained by her reading of the Derridean supplement as an *internalized* exteriority, one whose convoluted "attachments" return it to the realm of social reinscription.

Yet despite Butler's move here, and it is an important one, her commitment to a notion of lack or absence means that her question concerns the appropriateness of its location—either inside or outside the social. The identity of lack *as such* is not in question here. Consequently, her dilemma regarding the compatibility of the Derridean notion of supplementarity with the Lacanian notion of lack is based on the erroneous assumption that Derridean supplementarity never really leaves the social world. Although Derridean supplementarity is indeed about an internalized exteriority, Butler's need to locate reinscription and political possibility within an interiority that she names 'the social', as if the identity of 'the social' and the efficacy of reinscription could be contained, is precisely the problem.

The complexity of identity formation that Butler concedes to a word, to an individual, or to a particular social milieu, is not granted to 'entities' such as 'language', 'the social', or 'the cultural'. Although forces rupture and differentiate the respective interiorities of these identities, it seems that their identifying borders remain immune to this same disturbance. Butler conceptualizes the limit of these entities as separate supplements to those entities, supplements that are not themselves open to the logic of supplementarity. By foreclosing the domain of differentiation, productivity, and mutability in this way, Butler builds her critique of difference (as lack) upon the very logic that she contests; the logic that equates difference with absence. Put simply, the substance of nature and whatever else culture exteriorizes as properly outside itself, is rendered utterly absent by being placed under erasure.

A Derridean Intervention into the Conflation of Language with Culture

But what difference might the Derridean logic of the supplement effect upon this way of thinking? Is it inevitable that *différance* returns to lack, if not immediately, then in the final instance, as Butler assumes? There would be few scholars familiar with contemporary theoretical work on language who would be surprised to hear that Derridean *iterability*, or here, *supplementarity*, refigures temporality and spatiality such that our understanding of terms such as 'description', 'essence', 'origin' and 'ground' are riven within the differential of alter-ing. To put this another way, all of these terms assume a defined spatial and/or temporal locatability and fixity that Derrida's work disperses and makes peculiarly plastic. Given the assault of deconstruction upon foundational notions such as these, it is not much of a stretch to include the notions 'body' and 'matter' within the orbit of these interrogations. Yet does this assault involve corporeal substance?

As we have seen, Butler deploys the term 'matter' rather than 'substance' because the former is a synonym for significance/signification. To think of substance is to think of the very meat of carnality that is born and buried, the stuff of decay that seems indifferent to semiosis. Substance evokes the soil of groundedness itself; the concrete and tangible thing-ness of things. To avoid using the word 'substance' is surely a careful decision on the part of a writer whose stated interest is the materiality of bodies. What risk, then, is Butler's sustained avoidance of this term trying to minimize?

The concept 'substance' has a long history of philosophical engagement that certainly complicates any commonsense assumptions, assumptions that perceive the body's complex interior densities as self-evidently (made of) 'substance'. However, acknowledging complication is not necessarily achieved by dispensing with commonsense perceptions. Indeed, indifference to such perceptions fails to recognize that they are necessary ingredients in the very complication that should concern us. Interestingly, Butler's engagement with corporeality ignores this vulgar, lived sense of bodily substance as the sheer insistence and weight of the body's interiority. Instead, the body's surface becomes the site of engagement.

Butler reads the body as a shifting text, or discursive effect, such that the body's perceived outline is constantly changing. Butler regards these transformations of the body's morphology as a form of reckoning that 'contours the bodily matter of sex' and 'set[s] the limits to bodily intelligibility' (Butler, 1993, p.17). Butler draws on the work of several theorists in order to elaborate this notion of a contour/threshold, and renders it in terms of interpellation (Althusser), enunciation (Benveniste), body imago (Lacan), and inscription (Foucault). However, if her intention is to invest the surface/threshold itself with activity, Butler stops short of going all the way. Her intervention is limited to the surface of the surface because she assumes that the differentiation of contour-ing is given by/in signification. As signification is the play of form, substance is excluded from this activity. To question the identity of form in some depth by thinking *through* the body, that is, through the surfaces within surfaces which couple exteriority within interiority, does more than testify to the vagaries of signification.

To put this another way, *différance* is not the energy of attempted restitution propelled by its own failure, as the Lacanian model of difference assumes. According to Lacan, the break from the origin can never be repaired because the origin is irretrievably lost, such that substitution is the only consolation. Nor is *différance* a force whose 'productivity' or outcome can be confined to the model of power, discourse, or subject, which informs the work of Michel Foucault. And yet, although *différance* suggests something that is not at all compatible with the work of Foucault and Lacan, inasmuch as *différance* is not defined by exemption, it also embraces and inhabits these differences too. *Différance* is 'becoming itself'. It is a writing and reading whose many expressions include the workings of bio-logy in a conversation that reconfigures what and where 'intelligibility' is. If the logic of morphing is the complex mutation of limit-ing, then this re-articulation cannot be restricted to the polysemous possibilities and constraints of what is conventionally understood as language.[6]

Butler's commitment to an inarticulate lost origin denies the possibility that nature scribbles, or that flesh reads. For if nature is literate, then the question 'what is language', or more scandalously, 'who reads?', fractures the Cartesian subject to its very foundation.[7] The fiction of the self-conscious individual fully aware of his

---

[6] Although Rupert Sheldrake's argument is a far cry from this discussion and certainly has its own share of problems, it nevertheless opens the question of morphology in suggestive and tantalizing directions. See Rupert Sheldrake (1981), *A New Science of Life: the Hypothesis of Formative Causation*; and (1988), *The Presence of the Past: Morphic Resonance and the Habits of Nature*.

[7] In a recent interview with Judith Butler, I pressed this point by suggesting that Derrida's 'general writing' dislodges our assumption that writing is a human invention, a technology whose provenance marks the very definition of the cultural order. Her response was to

intentions and agent of his own destiny is quite clearly displaced here. However, if the humanist subject comes undone in the face of nature's literacy, this unraveling does not stop with the critique of humanism. Anti-humanism acknowledges a subject caught in the vicissitudes of language and constitutionally incapable of knowing himself. Yet the range or extent of this decentering is limited to the complexities of the cultural order and to its psychical and social determinations.

Much poststructural and postmodern criticism specifically addresses the complexities of language and discourse as expressions of power. If, however, the identity of culture and language is opened to an outside that reads, an outside that writes, then the identity of power is not synonymous with circumscription. Clearly, this has serious implications for Butler's thesis. Butler conceives power as 'constitutive constraint', coupling Foucault's notion of power as production with a poststructural attention to power as valuation. As we have seen, Butler wants to contest the black and white of abjection; the engendering of exclusions that work to guarantee that a whole(some) subject is different and separate from what is denigrated as deficient. She wants to contest the economy that invests a proper subject with the belief that he is not made of the same devalued matter, indeed, not made of matter at all. Homophobia, racism, and sexism feed on this conceptual legacy, a legacy that is corporeal and substantive because it is wrought with/in flesh.

Butler outlines the need for sustained contestation of the nature/culture division and why it matters, why this questioning is itself a political practice and why intellectual work at this interface will always be necessary. My reading of Butler's work has been an attempt to acknowledge this necessity and in a way that endorses many of her own perceptions. Given this, it seems appropriate to conclude with Butler's own representation of the importance of such contestatory readings of this problematic:

> The relation between culture and nature presupposed by some models of gender 'construction' implies a culture or an agency of the social which acts upon a nature, which is itself presupposed as a passive surface, outside the social and yet its necessary counterpart. One question that feminists have raised, then, is whether the discourse which figures the action of construction as a kind of imprinting or imposition is not tacitly masculinist, whereas the figure of the passive surface, awaiting that penetrating

---

reiterate that writing is a *model* or *metaphor* of the world, a human representation that should not be confused with the world itself. According to Butler, this model of life is by definition the *sign* of an inevitable failure of fit, a sign that the world is absent and elsewhere. There are two points to note here. Clearly, for Butler the world itself cannot *be* information. And related to the first point, human *being* is not *of* the world but rather *in* the world. By assuming that the technology of writing defines the human condition as something outside the world, as something that is not itself the production effect of a much larger field of forces (writings) than the conventional understanding of culture can concede, Butler reinstates the very problem that her intervention is meant to contest, namely, the political prescriptions of the nature/culture division. See the interview in Chapter 2 of this collection.

act whereby meaning is endowed, is not tacitly or—perhaps—quite obviously feminine. Is sex to gender as feminine is to masculine?

...This rethinking [of nature] also calls into question the model of construction whereby the social unilaterally acts on the natural and invests it with its parameters and its meanings. Indeed, as much as the radical distinction between sex and gender has been crucial to the de Beauvoirean version of feminism, it has come under criticism in more recent years for degrading the natural as that which is 'before' intelligibility, in need of the mark, if not the mar, of the social to signify, to be known, to acquire value. (Butler, 1993, pp.4-5).

If we agree with Butler that there are unfortunate and enduring political implications in this last assumption and that we need to dispute its logic, then it is imperative that we question Butler's insistence, a form of reassurance, that 'to return to matter requires that we return to matter as a *sign*' (Butler, 1993, p.49, emphasis in original). The enclosure of the sign's identity, if accepted, will not provide a fertile and generative departure point for thinking difference. However, by putting the sign into question and exploring and exploding identity on the atomic level of its constitution, matter may well become a curious subject.

References

Bohm, David (1980), *Wholeness and the Implicate Order*, Routledge and Kegan Paul, London.

Butler, Judith (1990), *Gender Trouble: Feminism and the Subversion of Identity*, Routledge, London and New York.

——— (1993), *Bodies That Matter: On The Discursive Limits of 'Sex'*, Routledge, London and New York.

——— (1997a), *Excitable Speech: A Politics of the Performative*, Routledge, New York.

——— (1997b), *The Psychic Life of Power: Theories in Subjection*, Stanford University Press, Stanford.

Davies, Paul and Gribbin, John (1991), *The Matter Myth: Beyond Chaos and Complexity*, Penguin, London.

Kirby, Vicki (1997), *Telling Flesh: The Substance of the Corporeal*, Routledge, New York.

Nancy, Jean-Luc and Lacoue-Labarthe, Philippe (1992), *The Title of the Letter: A Reading of Lacan*, David Pettigrew and Francois Raffoul (trans.), SUNY Press, Albany.

Sheldrake, Rupert (1981), *A New Science of Life: the Hypothesis of Formative Causation*, J.P. Tarcher, Los Angeles.

——— (1988), *The Presence of the Past: Morphic Resonance and the Habits of Nature*, Collins, London.

Weber, Renée, with Bohm, David (1982), 'The Enfolding-Unfolding Universe: A Conversation with David Bohm', in K. Wilbur (ed.), *The Holographic Paradigm*, New Science Library, Boston and London.

Chapter 5

Judith Butler and the Images of Theory

Mena Mitrano

Before Performativity: Snapshots from Mirò and de Kooning

There is a scene in Todd Haynes's homage to Douglas Sirk, *Far from Heaven* (2002), in which Raymond, the character of the African American gardener in Hartford, Connecticut, and Cathy, the character of a white housewife trapped in a conventional marriage, stand in front of Mirò's *Nightingale's Song* (1940).[1] 'It moves me', is all that Cathy can say to describe the effect of the image. She admits to the vagueness of her impression, but Raymond hurries to agree that that is exactly what abstract art does—it moves. For that reason, he explains, abstract art picked up where sacred art had left off. The scene captures the cultural situation of the 1950s: two people subjected to norms that decide how they can live and whom they can love, and for whom the future is no vista of cultural possibilities. For a while, in front of Mirò's nightingale something snaps, as if a motion were heard that does not change the norms and the arrangement of Cathy and Raymond's separate worlds of prohibited attachments but ends up weakening a bit the stomp of conventions and norms, temporarily undermining their authority. In the brief moment of the vague 'it moves me', social norms lose their hold a little, a slight shift occurs, a jolting is registered: nothing external; everything happens inside the spectator. There occurs 'a dramatic and contingent construction of meaning' (Butler, 1990, p.139), that makes the authenticity, the very reality of the conventions to which the two characters are subjected through and through seem preposterous, long enough for a shift of point of views to take place. What had been steely certainties are now consigned to the transitoriness of cultural constructions. Eventually, it becomes obvious that the history that has enforced those constricting certainties is the same history that will demolish them. What is at stake in Mirò's image is a refusal of forced immobility. Such refusal strikes us even more if compared to the fateful inaction of Kafka's man stranded before the law. Mirò's aesthetic abstraction seems to respond to Kafka's portrait of a cruel moral abstractionism. If the latter surges from the void of an absent law lodged inside the subject as a self-imposed injunction to prostrate before the gatekeeper, to

---

[1] Joan Mirò, *The Nightingale's Song at Midnight and the Morning Rain*, Perls Galleries, New York. A print of the painting may be found in Mink, 1994, p.69 and also on the web at abcgallery.com/m/miro/miro-4.html.

be starved by power relations, Miró's nightingale, by comparison, sings to the viewer of a green thought on a summer midnight. Even in his biography, Miró tried to depart from Kafka's imago of the modern European subject: he decided that the only guardian who could starve him would be himself. 'Where did I find the ideas for my paintings? I used to get back late at night to my atelier in rue Blomet and go to bed at times without a bit of food in my stomach. I saw things and annotated them in my sketchbook. I saw forms on the ceiling...' (Miró, in Mink, 1994, p.41, my translation). The energizing autonomy of his world of symbols comes from Miró's rejection of thresholds to cross as well as permissions or prerequisites to enter. His imagination moves the subject's stance beyond Kafka's ferocious anxiety of thresholds, declaring the moral abstractionism of the law, with its injunction to prostrate *before*, a bad dream.

Kafka's subject is closer to Freud's. It shares with Freud's a 'moral anxiety' (or anxiety of conscience—*Gewissenangst*) before an 'internal' authority, as 'imperative' as it is 'categorical' (Borch-Jacobsen, 1992, p.30). Kafka's man is kept before the gate of the law by the voice of conscience that Freud called ego ideal. In *Group Psychology* in place of the ego ideal he set up the Chief and painted the picture of a humanity fascinated by subjection, eager to prostrate before Chiefs, especially if they have been murdered or are absent. Like Freud's subject, Kafka's man asserts the summons of an abstract moral authority over political partaking. As Borch-Jacobsen writes, Freud's law rises from the void of its own absence (Borch-Jacobsen, 1992, p.31). This means that human society arises from an anxiety 'about nothing, about no one. It is when the powerful male is dead and no longer there to prohibit anything at all, in a perfectly disconcerting way, there emerge the alterity of duty and the debt of guilt, both of them all the more unbearable' (Borch-Jacobsen, 1992, p.31). As Borch-Jacobsen proceeds to ask: How does it happen that if Chiefs have been killed we are so eager to reinstate them at the center of society? Although his examples are the socialist humanity prostrate before Stalin, or the Volk 'fasciated' behind its Führer, obviously the list could easily be extended to our time.

The abstractionism of the law consists in its claim to the depth of an unbearable reservoir in the subject, a seemingly unchangeable, intractable void, which since Freud has engaged visual and verbal arts and critical thought alike. It was because Miró's world of symbols crossed the Atlantic that it could infect with its energy artists like de Kooning and the action painters. These, in their turn, formalized the cultural transition from Kafka's emblematic scene of subjection to a form of gestural language able to convey the sense of a passage from cultural immobility to the exhilaration of motion, emblematized by the activism of the hand.[2] Willem de Kooning was the first to achieve a sense of transition from Old World immobility to New World activism. His *Woman* series effectively scratches the archaic

---

[2] In 1941 a Miró exhibition was held at the Museum of Modern Art in New York. It exerted a lasting influence on the painters of the New York School, among them Willem de Kooning. *Song of the Nightingale*, however, is not listed among the paintings on show. Jenny Tobias, MOMA librarian, e-mail to the author, 20 June 2003.

immobility of Kafka's melancholy man, offering his viewer the relief of laughter at what once was feared as subjection.

De Kooning's *Woman I* (1950-1952) features a coarse sibyl in a domineering squat: she is the icon of a frightening, atavistic immobility.[3] It has also been described as a 'bad dream of nurture denied rendered with immense pictorial verve—imposing and commonplace and full of a power which flows from the slashing brushstrokes into the body' (Hughes, 1997, p.479). In *Woman II* (1952) there is a reprise of the paralysing female presence. Here, the aggressive fixity that emanates from her predecessor is spelled as something that has less to do with gender than cultural geography. It has not escaped art observers that de Kooning's *Woman II*, intended as a caricature of local movie stars, is actually pervaded by 'an Old World horror of empty space' (Janson and Janson, 2001, p.814). References to popular culture serve to mitigate the power of the female presence's injunction to immobility, just as in *Woman I*, kitsch is invoked to disfigure the atavism of a privative imperative that still stuck to de Kooning from his native Europe after he jumped ship in New York. De Kooning's images strive to move beyond the impasse of an impoverishing fear, of a failing nurture. From this light response to an Old World originary fear of the void comes de Kooning's 'tonic vitality' (Janson and Janson, 2001, p.814). The *Woman* series may belong to the painter's declining phase, but one hears in them an exhilarating sound, as if a door were closing with a loud finality, slamming on the presumption of outdated bonds, of ideas that lay claim to a form of a-historical authority by keeping their subjects in pain (the denied nurture in *Woman I*). The viewer of these images has the impression of someone getting out of a picture and breathing in fresh air. The images convey the sense of an awakening from an old subjection that, under the action of colors and brushstrokes, turns out to be...just a bad dream. The abstract gesture in de Kooning's expressionism has everything to do with such awakening, with the impression of a burden dropped, of a levity achieved. He makes way for a new dynamic composition in which energies are transmitted immediately on the canvas by the hand's gesture. Conceptually, the passage from fear to action is made possible by the working through of the tie to the European void, that is to say, to the abstract anxiety of the law theorized by Freud, to the threshold immortalized by Kafka, in brief to the scene of a subject before the law.[4]

---

[3] A print of *Woman I* may be seen in Hughes, 1997, p.478. The painting itself is in the Museum of Modern Art.

[4] Art historian Giulio Carlo Argan discusses de Kooning in a chapter titled 'La crisi dell'arte come "scienza europea"'. He argues that when in the 1940s the US began to replace Europe as the world's cultural center, this geographical move corresponded to a conceptual turn from the static world of Freudian anxiety to action painting. For Argan, Gorky and de Kooning stand out as the translators of the visual language of Europe, which becomes a new reinvented sign system. Although morphologically similar to the European one, the new system had a different semiotic thrust. See Argan, 1989, p.482.

Figure 1: De Kooning, Willem, *Woman II* (1952). Oil on canvas, 149.9 x 109.3 cm. Gift of Mrs. John D. Rockefeller 3rd. (332.1955). The Museum of Modern Art, New York, USA. © The Willem de Kooning Foundation/Artists Rights Society (ARS), New York. Digital Image © The Museum of Modern Art/Licensed by SCALA/Art Resource, New York.

Judith Butler's notion of performativity has exerted so much influence for the same reason that we continue to look at de Kooning's images: beyond the disfiguring going on, we hear a snap, something like the exhilarating sound of an exit. Though very different from Lacan's *passe*, it aspires to produce a similar sound of the passage from semblances to *désêtre*. It is described as the sound of a door hinge screeching, thus revealing that it had been rusty all along; it conjures up the sound of an exit from a constricting view, of a window frame collapsing.[5] One is relieved by the sound of a motion where fear and fixity once were. Our anthology testifies to the great impact of Butler's work in feminist and queer studies. It is a well-known fact, however, that her influential notion of performativity draws its energy from the Euro-American vicissitudes of the classic modernist immobility emblematized by Kafka's subject before the law. Butler's *Gender Trouble: Feminism and the Subversion of Identity* (1990) opens under the sign of the Kafkian subject's saturnine disposition to pine before the law and closes invoking Kafka's inspiring deconstruction of the inside/outside bar, resulting in a law written not before culture but with the body, on the surface of a body that, simultaneous with norms, repeats them rather than precedes them.

The scene of a man before the law makes its appearance in *Gender Trouble* through Derrida, as Butler notices in her second note. It is also ushered in by Althusser's interpellation, and by Foucault's own evacuation of the saturnine impasse with the notion of critique. Critique names a practice of knowledge that subtracts itself to commands, a form of self-making or *poiesis* that is simultaneous with the de-subjugation and the unveiling of the law's performative legitimacy (Butler, 2000). In Butler's writing, Kafka's subject irrupts once again on the critical scene to prove the gate a sham. In the following pages we shall see how, though the subject before the law evokes a poststructuralist constellation, Butler's writing exhibits an affinity to the visual reactions against European modernism of the de Kooning kind. The affinity affords a different angle on feminism and queer theory in that it places them on a continuum with the tradition of an American gestural, expressive poetics that reacts to European anxieties. Precisely because of its modernist pedigree, Butler's theory of the subject, I argue, can be seen, among other things, as a response to popular, hyperbolic representations of America abroad which, aided by contemporary international events, continue to be seduced

---

[5] Lacan thus describes *la passe*:

In this change of tack where the subject sees the assurance he gets from this fantasy, in which each person's window onto the real is constituted, capsize, what can be perceived is that the foothold of desire is nothing but that of a désêtre, disbeing.

In this désêtre what is inessential in the supposed subject of knowledge is unveiled, from which the psychoanalyst to come dedicates him- or herself to the *agalma* of the essence of desire, ready to pay for it through reducing himself, himself and his name, to any given signifier (Lacan, 1995, p.9).

by the spectacle of its bulky capitalist body but are much more timorous when it comes to accounting for the worth of its mind.

In *Gender Trouble* Butler talks of subjects who, regulated by notions of power, ('such structures') are 'by virtue of being subjected to them formed, defined, and reproduced in accordance with the requirements of those structures' (Butler, 1990, p.2). If later on, in Butler's *The Psychic Life of Power: Theories in Subjection* (1997), the focus will be on the requirements for entering sociality, in her first book the attention is on 'these structures' that subject, their vagueness asserting their pervasiveness. *Gender Trouble* will try and pinpoint those structures. As a result, gender and sex are chosen to prove the subject as the structural effect of the moral imperative of an anxiety of subjection that gapes out of absence and lodges in the profundity of man. In the absence of the law, the argument goes, one is before the law, kept there by this interior abstract anxiety. Perhaps, it could be described, with Gramsci, as the fear that the gap between the social and the psychic realms would close and thus bar any future possibility of change and of new thoughts.[6] As in Kafka's terse parable, Butler's structures are channelled in one impenetrable all-powerful law: 'In effect, the law produces and then conceals the notion of "a subject before the law" in order to invoke that discursive formation as a naturalized foundational premise that subsequently legitimates the law's own regulatory hegemony' (Butler, 1990, p.2).

As said earlier on, *Gender Trouble* is a feminist and queer book but it draws its classicist strain from the theoretical heritage of the moral anxiety described above. Among other things, Butler's subversion of identity responds to it, especially to its potential for spawning embarrassing, cruel ideas that keep people in their places. In this context, Butler's performativity proves influential because of its liberating effect: it sinks the anxiety of the threshold with the parodic laughter of a population of copies.

Although Butler's notion of performativity is well known, it bears repeating to stress the emancipatory potential from the theoretical inheritance that precedes it. Butler works with the notion of an intelligible identity (Butler, 1990, p.145). There are rules that make the assertion of an 'I' intelligible and they 'operate through *repetition*' (Butler, 1990, p.145, emphasis in original). She continues, 'Indeed, when the subject is said to be constituted, that means simply that the subject is a consequence of certain rule-governed discourses that govern the intelligible invocation of identity' (Butler, 1990, p.145). Because of repetition, an exit from a seemingly intractable structural subjection can be imagined: 'The subject is not *determined* by the rules through which it is generated because signification is *not a founding act, but rather a regulated process of repetition* that both conceals itself and enforces its rules precisely through the production of substantializing effects' (Butler, 1990, p. 145, emphasis in original). Repetition may restrict the domains of cultural intelligibility, but it also enables new ones through the subversive repetition of parody.

---

[6] See Gramsci, 1991. This notebook was originally written in 1934.

Because it exposes the failure of the copy, parodic repetition 'can serve to reengage and reconsolidate the very distinction between a privileged and naturalized gender configuration and one that appears as derived, phantasmatic, and mimetic' (Butler, 1990, p.146). But there is also a 'subversive laughter' built 'in the pastiche-effect of parodic practices' (Butler, 1990, p.146) such as drag, in which the natural, the authentic and the real are constituted as effects.

Feminism's Exhausted Outsiders

Before discussing further the reason why performativity proves to be, in Adam Phillips's definition, an 'exhilarating notion' (Phillips, 1997, p.153), I would like to suggest the role that feminism plays in it.

Butler's thought is heir to feminism's critical breakthrough. This consists in having established a secure communication between bodies and objects, on the one hand, and signs on the other.[7] But she does not share feminism's Apollonian view of the body according to which one attempts to use bodily energies and pleasures to shape better ideas. For example, in many cases sexual choice for feminism was a political choice, linked to the imagining of alternative communities. Butler's work reflects a rage at the abstract depth of subjection, whose signs are anywhere but which feminism ignores: feminism 'is itself a discursive formation and effect of a given version of representational politics' whereby subjects are produced by structures that subject them (Butler, 1990, p.2). Subjection is wider, deeper than feminism. Her critique of Kristeva finalizes the turn.

Kristeva features in Butler's reading as the guardian of an old immobility. She is attached to the threshold and thus to ideas produced by the fear of injury. Challenging Lacan and his prohibitive paternal law, Kristeva theorizes the semiotic, a realm of pre-paternal drives, original pleasures that she then makes coincide with a maternity reified as prior to the paternal law. But she 'fails to consider the way in which that very law might well be the *cause* of the very desire it is said to *repress*' (Butler, 1990, p.90, emphasis in original). Kristeva enjoys contemplating a subject before the law; she enjoys the productivity of it (witness her notion of the semiotic *chora*).[8] But with her enjoyment she participates in the reproduction of the old modernist immobility of the subject before the law: 'the female body that is freed from the shackles of the paternal law may well prove to be another incarnation of that law, posing as subversive but operating in the service of that law's self-amplification and proliferation' (Butler, 1990, p.93). By contrast, Butler is interested neither in the 'natural' past of the body nor in its original pleasures but in 'an open future of cultural possibilities' (Butler, 1990, p.93). To move toward the future means to move away once and for all from the seduction of

---

[7] For more see de Lauretis, 1984, pp.158-186.

[8] Kristeva borrows the term *chora* from Plato's *Timaeus* 'to denote an essentially mobile and extremely provisional articulation constituted by movements and their ephemeral stases' (Kristeva, 1984, p.25).

the requirements to enter the law, the seduction of a painful station in which the subject is kept. In Kristeva's work, if relinquished, the station threatens the subject with abandonment in a desert of madness. Yet Butler maintains that it is also revealed to be performatively established, as if coming from everywhere and nowhere.

Within this scenario, the externality of sex is felt as the epitome of imaginative constraints: 'This is not to say that any and all gendered possibilities are open, but that the boundaries of analysis suggest the limits of a discursively conditioned experience' (Butler, 1990, p.9). Performativity sees the externality of sex as the most intractable impediment to the freedom of cultural analysis, as the reinforcement of a general model to which feminism has been blind: this model has to do with 'substantive effect[s] performatively produced'—by discourse that does as it says—'and compelled by the regulatory practices of [gender] coherence' (Butler, 1990, p.24).

The line of communication established between bodies and the semiotic process leads to the evacuation of an abstract, disembodied ego and to imagining an unsurveilled practice of cultural analysis. But the emphasis on parodic repetition also helps dispose of feminism's expressive model in which the individual woman can bend the course of history and culture with her body, so that sexual choice is political partaking. If for feminism, too, sex is an apparatus of surveillance and restriction, it may also be put to a different political use, leading to new ideas, newly imagined worlds. By contrast, Butler's performativity (in which both gender and sex might be implicated), as she goes on to explain in *Bodies That Matter: On the Discursive Limits of 'Sex'* (1993) describes 'the forced reiteration of norms' (Butler, 1993, p.94). Otherwise explained: 'where there is an "I" who utters or speaks and thereby produces an effect in discourse, there is first a discourse which precedes and enables that "I"' (Butler, 1993, p.225). And she concludes: 'Thus there is no "I" who stands *behind* in discourse and executes its volition or will *through* discourse. On the contrary, the "I" only comes into being through being called, named, interpellated...and this discursive constitution takes place prior to the "I"' (Butler, 1993, p.225, emphasis in original). Performativity declares cultural opposition through life choices as itself submitted to a general, deeper force of which feminism remains unaware. One can only choose to repeat; one can only choose an enforced repetition. The enforcement comes from the moral depth of culture; it is about a subjection spread in discourse, uniting individuals in a sort of global promiscuity. Butler moves beyond the impasse of divisions within feminism by including its political aspirations in a larger canvas determined by the invisible hand of an irreducible subjection.

In Elizabeth Bishop's poem 'The Moose', a bus travels across a lovely North American landscape, carrying inside an old tale of death and sickness, a familiar and even gentle tale but with imponderable holes in it. As the tale reaches the speaker's ear, the lulling motion of the bus helps transform it into an 'auditory / slow hallucination' (Bishop, *The Complete Poems*, p.171). Similarly, as Butler redraws the boundaries of attachment, feminism's generational tale of silence and sorrow reaches her ear with its alternation of an assertive communal 'Yes' and gaping holes; her job is to transfigure those gaps from the prelude to a fall into an exhausted humanity abandoned to loss, linguistic death and madness, to points of empowering insertion. Butler's crowds may limit themselves to repeating a norm in which they come to believe, yet there is a sense in which their plunge in this sort of global discursive subjection appears as a glamorous negativity (especially when one considers the possibility of parodic laughter) when compared to feminism's abused population of neglected survivors. The glamour of a negativity that has no original to deny is a refreshing change from feminism's marginalizing identification with the rejected and abjected. If feminism's people are still haunted by the philosophical spectre of the defeated servant stranded before the law (therefore by an immobility that discouragingly verges on an abstract moral imperative difficult to bypass), the iterative alignment of Butler's performative crowd, like a pop art successful composition, generates a strange magnetic abstraction. Her canvas dislodges the anxiety of falling in a painful station with a mounting sense of aesthetic possibilities.

It was Tillie Olsen who in the 1960s paved the way for the image of the wreck, the human cargo whose beauty is lost to history. The premise of Olsen's classic, *Silences*, is that writing is a form of symbolic acknowledgment and thus it bears a direct link to the self. Olsen initiates what Butler will later call the revision of the subject as a philosophical trope, encouraging the examination of the requirements involved in the symbolic acknowledgment. Besides poems and stories, she speaks of circumstances and invites professional readers to take into account the alliance of circumstance and creation. The literary critic's focus shifts to 'the phenomenology of the act' (Olsen, *Silences*, p.263). The factors involved multiply: intimidations, anxieties, shamings, hidden injuries, 'the blood struggle for means' (Olsen, *Silences*, p.263). Olsen turns literary history inside out. In place of the piper's song and the charismatic fluency of the chosen ones—those who have been visited by the spirit of language—now quite another scene tantalizes the critical imagination: the scene of voices shut away as if in crypts, encrypted in the chronicles of creativity.

When voices are not silenced from the start, writing still remains a labour accomplished in the shadow of a privative principle. Words can be taken away, lost to constriction, submission, subjection (Olsen, *Silences*, p.151), and when not to them to the melancholy induced by the exhausting, difficult, slow labour of expression (Olsen, *Silences*, p.150). Where the green thought once was, now is only weakness. The mystery of writing's ephemeral privacy (which Stein refers to as 'I I': a relation of private love, an 'I' close to itself) lies in the fact that the felicitous semiotic bubble is at any time ready to pass into semiotic *aphanisis*.[9]

---

[9] Virginia Woolf's *A Room of One's Own* remains a classic description of this structural silence that is the partner of writing. I am referring to Woolf's portrait of the woman lost in thought; how easy it is to pass from the life of signs to their death, a death publicly amplified, it will be recalled, by the gesticulations of the Beadle who tells the woman to wait before the law (the university, the library). Besides a political allegory of

Olsen presents a world of exhausted writers hourly threatened by what she famously termed silences. There is no glamour to this people: they labour to produce the pearl of great price (writing), moved by an unflinching attachment to a love object that comes to coincide with the self. In Olsen's essay, writing is the equivalent of Cézanne's modernist embrace with painting, a state of being in the clutches of the medium. She deploys a patient notion of the self at one with the writing life, but this sort of long patience feels like immobility to Butler. The risk of relapsing in the pining of the subject before the law still remains. It is like looking at Mirò in Todd Haynes's movie: the nightingale's highly original song moves the viewers, taking them for a while beyond restrictions, beyond submission and subjections. But the motion is felt as melodramatic (as Haynes aptly shows), a temporary construction of meaning in an immobile world of boundaries and divisions, a beautiful bubble dissolved by the gesticulations of beadles and guardians bearers of painful and depressing ideas.

After Olsen, Adrienne Rich speaks of myths that are based on exclusion. Hence the responsibility to explore the denied, submerged humanity and the threadbare beauty of lost faces exhausted with the exhausting achievement of Olsen's people. Rich retrieves from the wreck a population of forgotten women; she celebrates them. In her turn, Audre Lorde speaks of a 'master's house' that can be dismantled only by an oppositional stance. Feminism's exhausted outsiders, though they struggle gloriously to write their names and thus cross into a culture that shuts them out, pass on a disturbing lesson: that of an intractable hatred at the heart of culture that can be shaken off only by placing oneself in the position of the outsider. But staying outside does not shake off the anxiety of the subject before the law, thus of a thought that attaches itself to servants stranded before the doors of the world.

Exhilaration

Performativity turns out to be an exhilarating notion because it dissolves the solitude of the outsider in an open public landscape of crowds. The singulars in the crowd are bound by the force of discourse that induces each to repeat a social norm simultaneously with the others. At the same time, they are made individually lighter by such general repetitive force. Indeed, *Gender Trouble* hinges on subversion not because sex is conceptually demonstrated to be written on the body, but because, if it is implemented by the cultural apparatus of gender, *sex may turn out* to be like gender, that is, culturally constructed. Like de Kooning's *Woman II*, gender as performative is a meditation in an emergency aimed at achieving a sense of relief, levity, and possibility. Its exhilaration lies in the style of subversion at work in the meditation: a suspicion is insinuated that has the force of a speech act; it warns that it does what it says. In such a subversive way Butler responds to an

---

discrimination, Woolf's woman is a reprise of Dürer's *Melancholia*, the image of a thought poised between the Dionysian surge and depression. See Woolf, 1978, pp.7-8.

existing theoretical field of illocutionary forces. These have to do not only with the old modernist injunction to melancholic immobility, but also with the constrictions of historical feminism. Against both, to overcome both, *Gender Trouble* warns that sex—supposedly the last bastion of the natural core of the subject—is, like everything else, a cultural-historical object.

The warning replaces the laborious etching of words, Olsen's lifetime of sublimation, with the glamour of a challenge to turn depth into surface, suggesting that the natural realm is discursive and, above all, asserting the semiotic consistence of the body:

> That the gendered body is performative suggests that it has no ontological status apart from the various acts which constitute its reality....[A]cts and gestures, articulated and enacted desires create the illusion of an interior and organizing core, an illusion discursively maintained for the purposes of the regulation of sexuality within the obligatory frame of reproductive heterosexuality (Butler, 1990, p.136).

While Butler always acknowledges her debts to feminism, her recourse to the European intellectual tradition, in particular to Foucault's, Nietzsche's and Kafka's view of the body as a blank page, provides relief from the maternalism of the feminist cultural narrative, which sought an exit by positing an alternative symbolic, dominated by the mother and supposed to be less punishing than the father's. By contrast, the notion of the body as a blank sheet proves critically liberating because it moves out of the straining dialectic of self and other (man/guardian, woman/man; homosexual/heterosexual), in which feminism participated, and toward the more open space of a dramatic situation that consists in the reenactment of socially established meaning, publicly heard, conceptually grasped. The scene changes from the combat of a dyad to the choral utterance of an audience, to something that implements itself via public loudness: gender is 'a performative accomplishment which the mundane social audience...come to believe and to perform in the mode of belief' (Butler, 1990, p.141). Performative acts are repeated acts, retrieved, that is, from an *oikos* of discourse, where the silence of nature before culture is supposed to dwell, and thrust in the open of public acts publicly seen. But if such emptying erases the cruel scene of a subject abandoned before a threshold, it nevertheless leads to another sort of problem: the image of a crowd seduced by subjection.

Even though now it is repetition to tie us to others, the social landscape of 'I's, interpellated by discourse, and relating to each other through that interpellation, still poses the problem of a mimeticism between inside and outside, the social and the psychic. The 'mundane social audience...come to believe and to perform in the mode of belief' (Butler, 1990, p.141) strangely recalls Freud's modernist crowd and the risk of a violent tautology between inside and outside.[10] Butler's performative people are obviously different from the modernist crowd. They are not subjected through the identification with a Chief. They are, however,

---

[10] See Mikkel Borch-Jacobsen, 1992, pp.15-35.

completely in the hands of the magnetic power of discourse. The mundane social audience are an assembly of 'I's who 'come to believe'; their repetition in the form of belief spells a seduction by the norms which discourse formalizes. As seen earlier, there is no 'I' who stands behind in discourse and executes its volition or will through discourse: 'the "I" only comes into being through being called, named, interpellated'. And this discursive constitution takes place prior to the 'I' (Butler, 1993, p.225). The point of discourse is in acting on the chorus of the named, the called, the interpellated.

To differentiate hers from Freud's crowd, Butler relies on Benjamin's technological reproduction, which fragments the compact mass into a chain of copies, in a series of 'I's called forth by discourse. Certainly, Butler's 'I's turn their back on the image of the pliable and pliant mass of men without qualities. As gender is 'moved off the ground of a substantial model of identity' (Butler, 1990, pp.140-141), the impermanence, even ethereality of norms (Butler, 1990, p.141), exerts their seduction. Discourse rises above old tales of punishment to include everyone via the groundlessness of the ground of identity revealed through the structure (a mass, a crowd?) of 'repeated acts that seek to approximate the ideal of a substantial ground of identity' (Butler, 1990, p.141). But the seduction of groundlessness comes with the unbearable lightness of attachment: the mundane social audience who come to believe and perform in the mode of belief do not know how to measure attachment. If the groundlessness of identity ties me to my neighbor through discourse, this tie is attended by a certain unreality or weightlessness of attachment: which attachments count? Which are real? Which losses are worthy of being mourned? How do I know by what I am affected?

These questions are an important contribution to contemporary critical thinking. With them Butler exits both the feminist tomb of human energies and the Old European haunted house of the law. She breaks the double shell with the image of a performative people seduced by the possibilities of discourse and bound by parodic laughter. But, having turned her back on feminist sorrow and European punishment, she is left with the task of a revisitation of the philosophical premises of the subject. It is no coincidence that in *The Psychic Life of Power*, in the same essay where she takes up the question of attachment, 'Melancholy Gender/Refused Identification', Butler also relinquishes the exhilaration of the logic of technical reproduction for a more 'traditional' descent in the depth of the subject.

From Abraham and Torok to Fear

The Psychic Life of Power begins under the aegis of the subject as a philosophical trope. If *Gender Trouble* had emphasized the body as surface, or the body as discursive, it had done so to subvert old conceptual constrictions, to open thought to the reality outside it.[11] In *The Psychic Life of Power*, the discursive substantiality

---

[11] *Bodies That Matter* shows criticism how to bridge this gap with readings of movies and texts.

of the body is not relinquished. But it becomes clear that, even when seen as a surface on which norms are written, this performative body aspires at some level to intervene inside the concept, in the interior of the notion of subject. Accordingly, Butler critiques 'the dismissal of the subject as a philosophical trope' (Butler, 1997, p.29) by critical currents such as structuralism with its impoverished account of the subject as linguistic category. As she observes, this dismissal 'underestimates the linguistic requirements for entering sociality at all' (Butler, 1997, p.29). To underestimate these linguistic requirements would mean to forget that we are not immediately in speech and social existence but must cross over to them. Not coincidentally it was Kristeva who had tried to give a psyche to Benveniste's linguistic subject. But with her unwillingness to give up the scene of a threshold to cross, she had ended up amplifying the fear of injury.[12] Importantly, Butler asks about the extent to which the scene itself empowers critical thought.

Still guided by the notion of the body as a blank surface, in *The Psychic Life of Power* Butler aspires to reconstruct conceptually what has been excised in the depth of the subject. In trying to do so, she moves from performativity to melancholia. Because melancholia in Freud determines the formation of the ego, inflecting the ego as a precipitate of lost objects and thus defining being as being like another, it permits her to raise the question of how we use others to become who we are and thus consider the work of attachment. As Adam Phillips has remarked, the recourse to psychoanalysis and melancholia 'give some gravity' to Butler's performativity (Phillips, 1997, p.153). To add to that, it gives some gravity to the levity of attachments, to the disorientation in telling their worth. In other words, it lends dignity to an idea that acts in the interior of concepts, and thus in the exterior of society, but might otherwise sound like a sociological truism: that we become who we are because of the fear of being injured.

In 'Gender Melancholy/Refused Identification' (1997), Butler reconsiders the notion of gender as performative in light of a critique of identification. Gender melancholy, the preservation of prohibited attachments, is posed thanks to the critique of Freud's notion of identification. Butler's re-reading of Freud revolves around the notion of the character of the bodily ego as 'the archaeological remainder, as it were, of unresolved grief' (Butler, 1997, p.133), because it preserves and contains the history of abandoned object choices. She notices how between 'Mourning and Melancholia' and 'The Ego and the Id' Freud reverses the formulation about resolving grief. In 'The Ego and the Id', he states that 'an object which was lost has been set up again inside the ego—that is, that an object-cathexis has been replaced by an identification', a process that determines the formation of character (Butler, 1997, p.133). If formerly he had maintained that attachment can be broken, now 'he makes room for the notion that melancholic identification may be a *prerequisite* for letting the object go. By claiming this he changes what it

---

[12] Through the case of women, Kristeva reminds us that without the crossing to the symbolic or paternal law, the subject would be abandoned 'to madness, to refusal, to the hysterical symptom' or collapse 'into psychosis or suicide' (Kristeva quoted in Sprengnether, 1990, p.215).

means to "let the object go" for there is no final breaking of the attachment' (Butler, 1997, p.134, emphasis in original). The formation of character *is* the process of melancholia. Butler's re-reading of Freud and her gender melancholy are modelled on Nicholas Abraham and Maria Torok's own re-reading of Freud and their notion of incorporation or inclusion.

Abraham and Torok re-read Freud's melancholia with particular attention to the recurrence of the images of the open wound. In Freud the melancholic is someone caught in a struggle as to 'whether or not one should keep investing the love object despite disappointments, ill treatment, and ultimately, despite the loss of the love object' (Abraham and Torok, 1994, p.135). After being struck by the image of an open wound 'that is said to attract the whole of the counter-cathecting libido', Abraham and Torok begin to see the melancholy as someone who tries 'to hide, wall in, and encrypt' *(*Abraham and Torok, 1994, p.135). The process takes place not in the unconscious but in the preconscious-conscious system and creates a supplemental topography where 'the wound is isolated and separated from the rest of the psyche and especially from the memory of what had been torn from it. Such a creation is only justified when reality must be denied all along with the narcissistic and libidinal import of the loss. We propose to call this supplemental topography *inclusion...*' (Abraham and Torok, 1994, p.135, emphasis in original). The melancholic 'cherish the memory of their lost object as their most precious possession even as it must be concealed by a crypt built with the bricks of hate and aggression' (Abraham and Torok, 1994, p.136). When faced with the danger of seeing the crypt crumble (because of the loss of some secondary love-object), 'the whole of the ego becomes one with the crypt, showing the concealed object of love in its own guise' (Abraham and Torok, 1994, p.136). They call the process 'preservative repression' (Abraham and Torok, 1994, p.135). In the chapter titled 'The Lost Object—Me: Notes on Endocryptic Identification', Abraham and Torok refer to the melancholic inclusion or incorporation as 'endocryptic identification' and further explain that this sort of identification refers to 'the memory of an idyll, experienced with a valued object and yet for some reason unspeakable. It is memory of an idyll that is forgotten, entombed in a fast and secure place, awaiting resurrection' (Abraham and Torok, 1994, p.141). Between the idyll and the forgetting a loss has occurred: 'a painfully lived Reality—untellable and therefore inaccessible to the gradual, assimilative work of mourning', that is, anti-metaphoric, waiting before the work of metaphor, 'since both the fact that the idyll was real and that it was later lost must in fact be disguised and denied' (Abraham and Torok, 1994, p.141). Abraham and Torok conclude that the self-governing mechanism of inclusion, 'leads to the establishment of a sealed-off psychic place, a crypt in the ego' (Abraham and Torok, 1994, p.141). They compare it to a cocoon around a chrysalis. The crypt is 'a form of anti-introjection, a mechanism whereby the assimilation of both the illegitimate idyll and its loss is precluded' (Abraham and Torok, 1994, p.141).

Butler's melancholic gender is a reprise of Abraham and Torok's crypt; it derives from the model of the refusal of the loss and the metaphoric failure (the failure to displace into words):

> When we consider gender identity as a melancholic structure, it makes sense to choose 'incorporation' as the manner by which that identification is accomplished. Indeed, according to the scheme above, gender identity would be established through a refusal of loss that encrypts itself in the body and that determines, in effect, the living versus the dead body (Butler, 1990, p. 68).

When applied to sex, Abraham and Torok's crypt serves even better Butler's aim of bridging the distance between gender and sex. Butler writes: 'As an antimetaphorical activity, incorporation *literalizes* the loss *on* or *in* the body and so appears as the facticity of the body, the means by which the body comes to bear "sex" as its literal truth' (Butler, 1990, p.68, emphasis in original). Indeed, Abraham and Torok's incorporation proves to be Butler's strongest demonstration that sex is, like gender, a cultural signifier: 'The localization and/or prohibition of pleasures and desires in given "erotogenic" zones is precisely the kind of gender-differentiating melancholy that suffuses the body's surface' (Butler, 1990, p.68). In Freud, in the case of homosexual identity not only is object lost but desire too (Butler, 1990, p.69), resulting in a triple never-never: 'I never lost that person and I never loved that person, indeed never felt that kind of love at all' (Butler, 1990, p.69). The more totalizing the denial the stronger the preservation (preservative repression in Abraham and Torok's terms). In other words, because incorporation or endocryptic identification implies anti-introjection, it places the subject and its prerequisites *before* the metaphorical work of mourning. Melancholia therefore testifies to the legitimacy, indeed to the urgency, of a theoretical revision of the subject.

Where Freud spoke of identification with the lost object, now Butler can speak of an incorporation of the attachment that appears as an identification: 'Insofar as identification is the psychic preserve of the object and such identifications come to form the ego, the lost object continues to haunt and inhabit the ego as one of its constitutive identifications' (Butler, 1997, p.134). From here on the story is well known: within the general law of compulsory heterosexuality masculine and feminine are not to be understood as dispositions; they are the result of labour; they are symbolic accomplishments, positions that come to be achieved through melancholic identification, an incorporation that masks as an identification. The positions 'are established in part through prohibitions which *demand the loss* of certain sexual attachments'. (Butler, 1997, p.135, emphasis in original).

Once plugged to the conceptual ground of psychoanalysis, the more evanescent concept of social fear can be outlined with some gravity; its effect on the bodily ego can be conveyed. Accordingly, threats, anxiety, the terror of social wounding and injurious interpellations hover over 'Melancholy Gender/Refused Identification' and, in general, in Butler's reconsideration of the subject as a philosophical trope in *The Psychic Life of Power*. The levity and laughter of performativity disappear from this later work. If performativity had put an end to the critical process of mourning a damaged humanity, whose beauty remains submerged in the recesses of ideas, now with melancholia we awake to a humanity shaped into a society by the profound force of fear and shame. Fear enters the theoretical scene to hollow out the subject, to do the work of the concept. Melancholy gender takes in the interior of the notion a social view of people who fear injury, are determined by it in their bodily egos, and aggregate because of it. Sexual attachments are a symbolic achievement accelerated by the fear of injurious interpellations. Naturally, Butler specifies, this is a 'stark and hyperbolic construction' (Butler, 1997, p.136), a hyper-realistic image, one could add, that only serves to highlight its fast grip on the imagination, and thus the rigidity of conventions and of a cultural style remote from life.[13]

The repetition of the performative population of *Gender Trouble* here modulates into a dull insistence; it eventually congeals in an assertion that protects the pain of a loss of philosophical dimensions: the power of fear as the other side of theories of subjectivity. Fear induces a radical refusal to identify with prohibited attachments: 'refusal suggests that on some level an identification has already been made and disavowed, whose symptomatic appearance is the insistence, the overdetermination of the identification that is, as it were, worn on the body that shows' (Butler, 1997, p.149). The laughter that, from Plato's *Theaethetus* to Bakhtin, has been the subversive weapon of those who remain spectators of the work of discourse now stops at the sight of a contemporary crowd bound by fear, shaped by it into a civility traversed by injury. Butler's reconsideration of the subject as a philosophical trope puts the work of fear back inside the subject; without its examination one builds indeed a cartoon image of society and the social tie.

Melancholy Theory

Certain attachments jeopardize the compactness of a whole, and the sense of belonging to a whole. Class and nation are the prime examples of wholes in Freud. In Butler's work, homosexual attachment features as the great interference. One is struck by how, as she gets to discussing the social effects of the fear of homosexual attachment (specifically, unmourned AIDS losses), Butler redraws the national landscape. Via psychoanalysis, melancholia theoretically comes to bind the nation around a core. She finds a structural foreclosure of sexual attachment (whether homosexual or heterosexual) at the heart of the subject. But if, on a social level, homosexual attachment jeopardizes America's sense of wholeness, this is theoretically reinstated via melancholia. The vista arises of a social body traversed by mourning, addressed by the activist injunction to value formerly unvalued losses. The aim of melancholy gender is to establish a fluid communication between the theoretical interior and the social landscape outside. It is with this aim in mind that the consideration of prohibited homosexual attachment leads to the

---

[13] Woolf's characters huddled together like birds on a bough (in *The Waves*) or Pound's petals come to mind as stylistic units of the fragility of the singular caught in the bond of discourse and, as such, classic precursors of Butler's people. Butler cuts the link with modernist images and begins to speak with the hyper-realism of American pop art.

structural foreclosure of attachment in the subject. The foreclosure of homosexual attachments questions the status of all attachments; it raises the problem of their worth:

> This problematic [ungrieved and ungrievable loss] is made all the more acute when we consider the ravages of AIDS, and the task of finding a public occasion and language in which to grieve this seemingly endless number of deaths. More generally, this problem makes itself felt in the uncertainty with which homosexual love and loss is regarded: is it regarded as a 'true' love, a 'true' loss, a love and loss worthy and capable of being grieved, and thus worthy and capable of having been lived? (Butler, 1997, p.138.)

Butler's incorporation masquerading as identification, as Adam Phillips notices, 'invites us to wonder what we use other people for and how other they are. In fact, it forces us to confront the question that exercised Freud and that object relations and relational psychoanalysis take for granted; in what sense do we have what we prefer to call relationships with each other?' (Phillips, 1997, p.152).

With a rippling effect, therefore, grief for homosexual losses extends to a wider, vaguer, more abstract loss that pervades the social body conjuring a cohesiveness through grief for lost attachments. What Butler says of sexual attachments is equally true of intellectual attachments. Attachments to ideas are like attachments to objects loved and lost; they form the critic (just as in Freud they form the ego). As Abraham and Torok put it, endocryptic identification describes a battle with phantoms (objects) 'that implore Heaven and demand of us their due' (Abraham and Torok, 1994, p.139). Phantoms may comprise ideas, valued ideas. Elsewhere I have discussed how the notion of endocryptic identification illuminates the passage from poetry to theory in the case of queer theorist Eve Kosofsky Sedgwick (Mitrano, 2000). It is shaped by historical circumstances from the 1960s on. In her autobiographical account, *A Dialogue on Love* (1999), Eve Sedgwick captures the critic's progress from feminism, to the socially oriented criticism of differences (multiculturalism, the class-race-gender axis), to a more capillary critique of power and how it colonizes individual consciousness, and finally to the love of gay men and queer theory as an object-choice. In Sedgwick's account, first the choice to give up poetry for theory, then the choice of devoting herself to theorizing homosexual attachments, bring up the issue of the loss of other intellectual attachments.

Sedgwick's career is representative of the path of many. The history of criticism from the post-Cold War era to the present has been dominated by a preoccupation with the notion of identity and its historical and cultural situatedness. One of the consequences is that the path of the critic has itself been a melancholy path, strewn with the phantom of objects left behind, with attachments to material differences left behind. From feminism on, criticism's engagement of differences has changed the old notion of identity as a self-possessed certainty of oneself. Such engagement has made the simultaneous action of multiple social differences felt in the abstract notion of the subject. This notion, which in part rises to repair the discomfort of the limited intellectual possibilities of identity and identity politics, strongly alludes to a mobile 'I' struggling against the fixity of conventions.[14]

Criticism's leaning toward the problematic of liberation has had two consequences. First, the main thrust of the discourse on identity and its deconstruction has been to acknowledge differences as if they were intellectual objects in serious risk of oblivion. They therefore have constituted the critic as the subject of an object that claims speech as if in a state of emergency. The critic is called to pay differences their due, to acknowledge them, to speak for them, to be their subject. It is this kind of critic that 'does' theory. But differences refer to specific sections of humanity: the gesture of the critic to speak the object that claims acknowledgment comes with a trail behind it. Like the feminist critic, the critic formed by the discourse on differences constantly feels the intimation of entire sections of humanity submitted to silence: mouths open ready for speech, only to be frozen on its verge. Theory has updated Munch's scream for the present. If literature has receded a bit in this state of emergency, it is because the image of mouths hungry for speech has interfered with the mythical private love that, in the reading experience, supposedly ties the reader to a chosen text or author.

Secondly, in the shift from identity to subjectivity differences have been acknowledged, wave after wave (class, race, gender, sex, queer theory). As the constricting hold of one has been undermined, another claims attention, the critic must make place for other differences that want to be acknowledged and need to be. The previous objects have not gone away, they continue to matter. Sedgwick's *A Dialogue on Love* makes this point. There is an embarrassing voice buried in Sedgwick's family history; it remains a phantom for Sedgwick the future queer theorist if only because to a certain extent the aspiring intellectual is conscious of having shaped her brilliant skills in English and critical theory in part to deny that embarrassingly marginal (marginalizing and anti-English) sound.

There seems to be a theoretical melancholy that preserves attachment to differences even when these have to be precluded. It is dictated by the times when one must say no to oppression and subjection. At such times, as one reads in Sedgwick's account, a transition occurs from the love of literature to the love of critical writing. The point is not that poetry or literature cannot say no to power; rather, each literary text becomes an abstraction in Miró's sense: the sign of something. One cannot pick up a specific text that the image of screaming mouths crowds one's mind, pairing reading with a difficult solitude. It makes the critic responsible for the acknowledgment of others before the universe.

Abraham and Torok open their essay on endocryptic identification with a quote from Hölderlin: 'The soul that in life did not its divine right/Acquire, has not even in Hades, repose' (Hölderlin, quoted in Abraham and Torok, 1994, p.139). This is the divine right of being acknowledged before the whole universe, say Abraham

---

[14] Criticism's mobile 'I' has a strong affinity with the psychoanalytic ego. As Adam Phillips writes: 'Freud glimpsed in the *Interpretation of Dreams* the ego's potential for promiscuous mobility; dreams in particular revealed that psychic life was astonishingly mobile and adventurous even if lived life was not' (Phillips, 1997, p.152).

and Torok. Somehow, this bears remembering when talking about theory. To a certain extent, theory is about the phantom of the unacknowledged that seizes the subject, making it paramount for critical thought to say 'No!', to stop the work of constriction, submission, and subjection. Such a 'No' comes to take precedence even over poetry or the love of literature. Did I ever love literature without this, without being a subject haunted by the phantom of an object that claims my speech?[15] There comes a point when, for a critic, choosing otherwise would mean only a half entrance into culture, the sense of an illegitimate, minor critical voice because an attachment to differences has to do with the conceptual labor of dissolving the strange anxiety that surrounds the linguistic act once one approaches it (an anxiety that formalism and structuralism preferred to ignore).

If her recourse to Foucault makes feminism's expressive model appear naïve, even Butler's theory of the subject bears the trace of the expressionist vocation that precedes it, if only because it feels compelled to halt the clamor around the dialectic speech/silence, insiders/outsiders. It switches off the image of the hungry mouths by confronting the critical sensibility with the challenge of a structural grief in literary and formal concerns.

The population bound in mourning at the center of Butler's essay 'Melancholy Gender/Refused Identification' is a significant leap from her earlier performative people. The connectivity that in the performative crowd was established by a global subjection to discourse here is secured by melancholia, a psychic mechanism of power:

> If melancholia appears at first to be a form of containment, a way of internalizing an attachment that is barred from the world, it also establishes the psychic conditions for regarding 'the world' itself as contingently organized through certain kinds of foreclosures. (Butler, 1997, p.143.)

The recourse to psychoanalytic melancholia allows Butler to paint a collective portrait that makes the reader pause because its massive mourning of deaths by AIDS anticipates the other more extended wave of mourning of deaths by terrorism. This latter mourning has divided the world between those who identify with America—and who feel 'American'—and those who do not. To a certain extent, it has publicly raised, even though often in the crude terms of the media, the question of the status of America as an object of attachment for others. Butler's inside portrait of a people formed by the fear of injury and bound by a structural grief, that therefore anticipates recurrent waves of grief, does not really square with the image of America outside. It seems to me important to consider the extent to which the American grief that Butler writes inside the theory of the subject is simultaneously an American grief written outside, projected on an outside, that is,

---

[15] The question remains of authors who haunt us, seeking acknowledgment, asking us to pay our dues. How are valued attachments to single authors formed?

that strikingly forecloses such grief with an imaginary America congealed in pre-Gramscian times,[16] in the image of a huge body without a mind.

Recent history has dragged us back violently to a world of modernist fear, to the injunction to stay put and to atavistic guardians of the Kafka and de Kooning type. In part, the recent fury against the free movement of human energies and people's increasing desire to use their resources, comes from impoverished ideas, attached first and foremost to cartoon-like images of cultures. The history of 'America' as one of such hyperbolic constructions was outlined by Dick Hebdige more than two decades ago. Taking his cue from Hoggart, Hebdige understood the fear of Americanization within the context of a visibly unbearable gulf between rich and poor, in the context of an internal class divide that 'was beginning to seem unacceptable or at the very least embarrassing to all but the most intransigent reactionaries' (Hebdige, 1988, p.46). But 'the spectre of Americanization' (Hebdige, 1988, p.47), Hebdige goes on to argue, depended largely on the context of national shame. In the form of glossy advertisements, big fridges and big cars, American culture seemed to numb class divisions. It seemed to put them beside the point, so to speak, thus depriving home culture not so much of an object of tradition but of an object of contestation of a home tradition, an internal dialectical object. In other words, Anti-Americanism has been embraced to exorcise embarrassing ideas at home, to mitigate local shame. As Hebdige remarks, people's desires in the invasion of American culture seem to have been completely disregarded. There does not seem to be a vocabulary for the complexity that attracted not only specific social groups—like the working class youth—but people in general to America. Not much has changed since Hebdige's analysis. If anything, recent history has exacerbated the modernist anxiety of Americanization.[17]

Rereading Butler's 'Melancholy Gender/Refused Identification' one senses the solitude of theory in the face of a history that prefers fear and immobility to the motion of ideas. From this point of view, Butler's national interior bound by fear but flaunted to the outside appears to interrupt the atavistic image of an America happily moving along its capitalistic path. Melancholia interrupts such a hyper-realistic image. Rising like a marble totem to lost attachments that conceptuality cannot recognize, Butler's melancholy subject says that if in the imagination of the outside the American crowd must be a body without a soul, it will at least be a body with a prohibited depth. But it would be wrong to view Butler's subject solely like a cenotaph, for it is not a nationalist marker.

With its interior of foreclosures, Butler's subject is more like de Chirico's melancholy statues. De Chirico's *La Statue Silencieuse* (1913) is modeled on

---

[16] In *Notebook 22* Gramsci sees the Fordist worker as a figure of future possibilities, of new thoughts.

[17] As corollary to Hebdige, on the topic of European cultural imperialism, see Richard Poirier, 1999.

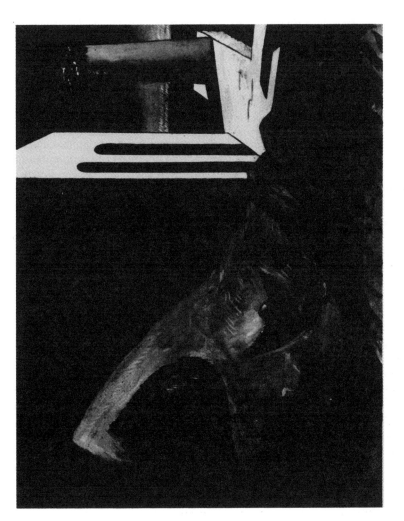

Figure 2 : De Chirico, Giorgio, *La Statue Silencieuse* (*Ariane*) (1913). Oil on canvas, 99.5 x 125.5 cm. The Kunstsammlung Nordrhein-Westfalen, Düsseldorf, Germany. Photograph by Walter Klein, Düsseldorf. © 2003 Artists Rights Society (ARS), New York/SIAE, Rome.

Dürer's *Melancholia*. Like her, she is poised on the verge of semiotic *aphanisis*—a withdrawal of signs—that might change any minute into productive fluency, making for exits out of the imprisoning labyrinths of embarrassing ideas. Significantly, de Chirico tropes Dürer's image for the ups and downs of thought with a marble Ariadne, the mythical interpreter, stranded in the midst of the public modernist *piazza* where no social tie is represented except for that intimated by the marble homage. To those who look at theory as an American thing, the inner foreclosures of Butler's subject signify an America caught in de Chirico's melancholy, affecting the interpreter left behind by those who have used her skills. There is a literary use to melancholy in Butler: it interrupts the modernist fetish status of the attachment of the outside *to* America. Her critical resources testify to this dialectic of a North American inside and a European outside as it deploys a European philosophical apparatus, with Benjamin and Kafka's moral vein in the foreground, to broach the issue of local 'wrecks'—abysses or archives—that conceptuality leaves out. Through her inquiry into homosexual attachment, Butler conjures a form of collective self-representation at work for the outside.

Butler's case shows that American theory has reversed old starving guardians into contemporary intellectual nurture. But, as her marble totem to grief suggests, while this theoretical spectacle is going on, history follows the opposite course, preferring (both on the inside and on the outside) the irrational, the easy warmth of old stuffy cameos to the loud life of new images.[18] We can feel beyond Kafka's man, but the question is whether we really want to move on from that scene of subjection. In the fragility of a wish lies a future of possibilities—and of critical thinking.

References

Abraham, Nicholas and Torok, Maria (1994), *The Shell and the Kernel*, Nicholas T. Rand (trans.), University of Chicago Press, Chicago and London.

Argan, Giulio C. (1989), 'La crisi dell'arte come "scienza europea"', in *L'Arte Moderna*, Sansoni, Florence, pp.467-601.

Bishop, Elizabeth (1983), 'The Moose', in *The Complete Poems: 1927-1979*, Farrar, Straus and Giroux, New York, pp.171-173.

Borch-Jacobsen, Mikkel (1992), 'The Freudian Subject: From Politics to Ethics', in *The Emotional Tie: Psychoanalysis, Mimesis, and Affect*, Douglas Brick et al (trans.), Stanford University Press, Stanford, pp.15-35.

Butler, Judith (1990), *Gender Trouble: Feminism and the Subversion of Identity*, Routledge, New York and London.

——— (1993), *Bodies That Matter: On the Discursive Limits of 'Sex'*, Routledge, New York and London.

---

[18] On history and the urgencies of theory see Laura Mulvey, 1993.

———— (1997), 'Melancholy Gender/Refused Identification', in *The Psychic Life of Power: Theories in Subjection*, Stanford University Press, Stanford, pp.132-150.

———— (2000), 'The Virtues of Michel Foucault', Talk at The School of Criticism and Theory, Cornell University, Ithaca, 14 July.

De Lauretis, Teresa (1984), 'Semiotics and Experience', in *Alice Doesn't: Feminism, Semiotics, Cinema*, Indiana University Press, Bloomington, pp.158-186.

Gramsci, Antonio (1991), *Americanismo e Fordismo*, Editori Riuniti, Rome.

Haynes, Todd (dir.) (2002), *Far From Heaven*, Universal, Los Angeles.

Hebdige, Dick (1988), *Hiding in the Light: On Images and Things*, Routledge, London.

Hughes, Robert (1997), *American Visions*, Alfred A. Knopf, New York.

Janson, H.W. and Janson, Anthony F. (eds) (2001), *History of Art*, Harry N. Abrams, New York.

Kristeva, Julia (1984), *Revolution in Poetic Language*, M. Waller (trans.), Columbia University Press, New York.

Lacan, Jacques (1995), 'Proposition of 9 October 1967 on the Psychoanalyst of the School', Russell Grigg (trans.), *Analysis*, vol. 6, pp.1-13.

Lorde, Audre (1983), 'The Master's Tools Will Never Dismantle the Master's House', in C. Moraga and G. Anzaldua (eds), *This Bridge Called My Back: Writings by Radical Women of Color*, Kitchen Table Press, New York, pp.98-101.

Mink, Janis (1994), *Joan Miró: 1893-1983*, Benedikt Taschen Verlag, Cologne.

Mitrano, Mena (2000), 'Che cos'è la teoria', *Anglistica: An Interdisciplinary Journal*, vol. 4, no. 2, pp.51-78.

Mulvey, Laura (1993), 'Some Thoughts on Theories of Fetishism in the Context of Contemporary Culture', *October*, vol. 65 (Summer), pp.2-20.

Olsen, Tillie (1980), *Silences*, Virago, London.

Phillips, Adam (1997), 'Keeping It Moving: Commentary on Judith Butler's "Melancholy Gender/Refused Identification"', in Judith Butler, *The Psychic Life of Power: Theories in Subjection*, Stanford University Press, Stanford, pp.151-159.

Poirier, Richard (1999), *Trying It Out in America: Literary and Other Performances*, Farrar, Straus and Giroux, New York.

Rich, Adrienne (1975), 'Diving into the Wreck', in B. Charlesworth Gelpi and A. Gelpi (eds), *Adrienne Rich's Poetry*, W.W. Norton, New York, pp.65-68.

Sedgwick, Eve Kosofsky (1999), *A Dialogue on Love*, Beacon Press, Boston.

Sprengnether, Madelon (1990), *The Spectral Mother: Freud, Feminism and Psychoanalysis*, Cornell University Press, Ithaca and New York.

Woolf, Virginia (1978), *A Room of One's Own*, Panther, London.

Chapter 6

The Plague of the Subject: Subjects, Politics, and the Power of Psychic Life

Kirsten Campbell[1]

Judith Butler is best known as a political thinker, as an inaugural figure in queer theory, and as a Foucauldian theorist of gender. Yet her book *The Psychic Life of Power: Theories in Subjection* (1997) appears to fit uneasily within this political and theoretical trajectory. Many discussions of Butler's work either ignore, or alternatively characterize, *Psychic Life* as her most 'psychoanalytic' and least Foucauldian theory.[2] However, *Psychic Life* should not be ignored or dismissed as a psychoanalytic aberration. The book presents a set of engagements that are integral to Butler's political and theoretical project. *Psychic Life* offers an important articulation of Butler's project of providing a political account of subjectivity. It presents a compelling argument for the importance of this project by contending that contemporary political thought needs to reconsider its emphasis upon a politics of identity, and instead should engage with the politics of the subjective performance of power. Central to this argument is Butler's development of her theory of the formation of the subject. Butler sketches such a theory in her previous work, *Gender Trouble: Feminism and the Subversion of Identity* (1990) and *Bodies That Matter: On the Discursive Limits of 'Sex'* (1993). However, she does not provide an elaborated theory of the constitution of the subject until *Psychic Life*.

The Problem of the Subject

Psychic Life opens with Foucault's injunction that '"[w]e should try to grasp subjection in its material instance as a constitution of subjects"' (Butler, 1997, p.1). This Foucauldian problematic of how power constitutes subjects frames Butler's

---

[1] A version of Campbell's essay appeared as 'The Plague of the Subject: Psychoanalysis and Judith Butler's *Psychic Life of Power*' in *International Journal of Sexuality and Gender Studies*, vol. 6, nos. 1-2 (April 2001). Reprinted with permission of Kluwer Academic.

[2] See, for example, the collection edited by V. Bell (1999), *Performativity and Belonging*. Lois McNay's piece 'Subject, Psyche and Agency: The Work of Judith Butler' in Bell's collection is a notable exception.

later theory of the formation of subjectivity. For Butler, the subject is a material instance of power, for 'if conditions of power are to persist, they must be reiterated; the subject is precisely the site of such reiteration' (Butler, 1997, p.16). Power thereby forms, and is performed by, the subject. For this reason, Butler argues that 'for power to act, there *must* be a subject' (Butler, 1997, p.203, emphasis in original). In order to understand the operation of power, it is also necessary to understand its subjective performance. A theory of the constitution of subjectivity is therefore integral to a theory of power, because it is not possible to theorize power without also theorizing the subject. The central theoretical problem of *Psychic Life* is how to understand the relationship between the operation of power and the formation of subjectivity. ·

Butler argues that this theoretical problem requires an examination of the relationship between the 'process of becoming subordinated by power' and 'the process of becoming a subject' (Butler, 1997, p.2). Butler contends that to understand the formation of the subject of power, it is necessary to understand these processes of subjection. However, if subjection constitutes the subject, then 'an account of subjection, it seems, must be traced in the turns of psychic life' (Butler, 1997, p.18). In this way, it becomes necessary to consider the question 'what is the psychic form that power takes?' (Butler, 1997, p.2).

While Butler begins with a statement of her Foucauldian problematic, she argues nevertheless that Foucault himself does not answer this question. Butler identifies three conceptual weaknesses in Foucault's account of power and subjectivity. First, he fails to 'elaborate on the specific mechanisms of how the subject is formed in submission'. Second, he fails to engage with the 'domain of the psyche'. Third, he fails to explore 'power in this double valence of subordinating and producing' (Butler, 1997, p.2). While acknowledging that 'Foucault is notoriously taciturn on the topic of the psyche', Butler argues that a theory of subjection requires a theory of the psyche (Butler, 1997, p.18). She contends that Foucault does not adequately address the question of subjection because he does not have an adequate theory of the psychic formation of subjectivity. Butler's argument is not that Foucault lacks a theory of that subject. Rather, she argues that he fails to theorize the constitution of the subject. With this crucial omission, Foucault fails to explain the psychic form that power takes.

Where, then, is an account of the psychic life of power to be found? Butler claims, 'one cannot account for subjectivation, and, in particular, becoming the principle of one's own subjection, without recourse to a psychoanalytic account of the formative or generative effects of restriction or prohibition' (Butler, 1997, p. 7). To theorize subjection requires a psychoanalytic theory of the constitution of the subject.

Butler's Theory of the Subject

In *The Psychic Life of Power*, Butler develops her own theory of the formation of the subject, drawing primarily on the psychoanalytic work of Freud and Lacan.

This theory is presented in three parts: first, the theory of the infantile passionate attachments; second, the theory of the normative regulation of those attachments; and third, the concomitant formation of the melancholic subject.

Passionate Attachments

Butler begins with the proposition that the infant has passionate attachments to its 'earliest objects of love—parents, guardians, siblings', who are objects of the infant's libidinal investments (Butler, 1997, p.8). However, because of its prematurity, the infant is also dependent upon those who care for it for its physical and emotional survival. Butler clearly draws upon the psychoanalytic idea that the child is born unable to care for itself, and, therefore, has a dependent attachment to others. Butler argues that because of this dependency, power always structures the relationship between infant and parent. The child exists in a relation of submission to its parents precisely because of its dependence upon them. The child's primary passionate attachments are to those upon whom it is dependent, and are thus structured as a relation of domination and submission. For this reason, Butler argues that the formation of the primary attachments of the subject occurs in relations of subordination and therefore subjection. From the beginning, we have passionate attachments to relations of power (Butler, 1997, p.7).

Foreclosed Attachments

In her first discussion of these primary 'passionate' attachments, Butler suggests that the structure of the infant's subjection to power forms him or her as a subject. She situates her subsequent discussions of passionate attachments, however, within the 'normative' formation of gendered identity. Butler compares the notion of passionate attachment to the Freudian conception of the drive, arguing that the concept of attachment always implies 'attachment *to* an object' (Butler, 1997, p.208, emphasis in original). Following psychoanalytic theory, Butler contends that these attachments are structured by an internalized prohibition on the drive (Butler, 1997, p.22). These internalized prohibitions are regulative norms that direct libidinal attachments. For Butler, 'foreclosure' is the psychic mechanism that 'structures the forms which any attachment may assume' (Butler, 1997, p.24). Butler takes up the psychoanalytic distinction between the disavowal of an attachment (the repression of an attachment) and the foreclosure of an attachment (the radical repudiation of an attachment) in her argument that foreclosure structures primary attachments by delineating certain objects as permissible aims of the drive and radically barring other objects. Foreclosure thus functions as the mechanism that regulates how attachments fix to objects.

In this account, Butler ties the psychoanalytic concept of foreclosure to 'the Foucauldian notion of a regulatory ideal', hence linking the psychoanalytic account of the psyche to Foucault's theory of the regulatory workings of power (Butler,

1997, p.25).[3] Butler reconceives foreclosure 'as an ideal according to which certain forms of love become possible, and others, impossible' (Butler, 1997, p.25). Foreclosure thus functions as an ideal that permits certain forms of attachment but not others, and so operates as an internalized social sanction upon object choice. For Butler, the regulatory ideal is that of heterosexuality, and the attachment that is foreclosed is a 'homosexual' same-sex object choice. The foundational prohibition that forms the subject is thus not the bar against incestuous oedipal desire that underpins classical psychoanalysis, for that desire is already heterosexual and hence based upon the preclusion of a homosexual desire. Rather, the foundational prohibition bars homosexual attachments to same-sex objects (Butler, 1997, p.135). Every heterosexual identity is founded upon a primary and foundational prohibition upon homosexual attachments.

The Melancholic Subject

Using the Freudian theory of melancholia (1984b), Butler argues that this heterosexual identity has a melancholic structure because of its formation through the foreclosure of homosexual attachment. Butler argues that this loss of the homosexual object founds the formation of femininity and masculinity. Heterosexual identity is thus constituted through a repudiation of homosexual desire and hence through the irresolvable loss of the homosexual object. That 'ungrieved and ungrievable loss' produces the melancholia of heterosexual identity (Butler, 1997, p.138). Because heterosexual identity disavows homosexual attachment, it cannot be acknowledged and hence cannot be named and so cannot be mourned. For this reason, Butler understands '"masculinity" and "femininity" as formed and consolidated through identifications which are in part composed of disavowed grief' (Butler, 1997, p.139). She argues that '[w]hat ensues is a culture of gender melancholy in which masculinity and femininity emerge as traces of an ungrieved and ungrievable love; indeed, where masculinity and femininity within the heterosexual matrix are strengthened through the repudiations which they perform' (Butler, 1997, p.140).

This theory of the subject offers a political account of the formation of subjectivity. That account is political because of its queer feminist critique of the relation between power and the production of 'normative' heterosexuality identity and the psychic and social cost of that formation. It is also political, however, in its description of the production of identity itself. In the final chapter of *The Psychic Life of Power*, Butler argues that the ego's 'I' of identity reproduces a psychic topography formed by power. This account does not claim that power acts unilaterally on the subject, such that power is internalized in the psyche. Rather, the psyche is itself an effect of power, because it is an effect of the regulatory, disciplinary, and normative operation of power. For Butler, power 'effects a

---

[3] The key Foucauldian texts that Butler draws upon for her account of the regulatory workings of power are *Power/Knowledge* (1980), *Discipline and Punish* (1977), and *The History of Sexuality, Volume 1* (1978) and *Volume 2* (1985).

melancholia that reproduces power as the psychic voice of judgement addressed to (turned upon) oneself, thus modeling reflexivity on subjection' (Butler, 1997, p.98). In this way, Butler offers a critique of the foundation of identity in power.

'Between Freud and Foucault'

In *Psychic Life*, Butler acknowledges that 'I am in part moving toward a psychoanalytic criticism of Foucault' (Butler, 1997, p.87). However, we should not characterize her theory of the melancholic subject as a 'turn' to psychoanalysis. *The Psychic Life of Power* represents neither Butler's first nor her most sympathetic engagement with psychoanalysis. Rather, psychoanalysis informs her account of gendered identity in *Gender Trouble* and *Bodies That Matter*. In these earlier books, Butler outlines her argument concerning melancholic heterosexual identity, which she subsequently develops in *Psychic Life*. While Butler provides a compelling feminist and Foucauldian critique of psychoanalysis, nevertheless, her critique is also a productive reading of the problems within psychoanalytic theory rather than a refusal of psychoanalysis.

Despite its psychoanalytic engagements, *The Psychic Life of Power* should not be read as a repudiation of Foucauldian theory. As in her earlier work, Butler's engagement with psychoanalysis is framed by a commitment to Foucault's theory of the historical production of the subject and to the Foucauldian problematic of theorizing the relation between power and the formation of subjectivity. Butler does not situate her work against Freud or Foucault but rather between them. She argues that to understand the relation between power and subjectivity necessarily 'requires thinking the theory of power together with a theory of psyche' (Butler, 1997, p.2). Butler locates her work at the intersection of these theories of power and the psyche, between Foucauldian and psychoanalytic thinking.

To 'offer a critical account of psychic subjection in terms of the regulatory and productive effects of power' (Butler, 1997, p.19), Butler provides a Foucauldian re-reading of psychoanalysis. In her re-reading, Butler develops the argument previously presented in *Subjects of Desire: Hegelian Reflections in Twentieth-Century France* (1987), *Gender Trouble*, and *Bodies That Matter*, namely, that the psychoanalytic postulation of a psychic 'law' needs to be reconsidered in terms of the Foucauldian theory of power. In *Psychic Life*, Butler returns to Foucault's critique of psychoanalysis as a juridical and repressive practice that continually reproduces the subject and its desires in terms of the operation of power. In her previous works, Butler argued that the Freudian and Lacanian formulations of that psychic law are repressive and juridical—hence the necessity for a Foucauldian theory of the productivity of power. In *Psychic Life*, however, her position is more ambivalent. Butler 'disputes the Foucauldian notion that psychoanalysis presumes the exteriority of the law to desire, for it maintains that there is no desire without the law that forms and sustains the very desire it prohibits' (Butler, 1997, p.103). Rather, 'one cannot account for subjectivation...without a psychoanalytic account of the formative or generative effects of restriction or prohibition' (Butler, 1997, p.87).[4] Instead of claiming that there is one repressive and normative 'law' as in psychoanalysis, Butler understands the normative constraints upon psychic production as an effect of networks of regulatory norms. These normative and regulating discourses produce the subject and generate desire.

While Butler situates her account of the psychic life of power at the intersection between Foucauldian and psychoanalytic theory, Foucault and Freud address different conceptual problems in the development of her account of the formation of subjects. For this reason, we should not follow Butler's characterization of her work as not situated *between* these theories because she deploys them for different purposes. For Butler, the problematic is Foucauldian and requires a theory of the operation of power. Foucault provides a theory of sociality and its production in power, whereas psychoanalysis provides a theory of the subject. Butler's theory presents a Foucauldian theory of power and a psychoanalytic theory of the subject. Psychoanalysis provides a supplementary theory of the subject, which addresses a gap in Foucault's work concerning a theory of the formation of subjectivity. Butler does not provide a psychoanalytic reading of Foucault that challenges, disrupts, or contests that theory. Rather, Butler seeks to address what she perceives as a 'missing' dimension to Foucault's work—a theory of the constitution of the subject—by supplementing Foucault with a psychoanalytic theory of the subject.

This strategy repeats earlier formulations of the relationship between social theory and psychoanalysis. For example, within psychoanalytic Marxism, notably the Frankfurt school, Marxism provides a theory of the social, and psychoanalysis provides a supplementary theory of the subject. Similarly, in certain strands of psychoanalytic feminism, the notion of patriarchy provides a theory of social relations, and psychoanalysis provides an account of the formation of sexual subjects. These formulations of the relationship between social theory and psychoanalysis posit psychoanalytic theory as a necessary but nevertheless supplementary theory of the subject. Psychoanalysis becomes necessary because the social theory in question lacks an adequate account of the subject. Butler reproduces this relation to psychoanalysis by using it as a theory of the subject that supplements Foucault's theory of social power.

Although these earlier traditions in social theory perceive psychoanalysis as necessary, nevertheless it is also perceived as inadequate. This failure of psychoanalysis occurs in relationship to the political, because psychoanalysis is characterized as either lacking or as refusing a political analysis of the social. An obvious example of this characterization of psychoanalysis can be seen in earlier feminist engagements with psychoanalytic theory. These critiques argue that if psychoanalysis is to be deployed as a theory of the subject, then it must undergo political critique and be reworked in relation to a critical and contestatory politics. Butler reproduces this critique, because she argues that psychoanalysis in and of

---

[4] Butler's term 'subjectivation' is a translation of the French, *assujetissment*, meaning 'subjection' or 'subjugation' (Butler, 1997, p.11). The Foucauldian concept of subjectivation— the process of becoming a subject and becoming subordinated to power—is central to *Psychic Life* (Butler, 1997, p.16).

itself cannot provide a *political* account of the constitution of the subject. In this way, Butler similarly posits psychoanalysis as necessary for her project, while also contending that it is inadequate.

Butler engages in a strategy that both appropriates, and provides a critique of, psychoanalysis. This strategy effects a series of theoretical displacements from Foucault, to psychoanalysis, to Butler's own theory. Butler's problematic is Foucauldian, not psychoanalytic. She appropriates psychoanalysis to that problematic, as she does not adopt psychoanalytic theory in its entirety, but rather reworks certain elements of Freudian and Lacanian theory in relation to a Foucauldian theory of power. Butler does not situate her account within psychoanalysis because she requires a political theory of the subject, which she argues that psychoanalysis does not provide. For this reason, Butler develops her own theory of the subject, which functions as a political supplement to the psychoanalytic theory that she appropriates. However, her supplementary use of psychoanalysis and in turn the supplementary nature of her own political account of the subject result in certain theoretical problems that are not worked through within her theory of subjection.

The Plague of Psychoanalysis

Butler's theory of subjection rests on three key ideas, which draw upon psychoanalysis: first, the concept of the infant's libidinal attachment to its parents; second, the idea of foreclosure; and third, the notion of the psychic subject. While Butler appropriates these psychoanalytic concepts to her account of psychic subjection, it is psychoanalysis that most troubles her theoretical desires.

The Subject of the Real

Butler provides an account of the fundamental passionate attachments of the child to understand the psychic effects of the operation of power upon the production of the subject (1997, pp.6-7). For Butler, that account is necessarily psychoanalytic. However, Butler's theory does not address the psychic relations of the child and parent, but rather focuses upon their 'real' empirical relations. For example, while Butler draws on Lacan's idea of the prematurity of the infant, she does not consider the infant's phantasmic relation to its specular others, nor its imagined relation to itself. Butler offers only the most attenuated description of the child's relationship to its 'earliest objects of love' (Butler, 1997, p.8). She characterizes 'parents, guardians, siblings' as empirical beings, which are undifferentiated in their psychical and social relation to the child. It is as if the psychical world of the child does not exist, so that those who care for it, and other members of its family, are simply empirical objects. For Butler, the relation between the carer and the child is always a real relation of power, which is not inflected through phantasmic object relations, nor the complexities of identification, nor troubled by the vicissitudes of sexuality. For example, Butler does not consider what psychic form these objects take for the child or how the child psychically constitutes these objects. She does not address the psychic life of the infant, and hence fails to provide a psychoanalytic account of the relation of the child to its parental objects. She privileges the seeming empirical reality of the infantile experience while not engaging with the psychical reality of these passionate attachments.

A consequence of this failure to address the psychic reality of the infant is that Butler does not provide a psychoanalytic theory of the relationship between the child and its 'family'. Such a theory would entail engaging with the complex attachments and disattachments—real, imagined, and symbolic—that form that relationship. Butler suggests that the relationship between the child and 'the earliest objects of its love' is a 'natural' and given fact of human existence (Butler, 1997, p.7). 'This situation of primary dependence' is ontological, in that it is a necessary condition of 'being' (Butler, 1997, p.7). The child 'must attach in order to persist in and of itself' (Butler, 1997, p.8).

By contrast, psychoanalysis argues that this relationship is *constituted* in the sense that psychical and social relations produce it. Despite her claim to provide a psychoanalytic theory of passionate attachments, Butler does not consider the complex psychical and social constitution of the parents as objects of passionate attachments. With this omission, Butler's theory of passionate attachment departs from psychoanalysis, and becomes instead a seemingly empirical and naturalistic account of the infantile subject.

The Foreclosure of the Subject

Butler conceives foreclosure as a regulatory ideal that forms the normative heterosexual subject. She attributes this notion of a fundamental 'order of prohibition' to Freud's distinction between 'repression and foreclosure, suggesting that a repressed desire might have once lived apart from its prohibition, but that foreclosed desire is rigorously barred, constituting the subject through a kind of pre-emptive loss' (Butler, 1997, p.23). However, as Laplanche and Pontalis (1973) point out, the concept of foreclosure is Lacanian, not Freudian. While Freud (1962) uses the concepts of 'repudiation' or 'disavowal' to describe the ego's refusal of an incompatible idea together with its affect, Lacan (1993) develops these ideas as a theory of foreclosure. Butler clearly uses foreclosure in the Lacanian sense of a foundational psychic exclusion that cannot be represented within the subject's symbolic economy. This deployment of Lacan in the name of Freud allows Butler to evade certain theoretical difficulties posed by Lacanian theory to her conception of foreclosure.

Lacan's theory of foreclosure concerns a basic fault in the operation of the paternal metaphor and, hence, in the production of the sexed subject. For Lacan (1977), foreclosure denotes the primordial expulsion of the fundamental signifier, the phallic signifier, from the subject's symbolic universe. Foreclosure, then, involves a failure of the production of sexed subjectivity. By contrast, Butler uses foreclosure to indicate both heterosexual norms (the regulatory ideal) and the regulatory mechanism of installation of those norms (the regulation of attachments).

In this way, Butler ascribes to foreclosure the successful constitution of heterosexual identity, while for Lacan it indicates a failure of the successful 'normative' production of sexed subjectivity. For Freud (1979) too, the concept of disavowal indicates a disruption in the constitution of the subject, for it is a psychotic defensive mechanism. In psychoanalytic theory, foreclosure indicates a fundamental disruption in the formation of the subject, whereas in Butler's theory, the concept is re-read as the mechanism of the production of normative (and coherent) subjects.

For Lacan, foreclosure is a defensive mechanism, which is situated in the register of the symbolic and, hence, in the register of sexual difference. However, Butler's account implies that the prohibition against the homosexual object is pre-oedipal, because it is prior to the constitution of the subject. This prohibition, however, *cannot be* pre-oedipal. If it is pre-oedipal, then it must be prior to sexual difference. If the prohibition is prior to sexual difference, then the object that is prohibited cannot be a homosexual object, because a homosexual object is defined by sexual difference. The definition of a same-sex object relies upon a notion of sexual difference because such a concept would be meaningless without an already established distinction between the sexes. In order for Butler's prohibition to operate against desire for same-sex objects, those objects must already be defined by sexual difference and, so, the prohibition described by Butler must be an oedipal prohibition in the register of sexual difference. The failure to address this problem of sexual difference entails that there is a lack of coherence in this theory of the formation of heterosexual identity.

Curiously, and perhaps more importantly for Butler's own theoretical and political project, her conception of foreclosure does not provide a theory of the formation of *homosexual* subjects. Rather, Butler's use of foreclosure precludes homosexual identity and desire. If there is a fundamental prohibition against an attachment to same-sex objects, then homosexual desire is always precluded and, thus, cannot exist. Indeed, Butler argues that to desire against this regulatory prohibition is to enter the realm of abjection and psychosis—and so to be outside the domain of social intelligibility. In order to provide an account of the formation of homosexual identity, it is also necessary to provide an account of the failure of this fundamental prohibition—which Butler does not. Butler's theory does not explain how it is possible to become anything other than a normative heterosexual subject—precisely the theoretical and political failure for which she criticizes Foucault (Butler, 1997). Ironically, Butler fails to provide an account of the constitution of homosexual desire within heterosexist norms because she does not properly engage with the insistence of psychoanalysis that such norms always fail, that normative identity is never fully established, and that the subject is not coherent. In the psychoanalytic account, the subject is never fully (and never can be) interpellated by social norms. For psychoanalysis, the 'normative' oedipal subject is a neurotic subject.

This critical examination of Butler's conception of foreclosure should not be mistaken for an argument that Butler is a poor reader of Freud and Lacan, and that therefore her theory has fundamental flaws. Rather, this analysis of Butler's concept of foreclosure reveals the problematic inconsistencies and implications of her account of the formation of the subject. The reinscription of the psychoanalytic conception of foreclosure shows the limitations of Butler's theory of the psychic life of power.

The Subject of the Unconscious

If Butler's account of the formation of the subject is not fully worked through in terms of her political and theoretical projects, so her theory of the subject itself suffers similar problems. Butler describes the subject as 'that viable and intelligible being' that is instituted by 'the normative demand'. Butler argues that this 'being' is an effect of 'the discursive demand to inhabit a coherent identity, to become a coherent subject' (Butler, 1997, p. 86). For Butler, the subject and identity are the same, for she conceives the subject as the individual's imagined self, the seemingly coherent identity that the subject misrecognizes as its being. This conceptual collapse between identity and subjectivity recurs throughout *Psychic Life* because Butler defines the subject as the conscious self. Butler argues that 'it is important to distinguish between the notion of the psyche, which includes the notion of the unconscious, and that of the subject, whose formation is conditioned by the exclusion of the unconscious' (Butler, 1997, p.206). According to this definition, the subject is that which is other to the unconscious. The psychic agency that refuses the unconscious is the conscious mind; and so, therefore, as Butler conceives it, the subject can only be the conscious self.

Butler's theory of the formation of the subject is in fact a theory of the formation of identity, because it theorizes the constitution of the conscious ego of the 'I' of the self. For this reason, it is not a theory of the psychoanalytic subject, which is the subject of the unconscious. Indeed, Butler does not address the unconscious in her theory of the formation of the melancholic subject. She confines her discussion of the unconscious to a consideration of the concept of the psychic resistance to power, which she argues should not be conflated with political resistance (Butler, 1997, p.98). Butler indicates that she understands the psyche as that which exceeds the normative demands of the social, and hence as that which includes an unconscious. However, she does not theorize this unconscious in relation to her theory of the formation of identity. For example, Butler describes the psyche in terms of the ego and the super-ego (Butler, 1997, p.86). However, it is not clear how this psyche includes a notion of the unconscious, as Butler does not discuss the id. Similarly, Butler's theory of the melancholic subject is primarily concerned with the psychic operations of the ego and super-ego as agencies of the reflexive conscious self, rather than with workings of the unconscious. For example, Butler characterizes the 'psychic instruments' of power as 'the declaration of guilt, the judgement of worthlessness, the verdicts of reality', which are conscious operations of the super-ego and the ego (Butler, 1997, p.197).

In this way, Butler reduces the subject to its conscious ego and so does not distinguish between the conscious ego that forms the 'I' of identity and the unconscious of the subject. Lacan (1977) argues that the subject cannot be reduced to the first person 'I' of consciousness. For Lacan, the confusion of subject and identity is a misrecognition of the ego as self, and the self as the subject, in a defensive operation that repudiates the unconscious. Without such a conceptual distinction, an account of the subject simply theorizes the subject of consciousness, not the psychoanalytic subject of the unconscious.

It appears that for this reason, Freud, and not Lacan, is the primary theoretical source of Butler's theory of the subject. For example, Butler appropriates Freud's (1984a) metapsychology of the ego and the super-ego, without referring to the third psychic agency: the id. In contrast, Lacan's return to Freud is predicated upon the unconscious, deploying his earlier schema of the division between conscious and unconscious. Although Lacan's work clearly informs much of Butler's theory, she rarely discusses his theory of the subject in *The Psychic Life of Power*. Instead, Butler's explicit discussions of Lacan most often address his conception of the symbolic paternal law. It seems that Lacan's absent presence permits an appropriation of his theory of the subject without the difficulty of engaging with the problem of the unconscious.

The irony of the predominant characterization of *The Psychic Life of Power* as Butler's (1997) most psychoanalytic work is that Butler's theory of the subject is not psychoanalytic. It is not psychoanalytic because it is not framed by the psychoanalytic problematic of that which is other to consciousness: the unconscious. The unconscious remains the unthought in Butler's theory, functioning as its *aporia*. This failure to engage with the psychoanalytic problematic produces an *aporia* within Butler's theory of the subject and prevents her from working through her own theoretical and political project.

The Subject of Philosophy

In 1999, Butler characterized her theoretical project as being fundamentally concerned with two questions: 'What is the relation between desire and recognition, and how is it that the constitution of the subject entails a radical and constitutive relation to alterity' (Butler, 1999, p.xiv). Butler argues that 'in a sense, all of my work remains within the orbit of a certain set of Hegelian questions' (Butler, 1999, p.xiv). These Hegelian questions frame *The Psychic Life of Power* (1997). For example, in *Psychic Life* Butler first articulates the problem of the constitution of the subject through Hegel, then re-reads Hegel on the unhappy consciousness, and ends with a discussion of melancholia as the reproduction of power in its modelling of reflexivity—one's relation to oneself—on subjection.

Lacan argues that the Hegelian model of the 'being conscious of self, the fully conscious self' produces a subject that is founded in the conscious and secured by consciousness (Lacan, 1977, p.296). This is a subject in the traditional philosophical sense of a conscious self. This subject projects consciousness and self as a unified identity. That unity of identity enables it to claim mastery and presence of self. It substantiates itself as a transparent, certain, and foundational consciousness. In his later work *L'Envers de la Psychanalyse* (1991), Lacan argues that the subject of consciousness founds philosophical discourse. Lacan (1991) contends that philosophy founds its knowing upon a conscious self, an 'I' that believes that what it perceives of itself represents its true self, that it can know itself and, hence, that it can master itself (Lacan, 1991, p.71). Philosophical knowledge continually reproduces this transcendental and illusory conscious self (Lacan, 1991, p.70). For Lacan, philosophy is a discourse of mastery.

In *Subjects of Desire*, Butler considers the implications of Lacan's critique of Hegelian philosophy. She briefly, but suggestively, discusses the implications of Lacan's critique of Hegel for philosophical thinking. Butler argues that:

> Inasmuch as philosophy savours the postulation of a self-adequate subject, philosophical discourse purports to say all that it means, and never to mean more than it actually says. The psychoanalytic deconstruction of philosophy would, then, consist in listening to the lacks and gaps in philosophical discourse, and theorising on that basis what kind of defence against desire the philosophical project seems to be (Butler, 1997, pp.196-197).

Considered in these terms, Butler's theory of the subject in *The Psychic Life of Power* reproduces philosophical discourse. It postulates the self-adequate subject of philosophy, a conscious self that is transparent, certain, and foundational. Her theory continually performs this subject, reiterating this transcendental and illusory conscious self of identity. If that theory is read symptomatically, this philosophical discourse of the conscious subject repudiates the unconscious. Because this subject takes up a defensive position against its unconscious other, it cannot know itself in its refusal of the unconscious. It repeats the philosophical defense against its unconscious other.

Butler's missed encounter with the psychoanalytic unconscious traps her theory of the subject within the philosophical discourse of the conscious self. The fundamental psychoanalytic distinction between the conscious and the unconscious reveals 'reason's inability to come outside of itself, to enclose and know itself from the outside: the inadequation of the subject and its other' (Grosz, 1993, p.189). *Psychic Life* continually repeats, and is haunted by, the impossibility of understanding the 'being conscious of self, the fully conscious self' without a theory of the unconscious. For this reason, the *aporia* of the unconscious in Butler's theory of the subject prevents her from working through a theory of the psychic life of power.

Psychic Life articulates an extremely important political and theoretical problematic for contemporary theory. Politically, it provides a critical account of the formation of identity in power. Theoretically, it deploys both Foucault and Freud to produce this critical account, opening the possibility of a powerful intersection of Foucauldian and psychoanalytic theory. However, Butler's repetition of philosophical discourse, and her failure to undertake a psychoanalytic discourse prevents her from developing this important theoretical and political project. Instead, like the return of the repressed, it continually suffers the plague of the (repressed) unconscious. In order to understand the psychic life of power, it is necessary to reconsider the problematic relationship between the political subject of Foucault and the unconscious subject of Freud. Such a reconsideration requires further engagement with the power of psychic life.

Acknowledgements

I am grateful to Parveen Adams, David Bausor, Steve Cross, and Kate Nash for their insightful comments on this paper.

References

Bell, Vikki (ed.) (1999), *Performativity and Belonging*, Sage, London.

Butler, Judith (1987), *Subjects of Desire: Hegelian Reflections in Twentieth-Century France*, Columbia University Press, New York.

———— (1990), *Gender Trouble: Feminism and the Subversion of Identity*, Routledge, London and New York.

———— (1993), *Bodies That Matter: On the Discursive Limits of 'Sex'*, Routledge, London and New York.

———— (1997), *The Psychic Life of Power: Theories in Subjection*, Stanford University Press, Stanford.

———— (1999), 'Preface', *Subjects of Desire: Hegelian Reflections in Twentieth-Century France*, Columbia University Press, New York.

Foucault, Michel (1977), *Discipline and Punish: The Birth of the Prison*, A. Sheridan, (trans.), Pantheon, New York.

———— (1978), *The History of Sexuality, Volume 1: An introduction*, R. Hurley (trans.), Vintage, New York.

———— (1980), *Power/Knowledge: Selected Interviews and Other Writings, 1972-1977*, C. Gordon (ed.), Pantheon, New York.

———— (1985), *The History of Sexuality: Volume 2: The Uses of Pleasure*, R. Hurley (trans.), Pantheon, New York.

Freud, Sigmund (1962), 'The Neuro-Psychoses of Defence', in *The Standard Edition of the Complete Works of Sigmund Freud*, J. Strachey (ed. and trans.), vol. 3, Hogarth, London, pp.43-61.

———— (1979), 'The Loss of Reality in Neurosis and Psychosis' in A. Richards (ed.), *On Psychopathology: Inhibitions, Symptoms, Anxiety*, J. Strachey (trans.), Penguin, Harmondsworth, pp.219-226.

———— (1984a), 'The Ego and the Id', in A. Richards (ed.), *On Metapsychology: The Theory of Psychoanalysis*, J. Strachey (trans.), Penguin, Harmondsworth, pp.339-407.

———— (1984b), 'Mourning and Melancholia', in A. Richards (ed.), *On Metapsychology: The Theory of Psychoanalysis*, J. Strachey (trans.), Penguin, Harmondsworth, pp.245-268.

Grosz, E. (1993), 'Bodies and Knowledges: Feminism and the Crisis of Reason', in L. Alcoff and E. Potter (eds), *Feminist Epistemologies*, Routledge, London and New York, pp.187-215.

Lacan, Jacques (1977), *Écrits: A Selection*, A. Sheridan (trans.), Norton, New York.

———— (1991), *Le Séminaire, Livre XVII, L'envers de la Psychanalyse, 1969-1970*, Jacques-Alain Miller (ed.), Seuil, Paris.

————— (1993), *The Seminar of Jacques Lacan. Book III. The Psychoses, 1955-1956*, Jacques-Alain Miller (ed.), R. Grigg (trans.), Routledge, London and New York.

Laplanche, Jean and Pontalis, J.B. (1973), *The Language of Psychoanalysis*, Donald Nicholson-Smith (trans.), Norton, London and New York.

McNay, Lois (1999), 'Subject, Psyche, and Agency: The Work of Judith Butler', in Vikki Bell (ed.), *Performativity and Belonging*, Sage, London.

Chapter 7

Excitable Speech: Judith Butler, Mae West, and Sexual Innuendo

Angela Failler[1]

What is so perilous, then, in the fact that people speak, and that their speech proliferates? Where is the danger in that? (Foucault, 1972)

Is that a gun in your pocket, or are you just glad to see me? (West, in Sherman, 1933)[2]

Mae West, American playwright, screenwriter, and classic Hollywood film star, became a figure of both controversy and popularity in the 1920s with the production of three off-Broadway plays titled *Sex* (1926), *The Drag* (1927), and *The Pleasure Man* (1928). The homosexual characters and narratives of West's plays incited criminal charges of obscenity, indecency, and immorality against West and her theatre crews, indicted by the Grand Jury of the county of New York (West, 1997, p.205). Censorship and celebrity followed West through her film career spanning from the 1930s to the 1970s, her television and radio appearances from the 1930s to the 1950s, and her return to playwriting and the theatre in the 1940s.

The brazen, buxom blonde West is famous for her sexual innuendo. With lines like 'Anytime you got nothing to do—and lots of time to do it—come on up' (*My Little Chickadee*, 1940), she established herself as a sharp-witted, provocative and transgressive *parleuse*. Her quips continue to be, irresistibly, repeated in various commercial and colloquial forms. To date, however, there has been little written explicitly about the connection of this kind of 'irresistible repeatability' to the performativity of speech acts. In this essay, the example of West's sexual innuendo becomes an irresistible occasion through which sexual innuendo and its performative repeatability are explored.

---

[1] A version of Failler's essay appeared under the same title in *International Journal of Sexuality and Gender Studies*, vol. 6, nos. 1-2 (April 2001). Reprinted with permission of Kluwer Academic.
[2] This is Mae West's well-known line from her film *She Done Him Wrong* (1933), directed by Lowell Sherman.

My discussion takes as its point of departure Judith Butler's *Excitable Speech: A Politics of the Performative* (1997a). In this work, Butler investigates the impact of speech acts and the qualities and conditions that render speech acts felicitous (successful)—whether injurious or pleasing. She begins by considering the social constraints and regulatory norms that condition our struggle for legitimacy as speaking subjects, arguing that these conditions constitute the speaking subject as vulnerable in the production of speech. Next to this, however, she carves out a theory of linguistic agency that rests upon a notion of 'discursive performativity'— that speech has the potential to resignify meaning and context against regulatory norms (Butler, 1997a). In this spirit, she offers an account of speech as a site of agency and political resistance for the subject in discourse.

Working alongside Butler, this essay pursues a series of questions about the performativity of speech acts, using Mae West's sexual innuendo as an example. Sexual innuendo provides an instance of 'excitable speech' to explore the possibility of speech as a site of political resistance. The questions that frame this discussion include the following. How are vulnerability and agency simultaneously produced in speech? What are the foreclosures or censors at work in producing speech and the speaking subject? What constitutes the 'force' of the performative speech act? How is the performative speech act made repeatable? And last, how are these conditions implicated in and by Butler's notion of linguistic agency as underpinned by a 'discursive performativity', where the act of speaking itself can serve to undermine linguistic conventions through resignification?

Linguistic Vulnerability, Linguistic Agency

Too many girls follow the line of least resistance—but a good line is hard to resist. (West, in Walsh, 1936)[3]

While as individuals we use language to compliment, seduce, demean, and dispute others, we are simultaneously vulnerable to the other's address. It is in both the agency and vulnerability accorded to us through the relation of address that we are constituted as subjects in discourse. Butler calls this Althusserian relation the 'linguistic condition of survivable subjects', where '[o]ne comes to 'exist' by virtue of this fundamental dependency on the address of the other' (Butler, 1997a, p.5). Essentially, recognition by others through verbal address legitimates our participation in discourse as agents of speech. But we are not, however, 'free agents', precisely because we are vulnerable to the regulatory norms and conventions of language.

Some theorists suggest that our vulnerability as agents of speech is a *prior* condition of becoming social, speaking subjects. Lacanians, in particular, argue that our entrance into the world of 'speakability' requires a foreclosure (refusal or denial) of the 'unspeakable'—those utterances that exceed the bounds of social

---

[3] Mae West speaks this line in *Klondike Annie* (1936), directed by Raoul Walsh.

norms (Butler, 1997a, p.135). Speaking subjects must practice this foreclosure in order to emerge as legitimate and intelligible participants in the symbolic order.[4] Here, as Butler notes, 'unspeakability' becomes as much a condition of subject formation as 'speakability' (Butler, 1997a, p.135); for what we are not allowed to say is, arguably, as formative as what we do say. In this regard, to speak the unspeakable is to risk social sanction or penalty and one's status as a legitimate participant in speech (Butler, 1997a, p.133).

Known best for her sexually 'aggressive' language and racy puns, Mae West transgressed both hegemonic American middle-class values and gendered filmic conventions that normalized passive female subjectivity. These transgressions resulted in the censorship of West's work, and further inflamed an already heated campaign against the representation of 'crime' and 'sex' in Hollywood movies as enforced, specifically, by the Motion Picture Production Code of 1934 (Curry, 1996, p.46). It was evident that West's provocative speech, especially as she insisted on sex as both pleasurable and economically beneficial for women, was the main offense in the eyes of the censors. So while West may have made some gains for sexual expression and representation of women's sexual agency, she was simultaneously vulnerable to industry regulations that succeeded in part to constrain her performance and limit her exposure to mainstream audiences.

As made apparent by West's catch-22, Butler is concerned with the kind of linguistic agency that can be had if subjects themselves are inextricably formed within the restrictive and regulatory conditions of language:

> If we are formed in language, then that formative power precedes and conditions any decision we might make about it, insulting us from the start, as it were, by its prior power...And how, if at all, does linguistic agency emerge from this scene of enabling vulnerability?" (Butler, 1997a, p.2.)

For my purpose, Butler's question might be reframed as such: if 'Mae West', as a cultural icon, necessarily performs within the restrictive censors of the American entertainment industry, how is West's risqué performance effective, if at all? Or, what allowed Mae West to be popular, even irresistible, in the face of insulting cultural critics and public organizations that fought to have her performances banned from public viewing? An investigation of the ways in which language constitutes the subject through restriction and foreclosure is required to take up this query further.

---

[4] The symbolic order, in Lacanian theory, is the social and cultural order in which we live our lives as conscious, gendered subjects. It is structured by language and the social institutions that language secures (Weedon, 1997, p.50).

Foreclosure and the Speaking Subject

Censorship made me. (West, in Jennings, 1971, p.6.)

Foreclosure refers to a forced loss or an exclusionary restriction—a shutting out of certain realities or possibilities. In regards to speech, we might think of foreclosure as a kind of censorship. Such censorship, however, does not happen after speech has occurred (like the banning of Mae West's plays/films/interviews after their initial showings); this censorship happens prior to speech, determining the very conditions of speakability (Butler, 1997a, p.41). According to Butler a certain foreclosure or 'implicit censorship' conditions the emergence of the speaking subject into the discursive world, limiting her/his agency in speech from the start. She notes Freud's distinction between the repression of thoughts and a prior kind of foreclosure as it is exercised upon the unconscious, as being important to an understanding of the pervasiveness of foreclosure: that which is repressed, Freud insists, might once have lived apart from its prohibition (and later censored through prohibition). In the foreclosure exercised upon the unconscious, however, desire has been rigorously, pre-emptively lost from the start, limiting even the capacity for desire, the capacity for thought (Butler, 1997b, p.23).

This analysis can be extended to explain the way that psychic foreclosure finds its expression in speech. When a person speaks, she/he always does so by excluding, censoring, and rejecting ideas and meanings. This is not solely a conscious or cognitive effort, but rather a process mediated by negation and psychic conflict.[5] Further, that speech is unconscious of its foreclosures means that, from a psychoanalytic perspective, the utterance of the speech act is not necessarily a statement of truth but rather, as Shoshona Felman says, a mode of indirect access to what speech cannot possibly say out loud (Felman, 1992, pp.15-16). This means that while it remains unsaid, the unspeakable lingers as a silent but animating presence or, put differently, as an active absence that is unconscious to both the speech act and its speaker but has implications nonetheless.

Gayatri Chakravorty Spivak offers an account of foreclosure using Lacan's (interpretation of Freud's) notion of foreclosure as a barring or blocking of ideas, but extends this analysis to metaphorize the barring of certain subjectivities from cultural intelligibility. Essentially, she argues that the production of the white Western subject is achieved through a foreclosure of the voice of the subaltern woman. For Spivak, the sense of foreclosure at work in this production is:

---

[5] In his essay on 'Negation', Freud describes how negation is invoked when there is a conflict between conscious and unconscious desire over an idea. As an 'intellectual substitute for repression' (Freud, 1925, p.438), negation functions to alleviate the pressure of psychic conflict by allowing us to dismiss certain (intolerable) thoughts in the pursuit of others. In other words, negation keeps the threatening or intolerable content of thought away from consciousness. This dismissed or discarded content, however, is not entirely lost. Instead, it comes to underlie and animate efforts like speech, for example, as the 'unsaid' of language.

[t]he sense brought to the fore by Lacan…[which is to be found] for instance, in [what] Freud writes…[about] 'a much more energetic and successful kind of defence. Here, the ego rejects [*verwirft*] the incompatible idea *together with the affect* and behaves as if theidea had never occurred to the ego at all' (Spivak, 1999, p.4, emphasis in original).

Spivak makes a parallel between Freud's notion of foreclosure by the ego with the way in which colonial violence serves to forcibly reject the subjectivity of non-Western or subaltern women and their place in the production of knowledge and culture. She argues that subaltern women are excluded as if they never existed at all, treated as incompatible with an idealized Western liberal-humanist notion of subjectivity, while the fact that the chimera of the white Western subject relies upon subaltern women's exclusion for its own façade, goes unacknowledged.

The representational foreclosure of the subaltern voice that Spivak describes is, for the most part, consistent with Butler's discursive notion of foreclosure where linguistic agency is made possible only through the constitutive constraints of cultural intelligibility. Within a Butlerian framework then, Spivak's account of colonial/racist exclusion can be used to understand the production of Mae West as a North American cultural icon. Particularly in West's films, African American actors appear in the roles of maid and/or attendant to West's character. These characters are typically at West's disposal as domesticated and/or exoticized servants. Their agency as subjects in speech is, for the most part, denied. Instead, their presence appears to reinforce West's position as the (sexually and racially) dominant figure of the scene. Ramona Curry observes this relationship:

…the maids clearly augment West's featured—and fetishized—status, enhancing the star's aura of power and sexual allure through their roles as servants and through their vividly contrasting visual presence, their dark skin, hair, and costumes setting off West's shimmering bleached-blonde whiteness (Curry, 1996, p.87).

Curry's analysis, in the spirit of Spivak's critique, suggests that West's character is effectual precisely because certain linguistic possibilities have been shut out and pushed underground—namely the linguistic agency of racialized 'others'. This foreclosed 'agency', then, becomes part of the unsaid of West's jokes and, I will argue, part of what gives her jokes their conventional force.[6]

---

[6] Cultural critic Dina Georgis notes that while Spivak rightly draws attention to the colonial and epistemic violence committed against subaltern women, her analysis remains melancholically invested in the un-recoverability of these voices (Georgis, 2003, p.14). Spivak herself forecloses the possibility of subaltern voices by limiting the notion of agency to one that conceptualizes 'speaking' only in terms of the capacity to have 'official resonance' (p.19). Georgis asks, does not the subaltern woman still 'speak' even if her voice comes from a place other than the 'agency' afforded non-colonized subjects? Do not her utterances still resonate even if they are in the register of otherness or difference? It is beyond the scope of this paper to fully draw out the significance of this critique; however, I will observe that the application of Spivak's analysis to the case of racialized characters in

Foreclosure is not only restrictive then—it is also productive since it determines what constitutes intelligible speech and the possibility of agency *upon* this foreclosure. In this sense, Butler explains, 'limitation [in language] is not fully negative in its implications' (Butler, 1997a, p.41). In a chapter from *Excitable Speech* called 'Implicit Censorship and Discursive Agency', she elaborates Foucault's idea of how pre-emptive or implicit censorship produces the conditions of discursive agency for the speaking subject: '[C]ensorship is not merely restrictive and privative, that is, active in depriving subjects of the freedom to express themselves in certain ways, but also formative for subjects and the legitimate boundaries of speech' (Butler, 1997a, p.132). When West claims 'I wasn't conscious of being sexy until the censors got after me' (West, 1975, p.87), and 'Censorship made me' (West, in Jennings, 1971, p.6), she points to this constitutive power of censorship as it shapes the reception of her speech and the production of her image. Curry too makes this relationship between censorship and West's success:

> Much of West's comedic appeal—like that of comedy more generally—derived precisely from her violating social mores in performance, even to the point of inviting censorship. Audience knowledge that West's performances had provoked censorship augmented her comic reception, for it alerted listeners and viewers to expect and catch possible sexual implications in almost every line and gesture. The threat of censorship enhanced, even yielded, the joke (Curry, 1996, p.81).

For West, censorship worked not only to reinforce her image as a defiant performer; it actually reiterated the force of her jokes. We might say then that West's talent was precisely her capacity to maintain the tension of simultaneous vulnerability and agency in speech.

Speech Acts and the 'Force' of the Performative

> It isn't what I do, but how I do it. It isn't what I say, but how I say it, and how I look when I do it and say it. (West, 1975, p.43.)

J.L. Austin wrote that performative speech acts are utterances that produce action or perform an operation in their speaking (Austin, 1962, p.32). Performatives work through the power of citation, meaning that they cite or invoke certain linguistic conventions thereby acquiring the power and legitimacy of social law (Butler, 1993, p.225). 'Felicitous' performatives are speech acts that achieve their intended actions or operation through this citation. The citation of conventions and social law accords them a certain 'force' that is recognized by the recipient(s) of the speech act as meaningful and legitimate, securing their success. On the other hand, 'infelicitous' performatives or 'misfires', to use Austin's terminology, fail to

---

Mae West's productions fails to account for the counter-discourse that might potentially be read from the 'speech' of these characters.

achieve their intended action and are experienced as 'void or without effect' (Austin, 1962, p.16). For instance, sexual innuendo that fails to be experienced as a sexual hint is rendered impotent by misrecognition.

Austin makes a further distinction between 'illocutionary' speech acts and 'perlocutionary' speech acts. In the case of the illocutionary speech act, the saying is itself a kind of doing, or, the speech is a performance of an act in itself (Austin, 1962, p.99). For example, 'I would like to apologize', conventionally, performs an apology—it does not only suggest an intended apology, as its literal meaning states, indeed, it *is* the apology. Distinctly, the perlocutionary speech act achieves certain *effects* by saying something (Austin, 1962, p.121). Althusser's famous example is the hailing of the pedestrian by the police officer's shout, 'Stop!' (Althusser, 1971). Here, it is assumed that the effect of the officer's shout is experienced after it has been heard. While the force of the illocutionary speech act is set in motion, simultaneous with its saying, by its situatedness within particular socially affirmed linguistic conventions (in the first instance, within the conventions of apology), the perlocutionary act is set in motion mainly by the subsequent actions it incites—in the second instance, by the pedestrian stopping and turning towards the call of the police officer.

Butler insists that Austin's distinction between illocutionary and perlocutionary speech acts is significant. Particularly, she is interested in his notion that the illocutionary speech act produces its effects *in the same time* as its utterance. For Butler, this distinction does not take account of how the meaning achieved by the speech act is produced historically and contextually – beyond the single moment of its articulation. She proposes that it is not only the conventional illocutionary force that renders a performative speech act felicitous, it is the *repetition of speech that recalls prior acts* that gives speech its performative power (Butler, 1997a, p.20):

> If a performative provisionally succeeds (and I will suggest that 'success' is always and only provisional), then it is not because an intention successfully governs the action of speech, but only because that action echoes prior actions, and *accumulates the force of authority through the repetition or citation of a prior, authoritative set of practices*. What this means, then, is that a performative 'works' to the extent that it *draws on and covers over* the constitutive conventions by which it is mobilized. In this sense, no term or statement can function performatively without the accumulating and dissimulating historicity of force (Butler, 1997a, pp. 226-227, emphasis in original).

The performative speech act, then, acquires its force through an accumulation of meaning over time, and through its relationship to its immediate discursive/temporal context. This relationship between speech and historicity, Butler maintains, is covered up, hidden through the conventions by which speech is mobilized—the structure of language. Somewhat paradoxically then, it is the repeated stifling of constitutive historicity in speech (and not the intentionality of the speaker) that allows the performative speech act to be understood.

Repetition and 'Discursive Performativity'

Women with 'pasts' interest men because men hope that history will repeat itself. (West, 1975, p.50.)

According to Butler, our simultaneous vulnerability and agency in language presents a paradoxical scenario: the speaking subject depends on restrictive regulatory norms and the aforementioned foreclosures in order to exercise linguistic agency. So, each time the subject 'enters' speech, she/he repeats these foreclosures, thereby reinforcing them, her/his dependency on them, and their constitutive restrictions:

> If the subject is produced in speech through a set of foreclosures, then this founding and formative limitation sets the scene for the agency of the subject. Agency becomes possible on the condition of such a foreclosure....Because the action of foreclosure does not take place once and for all it must be repeated to reconsolidate its power and efficacy....Thus, the subject who speaks within the sphere of the speakable implicitly reinvokes the foreclosure on which it depends and, thus, depends on it again (Butler, 1997a, pp.139-140).

What Butler effectively argues in the above passage is that the restrictive norms and foreclosures of speakability are maintained through discursive repetition—a repetition performed by the speaking subject who is *compelled* to repeat certain foreclosures in order to participate in speech. According to this reading, foreclosure and regulatory norms are not singular or final events; rather, they are 'reiterated effect[s] of a structure' (Butler, 1997a, p.138). On the double assumption, then, that foreclosure is not a final event and that it is the speaker who must reiterate its terms, Butler sees an opportunity to disrupt the chain of foreclosure's reiteration. Foreclosure's impermanence allows a space, somewhere between reiterations or repetitions, for the speaker to disrupt the conditions of speakability by *resignifying* meaning against or distinct from the terms of its prior usage.

There is another sense, however, in which repetition works in the production of language. While in the first sense, repetition works to reiterate foreclosures, in the second sense repetition works to accumulate and solidify meaning. In this sense, meaning is constituted through the repeated performance of the signifying mark—a process Butler calls 'discursive performativity'. Borrowed from Jacques Derrida, this notion of discursive performativity, the repetition of the signifying mark, is inherent to the production of language. For Derrida, the word or mark must be flexible enough to be recognized and understood in new and various scenarios, beyond its intended recipient, in order to function as a sign within communication. He writes, 'My communication must be repeatable—iterable—in the absolute absence of the receiver or of any empirically determinable collectivity of receivers' (Derrida, 1988, p.7). In other words, speech must be repeated and repeatable in order to work, and this repeatability 'presupposes that the formula [of the utterance] itself continues to work in successive contexts, that it is bound to no context in particular even as...it is always found in some context or another'

(Butler, 1997a, p.147). Speech, then, is never fully constrained or determined by its originating context. Rather, speech is transferable from one context to another. And while it never retains exactly the same meaning as in previous usages (which in Derrida and Butler's theorizing is because of the specific *discursive* conditions by which it is rendered meaningful in each subsequent repetition), it retains enough significance in order to be recognizable and felicitous in new situations. In fact, recognition of the old meaning in the new context is what gives the speech act its intelligibility even when resignified as something quite different from its 'original'.

Mae West used material repeatedly and often cited her own dialogue from one performance in another (Curry, 1996). These repetitions reinforced West's memorableness and 'quotability' by calling, to the viewer's attention, her performances over and over again. That West continues to be cited in various commercial and colloquial forms by others also proves her irresistible repeatability. A queer revision of one of West's notorious lines demonstrates this process of repetition and citation:

> Mae West sees a woman looking at her. West goes up to her and asks, 'Is that a puddle you're standing in or are you just glad to see me?' (Curry, 1996, p.xvii).

This joke, which Ramona Curry suggests circulated among media scholars in the early 1990s, is clearly fashioned after West's line 'Is that a gun in your pocket, or are you just glad to see me?' The original, spoken by West's (female) character to a male recipient, is rewritten here to make the line's recipient a woman, and the male-defined desire as signified in the original joke by the gun/erection gives way to a spillover of female (lesbian) desire as signified by the orgasmic puddle left by the woman.[7] Here, we notice that the substitution of the puddle for the gun is a significant break from the meaning of the old joke. The revised joke, however, is not entirely new, for it is still a play on the recipient's evident desire for West. Further, it is in recognition of the old joke that the new joke gains its effectiveness and, I would argue, its sense of humor. What is particularly irresistible about repeating/revising Mae West's sexual innuendo is not only the pleasure gained from the recollection of West's original text, but also the pleasure gained from recontextualizing the innuendo with new significance, meaning, and success. In this case, the revision undermines the conventions of the original joke, thereby breaking with the normative, heterosexual codes and articulations of desire. This is an example of Butler's 'discursive performativity' as it functions to resist; the repetition of the new joke (the puddle joke, in this case) confounds rather than consolidates the old joke's normative efficacy.

---

[7] Alternatively, this response might also be read as coming from a place of either gleeful, platonic adoration, or fear.

Sexual Innuendo and the Performativity of the 'Unsaid'

> A joke says what it has to say, not always in few words, but in *too* few words – that is, in words that are insufficient by strict logic or common modes of thought and speech. It may even actually say what it has to say by not saying it (Theodor Lipps, in Freud, [1905] 1991).

> Between two evils, I always pick the one I never tried before (West, in Walsh, 1936).[8]

Sexual innuendo presents a unique case by which to examine performative speech acts and the potential of discursive performativity because the meaning of sexual innuendo lies not in what is uttered, but rather in the effect of what is *unsaid* or what remains *unspoken*.[9] What is characteristic of sexual innuendo is its capacity for double meaning: first, a literal or uttered meaning that is, on the surface, non-sexual or platonic and, second, a suggested or underlying meaning that is characteristically sexual and unsaid. Simultaneity of meaning is thus required in order to produce the effect of an innuendo: what is said relies upon the unsaid meaning for its sexual suggestion, while the unsaid meaning relies upon the structure of the utterance for its articulation. Thus, the effect of innuendo relies upon the tension between the stated and the implied.

Sexual innuendo might also be characterized as a double entendre. The definition of 'double-entendre' that Freud gives is of a joke constructed on a double-meaning that relies upon a word or words not invoking their 'usual' meaning but, rather, in the context of the joke, having a 'sexual' meaning (Freud, [1905] 1991, p.75). On the other hand, speech act theorist John R. Searle would take up sexual innuendo as a metaphor or indirect speech act, '[an] utteranc[e] in which the speaker means metaphorically something different from what the sentence means literally...' (Searle, 1979, p.76). In addition to these, we can compare sexual innuendo to the categories of performative speech acts that Austin uses. Is sexual innuendo illocutionary? Does it perform something by its very saying? If so, what does it perform? Sex? Or is sexual innuendo better described as perlocutionary—that is, causing a certain effect (sexual interest?) in its saying? In the case of Mae West's performance of sexual innuendo, it is obvious that her speech was provocative, but we could also say that her speech performed and continues to perform something in its saying? In a sense, the reiteration of West's speech performs 'Mae West' and the complicated nexus of foreclosures and repetitions that typified her comedy. But let us examine how sexual innuendo, particularly, achieves its performative success.

We can start by asking, what constitutes a felicitous sexual innuendo? Or, how does sexual innuendo work? As Searle puts it, '[h]ow is it possible for speakers to communicate to hearers when speaking metaphorically inasmuch as they do not

---

[8] This is another one of Mae West's lines in *Klondike Annie*.

[9] Much of this analysis has derived from a reading of sexual innuendo alongside Linda Hutcheon's *Irony's Edge: The Theory and Politics of Irony* (1995).

say what they mean?' (Searle, 1979, p.76). When West says, 'Anytime you got nothing to do – and lots of time to do it – come on up', how do we recognize what she means by her invitation to 'do it'? At the very least, we can be sure that the performative force of the innuendo is *implicit* because the significance of the act lies in what is unsaid. But, then, how is the unsaid performative?

According to Butler's interpretation of Austin's felicitous performative, for sexual innuendo to 'work' it must resonate for the recipient with prior acts or signifiers of sexual desire. If it does not, the recipient experiences the utterance to be chaste. If this happens, the innuendo itself is seemingly infelicitous because it fails to repeat, for the recipient, something familiar enough to make the sexual intentions of the innuendo (and the speaker) understood. Note, however, that while sexual innuendo must repeat something 'prior', it need not repeat that prior thing *in the same way*. 'Is that a puddle you're standing in...?' does and does not recall its earlier version, 'Is that a gun in your pocket...?' While the puddle line's resonance with the earlier version of the joke constitutes its repetition, its difference from the earlier joke marks the moment where the speech act is resignified. We can consider the sexual innuendo *partially* resonant then, for it both does and does not recall prior structures of reference.[10] This partial or ambivalent resonance is characteristic of all speech acts, however; for any utterance, while it repeats a prior act, never does so *as precisely the same act*.[11]

The Queer West: Radical Resignifications

The best way to learn to be a lady is to see how other ladies do it (West, 1975, p.52).

Queer resignifications are one way that we can imagine 'discursive performativity' functioning as resistance to normative structures in language and discourse. This has been shown, for instance, by the queering of West's 'Is that a gun in your pocket...?' line (Curry, 1996, p.xvii). And we can queer this particular innuendo even further by shifting its structuring terms once again:

---

[10] I owe the articulation of this idea to Sharon Rosenberg in a personal communication in 2000.

[11] Perhaps it is worth noting here Gilles Deleuze's understanding of repetition where, distinct from Butler's understanding of repetition as presenting the *possibility* for resignification, for Deleuze, every repetition is already a resignification. He argues that while repetition is typically thought of in the terms of similarity, sameness, or equality, repetition is actually marked by an inherent *difference* or *variation* where that which is repeated is distinct from its previous articulation (Deleuze, 1994, p.xvi). For Deleuze, a repetition is not a repeating of something in exactly the same way because a repetition of an earlier articulation takes place in a different time than the last. Therefore, repetition, as it is marked by this temporal difference, is always, already a *re*signification or a new signification. Furthermore, and in congruence with Butler's notion of 'discursive performativity', Deleuze insists that there is no original that is being repeated in repetition; instead, repetition constitutes the term that it is said to repeat.

A woman sees another woman looking at her. The first woman goes up to the second woman and asks, 'Is that a gun in your pocket or are you just glad to see me?'

The rendition given here presents yet another shift in the joke's constitutive terms. From the earliest version, premised upon male desire as signified by the gun/erection, to the puddle version that represents female desire by the orgasmic puddle, this third version offers a possible 'lesbian phallus' as signified by the gun-suspected-to-be-a-dildo or some other form of female erection. While this version actually moves closer to the original in terms of its similitude of wording, it has turned the original on its head (so to speak) to expose the manipulability of the phallus as a strictly male signifier of heterosexual desire and, more generally, to demonstrate the transgressability of normative sexual codes through performative discourse.

A number of West's jokes also offer queer re-readings *without* changing the structure of the utterance: 'The best way to learn to be a lady is to see how other ladies do it', connotes lesbian sex whether West intended this or not. Alternatively, the line could be read as an offer of advice from one gay/drag queen to another.[12] 'They say gentlemen prefer blondes, but who says blondes prefer gentlemen?' (West, 1975, p.49) can be queered too. The first technique involved in queering this joke requires an understanding of the joke as it was originally intended: West begins with the common idiom 'gentlemen prefer blondes', which literally suggests that men prefer blonde *women* as sexual object choices. By introducing this idiom with the words 'They say', West marks 'gentlemen prefer blondes' as a conventional perception. Her intent, then, is to challenge the validity of this convention by reversing the terms as such: but do blondes prefer gentlemen, or perhaps some other kind of men? To un-straighten this line takes West's challenge one step further where 'who says blondes prefer gentlemen' comes to suggest 'who says blondes prefer *men* (at all)?' The queered line then both repeats and builds on West's original undermining of social convention and authority by asking 'who says?'—but this time challenging its heterosexual terms.[13]

In his analysis of jokes, Freud observes that often what is unspeakable, particularly criticism of social convention, is articulated through jokes as an undermining of social authorities. He writes, 'the object of the joke's attack may...well be institutions, people in their capacity as vehicles of institutions, dogmas of morality or religion, views of life which enjoy so much respect that objections to them *can only be made under the mask of a joke and indeed of a joke concealed by its façade*' (Freud, [1905] 1991, p.153, emphasis added). It is in this sense—that the joke functions to articulate an otherwise unspeakable criticism of authority—that Mae West is able to make her bold and defiant statements, for, arguably, they could neither be articulated nor heard outside of her comedic

---

[12] Thanks to Warren J. Blumenfeld, who in 2000 offered this reading.

[13] Thanks to Lesley Biggs, who in 2003, drew out the relevance of West's questioning of the 'who?'.

rendering. However, at the same time that West challenges sex, class, and gender conventions she relies upon these conventions by invoking them in her performances. Like the strategies of irony and parody, West's comedy must first erect social convention in order to subsequently undermine it. This has been demonstrated, for example, in the oppositional structure of the joke 'They say gentleman prefer blondes, but who says blondes prefer gentleman?'—where the first phrase introduces convention and the second undermines it. Only through invoking convention, then, is West able to set the stage for her rebellious speech and for the possibility of articulating a defiant female sexual agency.

Conclusion

> An ounce of performance is worth a pound of promises (West, 1975, p.71).

In *The Psychic Life of Power: Theories in Subjection* (1997b), Butler comes to rethink whether this process of 'discursive performativity' that she is committed to in *Excitable Speech*—whereby signification never occurs totally outside of discourse, but always within and sometimes against discourse—is actually capable of subverting the restrictive conditions of language and subjectivity. She writes, 'From a psychoanalytic perspective...we might ask whether this possibility of resistance to a constituting or subjectivating power can be derived from what is "in" or "of" discourse' (Butler, 1997b, p.94). In other words, she raises a question about the possibility of resisting the conventions of speakability from within language; for as demonstrated earlier, the foreclosures that constitute the impossible 'outside' of linguistic intelligibility also secure our entrance into and intelligibility within discourse as speaking subjects. In *Excitable Speech* she argues that speech is never fully constrained by its context (thereby allowing the speaker opportunities for agency within speech). But speech can never be fully constrained by its speaker either. So while the indeterminacy of language might allow for certain linguistic possibilities, there is also psychic ambivalence that imbues speech with meaning that cannot be known in advance for both the speaker and recipient of speech. In this sense too, we are never guaranteed transparency or intentionality in language.

Next, Butler poses an even more difficult question: what does it mean that discourse not only produces the domains of the speakable, but is itself 'bounded through the production of a constitutive outside: the unspeakable, the unsignifiable?' (Butler, 1997b, p.94). In other words, what does it mean that language is constituted by discursive contests and psychic turns that are ultimately unknowable ('outside') and incomprehensible to us as speakers and interpreters of discourse? How can we know the ways, for instance, by which sexual innuendo is rendered psychically meaningful for the participants involved? Or, how can we predict the discursive significance that will be attached to the uttering of a sexual innuendo in any particular or specific context? While it is beyond the scope of the present discussion to pursue these questions in any depth, they serve to further reiterate the idea that the performativity of language and the relations between any subject and its utterance are ultimately 'contingent and radically *heterogeneous*, as well as...contestable' (Parker and Sedgwick, 1995, p.14). Moreover, to begin to consider psychic ambivalence and the role of the unconscious raises more questions (largely unexplored by Butler in *Excitable Speech*) about our understanding of the play of language and our assumed 'agency' in speech.

That the performative speech act is not limited to any single context—indeed that it is transferable and contestable through this transferability—also means that speech proliferates beyond itself and its own intentions. Shoshana Felman writes, most often in speech 'the utterance performs meanings that are not precisely the ones that are stated or, indeed, capable of being stated at all' (Felman, in Butler, 1997a, p.10). This potential, then, for the utterance to perform meanings other than the ones that are stated, is the 'danger' Foucault speaks of when he asks, 'What is so perilous, then, in the fact that people speak, and that their speech proliferates?' (Foucault, 1972, p.216). But while Felman is drawing attention to the unknowability of the unconscious and psychic ambivalence as it comes to figure in speech, Butler's aim in *Excitable Speech* is to explore the indeterminacy of discourse that characterizes this 'proliferation', allowing for the possibility for speech acts to resignify conventional meanings, to function as resistance. It is from within Butler's framework, then, that we might be seduced by Mae West's claim that 'an ounce of performance is worth a pound of promises'—a promise that speaks to the potential for performative resignifications to speak louder than words themselves toward challenging the normative conditions of speakability.

References

Althusser, Louis (1971), 'Ideology and Ideological State Apparatuses', in *Lenin and Philosophy*, B. Brewster (trans.), Monthly Review Press, New York and London, pp. 170-186.

Austin, J.L. (1962), *How to do Things with Words*, Harvard University Press, Cambridge, Mass.

Butler, Judith (1993), *Bodies That Matter: On the Discursive Limits of 'Sex'*, Routledge, New York.

———— (1997a), *Excitable Speech: A Politics of the Performative*, Routledge, New York.

———— (1997b), *The Psychic Life of Power: Theories in Subjection*, Stanford University Press, Stanford.

Curry, Ramona (1996), *Too Much of a Good Thing: Mae West as Cultural Icon*, University of Minnesota Press, Minneapolis and London.

Deleuze, Gilles (1994), *Difference and Repetition*, Paul Patton (trans.), Columbia University Press, New York.

Derrida, Jacques (1988), *Limited Inc.*, Northwestern University Press, Chicago.

Felman, Shoshona (1992), 'Education and Crisis, or the Vicissitudes of Teaching', in S. Felman and D. Laub (eds), *Crisis and Witnessing in Literature, Psychoanalysis and History*, Routledge, New York, pp.1-56.

Foucault, Michel (1972), *The Archeology of Knowledge and the Discourse on Language*, A.M. Sheridan Smith (trans.), Pantheon Books, New York.

Freud, Sigmund ([1905] 1991), *Jokes and Their Relation to the Unconscious*, J. Strachey (trans.), A. Richards (ed.), Penguin Books, London.

————— (1925), 'Negation', in Freud, Sigmund, *On Metapsychology: The Theory of Psychoanalysis*, J. Strachey (trans.), A. Richards (ed.), Penguin Books, London, pp.435-442.

Georgis, Dina (2003), *Trauma's Narratives: Diasporic Histories and Ineffable Truths*, Diss. York University, Toronto.

Hutcheon, Linda (1995), *Irony's Edge: The Theory and Politics of Irony*, Routledge, New York.

Jennings, R.C. (1971), 'Mae West: A Candid Conversation with the Indestructible Queen of Vamp and Camp', *Playboy*, January.

Parker, Andrew and Sedgwick, Eve K. (1995), 'Introduction', in A. Parker and E.K. Sedgwick (eds), *Performativity and Performance*, Routledge, New York and London, pp.1-18.

Searle, John R. (1979), *Expression and Meaning: Studies in the Theories of Speech Acts*, Cambridge University Press, Cambridge.

Sherman, Lowell (dir.) (1933), *She Done Him Wrong*, Paramount, Los Angeles.

Spivak, Gayatri C. (1999), *A Critique of Postcolonial Reason: Toward a History of the Vanishing Present*, Harvard University Press, Cambridge and London.

Walsh, Raoul (dir.) (1936), *Klondike Annie*, Paramount, Los Angeles.

Weedon, Chris (1997), *Feminist Practice and Poststructuralist Theory*, 2nd edition, Blackwell Publishers Inc., Malden, MA.

West, Mae (1975), *Peel Me a Grape*, J.W. Weintraub (ed.), Futura Publications Limited, London.

————— (1997), *Three Plays by Mae West: Sex, The Drag, The Pleasure Man*, L. Schlissel (ed.), Routledge, New York.

PART III
BODY MATTERS:
ARCHAEOLOGY, LITERATURE,
AND PEDAGOGY

Chapter 8

Past Performance:
The Archaeology of Gender as
Influenced by the Work of Judith Butler

Elizabeth M. Perry and Rosemary A. Joyce[1]

Introduction

Recent archaeological work on gender and sexuality has drawn on Judith Butler's (1990, 1993) discussions of such concepts as gender performance and abjection. Butler's focus on the social mechanisms through which gender is produced, performed, and regulated shift attention from presumptions of innate biological difference towards an emphasis on the fluidity of gender constructions. For archaeology, a materialist discipline that treats residues of human behavior as the basis for representations of cultural identities, the confrontation with issues concerning the stability of identity and its relationships to materiality that Butler's work requires is critical. Without such a critique, archaeological materialism could represent biological residues as somehow prior and natural bases for the social categories of gender. While Butler's work is as yet used only by a small number of archaeologists, these contributions represent an important direction within the archaeology of gender. Such archeological studies promise to contribute to explicating the more general applicability of Butler's concepts of performance and abjection through attention to their relationships to practice, regulatory regimes, and materiality. In this paper we provide an overview of this recent archaeological writing, with an emphasis on the ways it draws on, critiques, and extends Butler's work. At the same time, we offer an analysis of the importance of Butler's work to redirecting research on gender within archaeology.

Representations of the past, like those produced by archaeologists, have the potential to lend the illusion of time depth, and thus cultural legitimacy, to contemporary social phenomena. Initially, the archaeology of gender did not critically interrogate its beginning concepts (Claassen, 1992; Joyce, 1995; Joyce and Claassen, 1997; Knapp and Meskell, 1997; Meskell, 1996, 1999).

---

[1] A version of Perry and Joyce's article appeared under the same title in *International Journal of Sexuality and Gender Studies*, vol. 6, nos. 1-2 (April 2001). Reprinted with permission of Kluwer Academic.

Consequently, it could be used to reinforce static, natural, and binary representations of gender in reconstructions of the past and their use in conservative ways in the present (Conkey and Williams, 1991).

The archaeology of gender involves a complex balancing act that requires a critical awareness and deconstruction of how gender operates in the present, the influence of present gender relations on interpretations of the past, and the task of describing the nature of gender and gendered processes in past societies that may have been very different from any known to written histories or ethnographies. Archaeologists may uncover material traces of gender relations that may have no clear modern, historical, or ethnographic counterparts. Gender theory that is not reliant on deterministic views of what constitutes 'male' and 'female' in all societies ultimately proves to be the most fruitful for archaeologists seeking to explore such unknown terrain, since unanticipated diversity in past gender expression may be conflated into socially preconceived categories of 'feminine' and 'masculine'.

As Butler's views of gender focus on the social mechanisms through which gender is produced, performed, and regulated in a society, rather than departing from assumed natural and universal gendered categories or roles, her concepts have proven invaluable for the description and interpretation of (unobserved) prehistoric social systems known only from their material remains. Models of gender that assume (implicitly or explicitly) that gender emerges in a more or less cross-temporally predictable way from 'sex' run the risk of obscuring gender variability in archaeological cultures. Archaeological explanation is bound to an interpretive spiral, in which cultural assumptions frame particular observations as evidence with respect to particular theories. Unexamined assumptions taken for granted can simply be reified, and given an undue sense of reality by the materiality of archaeological remains. When the topic at issue is something like gender, which is so thoroughly biologized in contemporary Western thought, the danger of treating certain material as simply reflective of natural, adaptive, or otherwise inescapable characteristics is high. This would be especially unfortunate in archaeology, where we know that most of human history was not documented in Western sources and where we can assume a variety of social and political relationships once existed that may never have been seen by Western observers. Thus, the deconstruction of the influence on interpretation of current or historically observed social and political conditions facilitated by gender theory like that outlined by Butler is essential to understanding the operation of gender and power in prehistoric communities.

Recently, archaeologists have begun to focus on the regulatory modes through which gender was produced and reproduced in prehistoric communities (Joyce, 1996, 1999, 2001a, 2001b; Meskell, 1999). Judith Butler's work on gender, uniquely appropriate to this task, has been fruitfully employed in this work. Archaeologists have been especially successful in examining the material dimensions of gender performance (Joyce 1996, 1998, 1999, 2000; Knapp and Meskell, 1997; Meskell, 1999). By providing discussions of how materiality can be shaped by regulatory regimes and recursively shape them, this archaeological work addresses one of the repeated criticisms of Butler's concept of performance: its apparent idealism and potential erasure of the physical experience of difference (compare to Conkey and Gero, 1997 and Meskell, 1999).

Gender Performance and Archaeology

Butler's (1990) concept of performance relies on rejecting the assumption that gender possesses inherent natural or pre-social meaning. Prior to the influence of third-wave feminism in anthropology, gender was widely understood as the social manifestation of the immutable and biologically determined 'sex' (Rubin, 1975; compare to Butler, 1993, di Leonardo, 1991, and Moore, 1994). In this view, gender is static, a state of being rather than an act of doing (Hawkesworth, 1997). For Butler, in contrast, gender is more than culturally specific meanings that are inscribed on the passive, always/already sexed body (Butler, 1990). 'Doing' gender describes an ongoing, dynamic process that involves the '*stylized repetition of acts*' through time (Butler, 1990, p.140, italics in original). The act, or activity, of gender is 'both intentional and performative, where "*performative*" suggests a dramatic and contingent construction of meaning' (Butler, 1990, p.139, italics in original).

Gender performance involves public, repetitive actions of movement, gesture, posture, dress, labor, production, interaction with objects, and the manipulation of space (Butler, 1990). As a result, archaeologists are in a position to document gender performance through exploration of these material media. Since gender performance is by definition a repetition or citation of a precedent (Butler, 1993), the kinds of material regularities that archaeologists document in the media of performance can profitably be viewed as mechanisms for the regulation of gender. The character of gender performance will vary across time and space, as gendered meaning is negotiated differently across cultures (Gillespie and Joyce, 1997).

Both formalized ritual performance and the embedded 'performance' of repetitive everyday activities contribute simultaneously to the social regulation of gender. In the overlapping of aspects of ceremonial performance and the performance of everyday life, mechanisms of social power that structure the possible fields of gendered action and representation are most persistent and flexible. The inextricable connections between ceremonial and domestic performance embed power-laden constructions of gender firmly in social life. A critical question in the archaeological examination of gender performance is 'how and why certain kinds of action came to be *representative* of certain kinds of gender' (Joyce, 2001a, p.11). Ritual or ceremonial performances provide one site within which certain kinds of gender performance are presented as precedents for citation in individual, everyday performance. The regulatory effects of such formalized performances include an often public, and always sanctioned, evaluation of the conformity of individuals to ideals.

For Aztec youth in pre-Hispanic sixteenth-century Mexico, for example, communal training in songs and dances was tested by participation in public rituals, which exposed young men to the gaze and comments of young women, the elder males who had trained them, and the men and women of their families of birth (Joyce, 1999). The highly formalized performances on which Aztec boys were judged were formative of gendered subject positions that were desired by central Aztec authorities, in theory leading young men to seek achievement in battle in order to affirm their manliness. Achievement in battle served as a base from which young men could later contract heterosexual unions with the girls who were taught their socially-approved gendered subject position through the same formal ritual performances. In these ceremonies, women impersonating mythical beings reenacted the socially approved lives of Aztec women, as mothers of warriors who literally sacrificed themselves for the good of the state.

In the late pre-Hispanic American Southwest, changes in architectural plans of settlements and the distribution of tools used in tasks that in historic periods were strongly associated with gender materially attest to the embedding of everyday gender performance in spatial contexts charged with the regulatory norms of formalized ritual performances. In contrast to weak evidence for a gendered division of labor prior to 1150 CE (Common Era), spatial segregation of different craft production areas, and the dualistic distribution of production tools in burials after this time in some communities materially documents a division that may be seen as evidence of a newly developed gendered performance of labor (Mills, 2000).

A trend that begins around 1275 CE across the Southwest involves the construction of large, aggregated settlements with central plazas, which may have been open performative spaces at this time. Plazas may have become the dominant spaces for new, integrative communal rituals (Adams, 1989), as some aspects of ritual become public and performance oriented for the first time (Cordell, 1997). During this period, some nucleated sites in the Zuni region were completely enclosed from their inception (Potter and Perry, 2000). These plaza spaces promoted social integration and structured performative possibilities. Plazas were the focal spaces of both discrete ceremonial ritual acts and repetitive everyday activities.

With the emergence of plaza architecture, everyday labor activities historically associated with women in pueblo communities, such as corn grinding, tended to shift from locations inside rooms to communal spaces such as plazas (Ortman, 1998). Plazas were the locus of both ceremonial and domestic performances, partitioned in various ways. At the late prehistoric pueblo of Homol'ovi I in central Arizona, for example, the east side of a large central plaza was intensively used for domestic activities, while the west side contained at least three kivas and seems to have been reserved for ceremony (Adams and Adams, 1999). The probability that 'domestic' activities, such as corn grinding and food preparation, that occurred in the east side of the plaza were tied to ritual activities, such as food preparation for ceremonies, underscores the conceptual connection between ceremonial and domestic life. Potter (2000a) has demonstrated that in the Zuni region, central plazas at pueblo sites of this period were the locus of communal feasting, an activity that linked domestic food production with public ceremonial obligation and presentation. These trends occurred within a potentially dualistic gendered system of production after 1275 CE that is reified though the connection between everyday and ceremonial performance. While gender is performed in repetitive, publicly visible divisions in labor, this dualism is embedded in ritual practice as well. Bunzel ([1932] 1992) has pointed out that at Zuni, ritual responsibilities mirrored economic dualisms; women feed the gods, while men clothe the gods:

> Prayer sticks are especially male offerings. Although women frequently offer prayer sticks they never make them. Their male relatives (actual or ceremonial) make them for them. So also, although men offer food and corn meal, it is always prepared for them by the women. This division in ritual is a reflection of the general economic pattern, in which the females supply food and the males the clothing of the household. So also women furnish the food of the gods and men their clothing (Bunzel, [1932] 1993, p.501).

The movement of 'everyday' activities, such as corn grinding, into open spaces and the co-incidence of ritual performance in those spaces links ritual performance to the gendered performances of everyday life. This merging of the ceremonial and the domestic materially constituted gendered persons, as gender-segregated ritual performances were naturalized though their visceral connection to and alignment with repetitive daily activities.

Materiality and Gender Performance

Gender performance as repetitive activity is strongly material. Its material dimensions in archaeological contexts include architecture, human figural representations, distributions of artifacts, indications of repetitive action or differences in habits discernible from human skeletal remains, treatment of human burials, and in some times and places, contemporary written documents. The articulations among different materials and their engagement in gender performance are highly culturally contingent. Types of performance and practice that may be situationally associated with a particular gender can change drastically within and across cultures.

For example, Joyce has traced the conditions under which spinning and weaving became representative of adult female gender in Mesoamerica, demonstrating the dependence of constructions of gendered labor on class and on associations between the product of weaving (cloth) and the body (Joyce, 2001a, b). In pueblo communities of the North American Southwest (both pre-Hispanic and post-colonial), the practice of weaving has been socially regulated as a male activity, tied heavily to the subterranean architectural structures in which it commonly occurred (kivas), and engaging a formal ritual component (Potter, 2000b). In both regions, the embedded association between labor practices and particular genders may have been experienced as an entirely natural phenomenon. The reversal of associations in these cases underscores the idea that various social factors collide to produce 'natural' representations of gender. One of the crucial questions addressed by archaeologists using Butler's work is how a sense of naturalism is created for culturally specific regulatory regimes of gender.

Visual representations of idealized human action can serve as powerful material media through which gender performances are naturalized. By embedding apparently realistic depictions of specific gendered behavior, such as postures and movements, in compositions whose surface message was a record of historical incident or everyday activity, Classic Maya (c. 250-1000) artists produced enduring precedents for citation in gendered performance (Joyce, 1996, 2000, 2001a, 2001b). Much as films and advertising photographs provide a source of images against which contemporary North Americans evaluate themselves, ancient visual representations reproduced static, and in most cases highly exclusionary, visualizations of human existence. Unlike the more ephemeral visual media that surround North Americans, in many ancient societies like that of the Classic Maya, human representations were produced in materials that were highly resilient, outlasting their actual makers and users (Joyce, 1998).

Visual representations of highly idealized human action executed in permanent materials, such as stone and pottery, are only the most obvious medium for the production of regulatory regimes of gendered performance that archaeologists can document. As with the interpenetration of formalized and everyday performances, the more visible material media that provide images of regulatory ideals may be systematically related to the everyday experience of individuals within a society through other material means. In a number of societies in Central America, spanning a period from at least 1200 BCE (Before the Common Era) to 1521 CE, gender performance was also shaped by the use of particular forms of dress, both perishable clothing and body ornaments of more permanent materials (Joyce, 1998, 1999, 2001a, 2001b). Ear ornaments that required a long sequence from initial piercing through gradual expansion of the opening in the ear lobe, for example, are remarkably consistent in size and shape from the earliest pottery examples to the latest fine carved stone sets. They imply a conservatism in practices of body modification that itself would have materially shaped the experience of the body as a gendered performance in similar ways over three millennia.

The sheer permanence of architecture and the spaces it shapes, visual representations in stone and pottery, and items of costume provide an abundant body of material through which fleeting gender performances could be permanently inscribed, constrained, and judged against other, represented, performative precedents (Joyce, 1998). It would be easy, given the material bias of archaeological investigations, to be persuaded to a normative view of past societies as inhabited by persons who all were always engaged in tightly regulated gender performances, with little variation. It is this potential for archaeology to overstate regularity that is most dangerous when coupled with investigations of human subjectivity (Conkey and Gero, 1997; Conkey and Williams, 1991). Archaeologists who have actually employed the theoretical concepts of Judith Butler have consistently avoided this pitfall by recourse to other aspects of her work, which directs attention to the boundaries created by performativity. Examples of the archaeological exploration of gender transgressive performance, the materialization of sexuality, and the marking of boundaries of abjection, details of which are discussed in the following pages, provide illustrations of the way attention to these concepts can redirect interpretation of material remains.

Gender Transgressive Performance That Matters

After around 1275 in the pre-Hispanic North American Southwest, gender performance was taking shape seemingly as a binary social phenomenon, reflected in multiple contexts of labor and craft production, architecture, and ritual organization. Viewing gender in terms of its performative character, and exploring the range of social possibilities for its expression exposes degrees of gender fluidity in the same material remains that can be superficially interpreted as always naturalizing normative binary gender. Specific forms of gender transgressive performance, however, both domestic and ceremonial, documented in historic period Zuni communities (Roscoe, 1988, 1991) may have first taken shape during this period of widespread social change.

Public, integrative aspects of ritual and domestic life are particularly relevant to the identification of gender transgressive performance. The movement of domestic activities requiring women's labor into open spaces, and the coexistence of ritual performance in those spaces, enhanced the performative nature of both by virtue of their visibility. In turn, visibility and surveillance constrained and regulated possibilities for expression of gender performance. Since what was ceremonial and what was domestic constituted a fuzzy boundary, the possible avenues for gender expression were continually enforced and reinforced in formal and informal ways. New architectural patterns at this time contributed to the increased visibility of both ritual performance and the performance of everyday activities.

Historically, the status of lhamana, or transgendered person, in historic Zuni communities was tied up with both the performance of domestic labor (which was infused with culturally specific gender significance) and the public, ritual performance of the transgendered Katsina called *Kolhamana* (Roscoe, 1991). For the purposes of this discussion, the term 'lhamana' is used to refer to the gender transgressive person in a general sense, while 'Kolhamana' describes a particular Zuni ritual and religious figure who was, on certain occasions (such as public dances), represented by lhamanas in the community. Lhamanas were primarily identified by ethnographers and other observers who visited Zuni pueblo during the historic period by dress and gesture. Parsons (1939) referred to lhamanas as transvestites, and described in detail the culturally specific feminine clothing, jewelry, hairstyle, speech, and mannerisms of individuals who she perceived to be biologically male (Parsons, 1916). Similarly, some individuals perceived to be biologically female were described as 'girl-boys' primarily based on such characteristics as gait, movement, and attitude (Parsons, 1916, p.525; Roscoe, 1991, p.28). Although individuals described as 'lhamanas' in the historic literature are almost without exception documented as participating regularly in the economic labor stereotypically associated with the 'opposite sex' at Zuni (Parsons, 1916), it seems that there was a tremendous amount of diversity in the types of labor performed by lhamanas. The famous Zuni lhamana, We'wha, was a farmer, weaver, potter, and housekeeper—a mixture of occupations with both female and male contextually contingent gender significance (Roscoe, 1991). Female-bodied lhamanas were described in a sweeping manner as 'mannish', but their labor tended to cross gender lines as well (Roscoe, 1991, p.27).

Lhamanas tended to take the role of Kolhamana, the transgendered Katsina, in public ritual performances, a role for which they were prepared by their transgressive gender performance in domestic settings, in many cases beginning in childhood (Parsons, 1916). In 'one of the most important and elaborate of all Zuni dances' (Roscoe, 1991, p.147), Kolhamana figures prominently in a public ceremony that reflects and performs elements of Zuni origin stories. Parsons (1916) reports some dispute among her Zuni consultants regarding the specifics of Kolhamana's story. Roscoe (1991), however, discusses Cushing's (1896) description of Kolhamana as the first of ten supernatural offspring of a brother and sister, situated in an account of an important Zuni migration. Roscoe (1991) cites Cushing's description of the Zuni's interpretation of these offspring, which become important ritual figures in Zuni religion: 'Neither man-children nor woman-children they! For look now! The first was a woman in fullness of contour, but a man in stature and brawn' (Cushing, 1896, p.401 cited in Parsons 1916, p.524 and Roscoe, 1991, p.153). Due to his role in Katsina origin stories, Kolhamana figured in public ceremonial performance (Parsons, 1916).

Ritual practice in the Zuni region underwent a shift during a period of social transition and reorganization beginning around 1275 CE. The regional pattern of the construction of large, planned, plaza oriented settlements is particularly striking at Zuni (Potter and Perry, 2000). Adams (1989, 1991) suggests that this was associated with the emergence of new ritual and religious ideologies that would have facilitated the integration of diverse groups. If Katsina religion did crystallize at this time, or at least if public performances like those of Katsina religion were formalized, the social status of lhamana may have its roots in this period as well. If gender transgressive performance (both ceremonial and domestic) developed within the context of a highly structured ritual system at the same time that a dualistic gendered organization of labor is evident in social life, this alternative gender performance should also be archaeologically accessible.

For instance, a dualistic gendered division of labor has been suggested for the pre-Hispanic site of Grasshopper pueblo in east-central Arizona, where evidence was discovered for the spatial segregation of manufacturing activities. Two rooms seem to have been devoted to weapons production, while tools for ceramic production were found on other room floors (Mills, 2000; Whittaker, 1987). Mortuary contexts also demonstrate a separation of these tasks. Individuals seem to be buried either with items associated with ceramic tool kits or with weapon-related tools, but not both (Mills, 2000, p.32).

Divisions of labor such as this are examples of what Butler called 'regulatory schemas that produce intelligible morphological possibilities' (Butler, 1993, p.13).

The performance of specific tasks produces skeletal traces that can be identified by archaeologists. For example, analysis of human skeletal material recovered from prehistoric communities in the Midwest and Southeast US has demonstrated that participation in repetitive activities may be evident on the skeleton. In some cases, male skeletons tended to show asymmetrical arm sizes, a result of the use of bow and arrow, while female skeletons possessed symmetrical arm sizes as a result of grain processing with a mortar and pestle (Claassen, 1997). While divisions of labor are one means through which gender and the techniques of regulatory power become inscribed on the skeletal body, another poignant example involves physical evidence for violence against women in prehistoric contexts. Martin and Akins (1994) have documented cranial and skeletal trauma, irregular burial patterns, evidence of short life spans and infection, and extreme occupational stress on the remains of women from the La Plata river valley in northwestern New Mexico. These examples underscore the idea that the materiality of gender in prehistory can be expressed in ways that are highly linked to structures of power.

In communities where gender performance includes labor, individuals who carry the physical inscriptions of gender of the 'opposite' sex may be isolated. Holliman (1997), in a study of Chumash burials, has suggested that where gender is marked by grave goods that fall into two categories, individuals who share grave goods with those of the apparent 'opposite' sex may be transgendered individuals. This type of analysis has potential for pre-Hispanic pueblo sites where later ethnography leads us to suspect the pre-Hispanic existence of transgendered performance. Where craft production is spatially segregated within the site, and burial goods demonstrate a dualistic pattern, individuals that deviate from these patterns in terms of skeletal sex would be candidates for consideration as performing alternative genders. In communities where gendered acts were structured as dualistic and entwined in the perhaps inseparable dimensions of the ceremonial and the domestic, and all realms of performance became increasingly public and visible, transgressive gender performance may have been visible as well. And again, due to the materiality of the performance of gender, transgressive gender performance is potentially as evident as other social practices in the past, once archaeologists reframed their expectations in light of these concepts.

Performance and the Archaeology of Sexuality

Butler's work has by no means been uniformly adopted by archaeologists involved in the burgeoning new subfield of the archaeology of gender (Conkey and Gero, 1997), but it has had particularly strong influence on those archaeologists who are concerned with questions of ancient sexuality (see Schmidt and Voss, 2000). For archaeologists concerned with questions of individual experience of the sexed body, Butler has provided a crucial conceptual vocabulary without which it would be difficult to propose investigations of this topic based on archaeologically recovered remains.

In her discussions of gender performances in the late pre-Hispanic Aztec capital city, for example, Tenochtitlan, Joyce (1999, 2001a) employs a conceptual vocabulary derived from Butler to make sense of practices described in sixteenth-century texts, and relates them to the objects archaeologists working on Aztec society recover. Where standard approaches to these materials relate them almost exclusively to social and economic organization, Joyce is inspired by Butler to consider the subjectivities that were variously shaped by distinct material practices related to the body. The gendered performances she describes include some that contrast with those of both young adult heterosexual women and young adult heterosexual men. Instead of simply describing a dualistic gender system, Joyce is led by Butler's attention to embodied performance to describe an alternative form of gendered performance, that of celibate males and females dedicated to religious service. The same material media—particularly hair dressing and body ornaments—marked this alternative embodied gender performance.

Joyce notes that the earliest performative materialization of gendered bodies in this society was the permanent marking of the bodies of infants destined to such religious service, a gender status that conforms not to a dichotomy of genital sexuality, but to a division based on sexuality that crosses sexed categories. Without the benefit of Butler's concept of performative gender, the significance of body markings and ornaments in establishing Aztec gender performances would not have been identified, and the distinction of a sexual status that crosses biological sexual categories would have been difficult.

Joyce (2000) further explores the materialization of sexuality in a study of Classic Maya (c. 500-1000 CE) male-male sociality. Drawing on the concept of gender performance as citations of precedents (Butler, 1993), Joyce calls attention to the predominance in Classic Maya visual imagery of all-male groups in which young men whose bodies are largely exposed engage in competitive games, dances, and raids, often under the watchful eye of older male figures. Viewing these images as providing precedents for citational gender performance, Joyce argues that the embodied experience of gender they support is one of male-male sexuality. She notes the use of drawings of male genitalia in the Classic Maya writing system as the main component of the word for 'young man' and of a title displayed by some noble men. With the concept of citational precedents for performance in mind, she re-examines the significance of the production of monumental (up to 3 meters) three-dimensional phallic sculptures as evidence not of a 'cult of the phallus', but of the imposition on young men of an idealized citational precedent of adult maleness.

Joyce (2001a), following Butler, notes that regulation of the performance of sexualized genders also marks out the dimensions of abjection, where individual subjectivity is neither recognized nor produced. Bodies that fail to conform literally do not matter, their physical difference is rendered unrecognizable. Joyce argues that visual representation in Mesoamerica provided a mirror against which individual performance could be evaluated against the idealized precedents represented. Butler (1993) argues that performances always fail to adequately conform to the citational precedent. Performance never completely forecloses the difference between a norm and its citation in action.

Joyce (2001a) argues that just as Butler suggests, in Mesoamerica, materialization of the body simultaneously created a domain of bodily abjection that is specific to that context. While in the Euroamerican tradition the domain of the abject is provided by same-sex desire, in Mesoamerica, mixed performances, inter-species hybrids, and the dwarf—beings presented as incompletely human—occupy the edges of embodied abjection. Joyce argues that based on the testimony of regulatory regimes given material form in Mesoamerican representations of anthropomorphic beings, the anxiety of the Mesoamerican tradition is engaged not with sexuality, but with humanity. The repeated representation of dwarf figures as counterparts of idealized male figures (and more rarely, of male and female figures depicted together) in Classic Maya monuments and painted pottery produced for noble households is, from this perspective, a juxtaposition of citational precedent with its unspeakable alternative, a juxtaposition that reinforced this specific regulatory regime.

Conclusion

Archaeology, as practiced in North America, has its theoretical and historical roots in anthropology. Like its maternal discipline, archaeology has seen a significant shift in emphasis since gender difference, rather than gender identity, has been taken as the object of investigation (di Leonardo, 1991; Moore, 1994). The results of engagement by archaeologists with issues of gender difference are voluminous and represent an astonishing range of theoretical, methodological, and empirical studies (Conkey and Gero, 1997).

Within the diverse body of works that make up the contemporary archaeology of gender, the work of Judith Butler is clearly neither uniformly seen as useful nor employed as the theoretical basis for analysis. We, and others who employ Butler's conceptual vocabulary, do so because we are concerned with the social creation of subjectivity, with sexuality, and with exploring the probabilities that alternative sexed positions and alternative conceptions of subjectivity existed in the past. Many other archaeological approaches provide tools to conduct a corrective search for women in the past, or to document the nature of gender hierarchies. But Butler's work is distinct as a resource for archaeologists because it foregrounds topics that until very recently have received no attention precisely because they were believed to be unrelated to material remains: sexuality, the subjective experience of gendered positions, and the processes of embodiment. Our experience in employing conceptual approaches grounded in Judith Butler's work has been to find that material remains usually used as evidence for interpretations distanced from subjectivity are equally, or even more, useful in talking about embodiment, sexuality, and gender.

Because we, as archaeologists, depend on things to talk about social relations, have of necessity had to confront the apparent elision of material experience that has been criticized in Butler's work (Conkey and Gero, 1997; Meskell, 1999; Moore 1994). Archaeologists can, we believe, contribute new perspectives on how performance of gender can be constrained, on where and how precedents for performance could be created and disseminated, and on how they might gain the power to discipline individual experience in societies much removed from the contemporary Euroamerican tradition that is the subject of Butler's analysis. The kinds of material objects, material settings, and material relations that we have identified as useful for our archaeological understanding also have the potential to point towards analogous objects, settings, and relations in the contemporary context, helping to identify the forms of materiality that shape and mask gender performance today as well.

References

Adams, E.C. (1989), 'Changing Form and Function in Western Pueblo Ceremonial Architecture from A.D. 1000 to A.D. 1500', in W.D. Lipe and M. Hegmon (eds), *The Architecture of Social Integration in Prehistoric Pueblos*, Crow Canyon Archaeological Center Occasional Paper no.1, Cortez, CO., pp.155-160.

———— (1991), *The Origin and Development of the Pueblo Katsina Cult*, University of Arizona Press, Tuscon.

Adams, Jenny L. and Adams, E. Charles (1999), 'Inferences about Use from Deposits in Open Spaces of Pueblos in American Southwest', Paper Presented at the 64th Annual Meeting of the Society for American Archaeology, Chicago.

Bunzel, Ruth L. ([1932] 1992), *Zuni Ceremonialism*, University of New Mexico Press, Albuquerque, originally published Washington, DC: Smithsonian Institution Press, Washington, DC

Butler, Judith (1990), *Gender Trouble: Feminism and the Subversion of Identity*, Routledge, New York.

———— (1993), *Bodies That Matter: On the Discursive Limits of 'Sex'*, Routledge, New York.

Claassen, Cheryl (1992), 'Questioning Gender: An Introduction', in C. Claassen (ed.), *Exploring Gender through Archaeology: Selected Papers from the 1991 Boone Conference*, Prehistory Press, Madison, WI, pp.1-9.

———— (1997), 'Changing Venue: Women's Lives in Prehistoric North America', in C. Claassen and R. Joyce (eds), *Women in Prehistory: North America and Mesoamerica*, University of Pennsylvania Press, Philadelphia, pp.65-87.

Conkey, Margaret W. and Gero, Joan M. (1997), 'Programme to Practice: Gender and Feminism in Archaeology', *Annual Review of Anthropology*, vol. 26, pp.411-437.

Conkey, Margaret W. and Williams, Sarah (1991), 'Original Narratives: The Political Economy of Gender in Archaeology', in M. di Leonardo (ed.), *Gender at the Crossroads of Knowledge: Feminist Anthropology in the Postmodern Era*, University of California Press, Berkeley, CA, pp.102-139.

Cordell, Linda (1997), *Archaeology of the Southwest*, Academic Press, New York.

Crown, Patricia L. (1994), *Ceramics and Ideology: Salado Polychrome Pottery*, University of New Mexico Press, Albuquerque.

Cushing, Frank H. (1896), 'Outlines of Zuni Creation Myths', in *Thirteenth Annual Report of the Bureau of American Ethnology, 1891-1892*, Government Printing Office, Washington, DC, pp.321-447.

Di Leonardo, Micaela (1991), 'Gender, Culture, and Political Economy: Feminist Anthropology in Historical Perspective', in M. di Leonardo (ed.), *Gender at the Crossroads of Knowledge: Feminist Anthropology in the Postmodern Era*, University of California Press, Berkeley, pp.1-48.

Gillespie, Susan D. and Joyce, Rosemary A. (1997), 'Gendered Goods: The Symbolism of Maya Hierarchical Exchange Relations', in C. Claassen and R.A. Joyce (eds), *Women in Prehistory: North America and Mesoamerica*, University of Pennsylvania Press, Philadelphia, pp.189-207.

Hawkesworth, Mary (1997), 'Confounding Gender', *Signs: Journal of Women in Culture and Society*, vol. 22, no. 3, pp.649-687.

Holliman, Sandra E. (1997), 'The Third Gender in Native California: Two-Spirit Undertakers among the Chumash and Their Neighbors', in C. Claassen and R.A. Joyce (eds), *Women in Prehistory: North America and Mesoamerica*, University of Pennsylvania Press, Philadelphia, pp.173-188.

Joyce, Rosemary A. (1995), 'Comment on "Engendering Tomb 7 at Monte Alban: Respinning an Old yarn"', by Geoffrey and Sharisse McCafferty, *Current Anthropology*, vol. 35, no. 3, pp.284-285.

——— (1996), 'The Construction of Gender in Classic Maya Monuments', in R.P. Wright (ed.), *Gender and Archaeology*, University of Pennsylvania, Philadelphia, pp.167-195.

——— (1998), 'Performing the Body in Prehispanic Central America', *RES: Anthropology and Aesthetics*, vol. 33 (Spring), pp.147-166.

——— (1999), 'Girling the Girl and Boying the Boy: The Production of Adulthood in Ancient Mesoamerica', *World Archaeology*, vol. 31, no. 3, pp. 473-483.

——— (2000), 'A Precolumbian Gaze: Male Sexuality among the Ancient Maya', in R. Schmidt and B. Voss (eds), *Archaeologies of Sexuality*, Routledge, London, pp.263-283.

——— (2001a), *Gender and Power in Prehispanic Mesoamerica*, University of Texas Press, Austin.

——— (2001b), 'Negotiating Sex and Gender in Classic Maya Society', in C. Klein (ed.), *Gender in Pre-hispanic America*, Dumbarton Oaks, Washington, DC, pp.109-141.

Joyce, Rosemary A. and Claassen, Cheryl (1997), 'Women in the Ancient Americas: Archaeologists, Gender and the Making of Prehistory', in C. Claassen and Rosemary A. Joyce (eds), *Women in Prehistory: North America and Mesoamerica*, University of Pennsylvania, Philadelphia, pp.1-14.

Knapp, A. Bernard and Meskell, Lynn M. (1997), 'Bodies of Evidence in Prehistoric Cyprus', *Cambridge Archaeological Journal*, vol. 7, no. 2, pp.183-204.

Martin, Debra L. and Akins, Nancy J. (1994), 'Patterns of Violence against Women in the Prehistoric Southwest', Paper presented at the Southwest Symposium, Tempe, Arizona.

Meskell, Lynn M. (1996), 'The Somatisation of Archaeology: Institutions, Discourses, Corporeality', *Norwegian Archaeological Review*, vol. 29, no. 1, pp.1-16.

——— (1998), 'The Irresistible Body and the Seduction of Archaeology', in D. Montserrat (ed.), *Changing Bodies, Changing Meanings: Studies on the Human Body in Antiquity*, Routledge, London, pp.139-161.

——— (1999). *Archaeologies of Social Life: Age, Sex, Class, etc. in Ancient Egypt*. Oxford: Blackwell, Oxford.

Mills, Barbara J. (2000), 'Gender, Craft Production and Inequality in the American Southwest', in P.L. Crown (ed.), *Women and Men in the Prehispanic Southwest: Labor, Power and Prestige*, SAR Press, Santa Fe, pp.301-343.

Moore, Henrietta (1994), *A Passion for Difference*, Indiana University Press, Bloomington.

Ortman, Scott G. (1998), 'Corn Grinding and Community Organization in the Pueblo Southwest, A.D. 1150-1550', in K.A. Spielmann (ed.), *Migration and Reorganization: The Pueblo IV Period in the American Southwest*, Arizona State University Anthropological Research Papers, no. 51, pp.165-192.

Parsons, Elsie Clews (1916), 'The Zuni La'mana', *American Anthropologist*, vol. 18, no. 4, pp.521-528.

———— (1939), 'The Last Zuni Transvestite', *American Anthropologist*, vol. 41, pp.338-339.

Potter, James M. (1997), 'Communal Ritual, Feasting and Social Differentiation in Late Prehistoric Zuni Communities', Unpublished PhD Dissertation, Department of Anthropology, Arizona State University, Tempe.

———— (2000a), 'Pots, Parties and Politics: Communal Feasting in the American Southwest', *American Antiquity*, vol. 65, no. 3, pp.471-492.

———— (2000b), 'The Technology of Metaphor: Architectural Changes across the Pueblo III to Pueblo IV Transition in the El Morro Valley, New Mexico', Paper presented in the Symposium 'Lines of Evidence for Understanding Prehistoric Technology in the Southwest', in the Southwest Symptom, Santa Fe, New Mexico.

Potter, James M. and Perry, Elizabeth M. (2000), 'Ritual as a Power Resource in the American Southwest', in B.J. Mills (ed.), *Alternative Leadership Strategies in the Prehispanic Southwest*, University of Arizona Press, Tucson, pp.60-78.

Roscoe, William (1988), 'We'wha and Klah: The American Indian Berdache as Artist and Priest', *American Indian Quarterly*, vol. 7, no. 2, pp.127-150.

———— (1991), *The Zuni man-woman*, University of New Mexico Press, Albuquerque.

Rubin, Gayle (1975), 'The Traffic in Women: Notes on a "Political Economy" of Sex, in R.R. Reiter (ed.), *Toward an Anthropology of Women*, Monthly Review Press, New York.

Schmidt, Robert and Voss, Barbara (2000), *Archaeologies of Sexuality*, Routledge, London.

Whittaker, John C. (1987), 'Individual Variation as an Approach to Economic Organization: Projectile Points at Grasshopper Pueblo, Arizona', *Journal of Field Archaeology*, vol. 14, pp.465-479.

Chapter 9

Renaissance Body Matters:
Judith Butler and the Sex That is One

Belinda Johnston[1]

This essay explores the potential impact of Judith Butler's work on the study of gender in Renaissance England. In particular, it looks to the theatre, which has proved an especially productive site for discussions of Renaissance gender. As evidenced in the anxieties of its opponents, Renaissance theatre called into question the ontological status of gender, suggesting instead a performative model. Meanwhile, however, at other cultural locations, gender was being increasingly naturalized: in the practice of witch-hunting for instance, we see an intensified concern with the 'nature' of the female body.

Moving from an examination of debates about the staging of Renaissance gender to a reading of the staging of female witchcraft, this paper explores the possible readings generated by Judith Butler's observations about the performativity of gender. If *Gender Trouble: Feminism and the Subversion of Identity* (1990) offers a framework for thinking about Renaissance practices of theatricality, then it is *Bodies That Matter: On the Discursive Limits of 'Sex'* (1993) that offers a framework for questioning those notions and for negotiating one of the most vexing of issues in Renaissance studies: the sexed body. This essay thus has, at the very least, a double focus. It performs a Butler-inflected reading of stagings of female witchcraft in Early Modern England across a number of sites. Further, it performs this reading in order to end with what can only be the beginnings of a discussion about the enormous usefulness of Butler's work to Renaissance scholars, struggling to find a language that can describe the processes of gendering four hundred years ago.

While focusing on the configurations of the sexed body in postmodernity, Butler's concerns bear a striking similarity to those of postmodern theories of Renaissance gender and sexuality. Explorations of the body, of cross-dressing, and of the homoerotics of Renaissance culture, have resulted in a questioning of the models of sex, gender, and sexuality that critics have traditional relied on in reading the Renaissance. This has proved a mixed blessing for feminist critics,

---

[1] A version of Johnston's essay appeared under the same title in *International Journal of Sexuality and Gender Studies*, vol. 6, nos. 1-2 (April 2001). Reprinted with permission of Kluwer Academic.

particularly those most keenly aware of the struggle, both within the academy and without, to put sex, gender, and sexuality on the agenda at all. Having achieved that goal to a considerable extent within the field of Renaissance studies, there are times when that political project appears under threat, particularly when those categories are questioned for their capacity to address the actual discourses and practices of the Renaissance. This essay considers both the losses and the gains that emerge from that questioning.

One-Sex, Two-Sex: Early Modern Gender Trouble

Along with writers such as Anne Fausto-Sterling (1992, 2000), Butler (1990) played a significant part in the profound, cross-disciplinary revaluation of notions of gender that took placed in the early 1990s. Both writers called into question the 'foundational' status afforded the binary, male/female model of sexual difference. In the area of history, Thomas Laqueur's *Making Sex* (1990) raised similar concerns: indeed it is, perhaps, an indication of the impact of this book that it seems almost redundant to rehearse his observations about the Renaissance body. Laqueur (1990) suggests that the binary model of sexual difference through which twentieth-century critics often read Renaissance texts fails to account for the historical differences between Modern and Early Modern constructions of the sexed body. He argued that the Renaissance imagined the body as a 'one-sex' body. Masculinity and femininity were not simple opposites, but rather existed on a sliding scale: the result of different balances of heat and fluids within what was morphologically the same body. In this one-sex body, the same four humours, or bodily fluids, existed in different amounts and temperatures. So, Laqueur states:

> In the blood, semen, milk, and other fluids of the one-sex body, there is no female and no sharp boundary between the sexes (Laqueur, 1990, p.35).

It was the differential balance of these fluids that would determine whether genitals would be exterior or interior to the body. The penis was inverted in the female body because of its colder, clammier constitution, whilst in the much warmer male body the same organ was outside the body. Thus masculinity and femininity were the hierarchically organized characteristics of a single model of the body. Laqueur argued that in the West, the essentialist model of a division of bodily sex into male and female did not come about until the eighteenth century. By the nineteenth century, the bodily differentiation between male and female had come to be seen as fixed in and by nature rather than the hierarchical cosmologies of earlier orders.

Stephen Greenblatt's reading of Shakespeare's *Twelfth Night* in the essay 'Fiction and Friction' (1988) draws on similar material to that of Laqueur. Challenging the idea of Shakespearean comedy as offering a stable marital resolution to the free play of desires, Greenblatt points out the instability inherent in Renaissance gender:

I would suggest that *Twelfth Night* may not finally bring home to us the fundamental distinction between men and women; not only may the distinction be blurred, but the home to which it is supposed to be brought may seem less securely ours, less cozy and familiar, than we have come to expect (Greenblatt, 1988, p.72).

The 'one-sex' model quickly achieved a critical orthodoxy. Peter Stallybrass (1991), Stephen Orgel (1989) and Alan Sinfield (1992) have all referred to this model as more or less a 'fact' of Renaissance gender perception. However, recent feminist critics of the one-sex model have noted the reliance of its proponents on a limited range of texts. Both Greenblatt and Laqueur build their arguments through stories of young women's unexpected genital transformations into men, which appear in Montaigne (1983), Paré (1968), and other sixteenth-century medical or legal texts. Elizabeth Harvey also appears to take for granted the hegemony of the medical model:

Our notions of bodies are, after all, constructed primarily through their descriptions in the discourses of medicine and science, representations that are themselves implicated in and serve to perpetuate ideological structures (Harvey, 1992, p.4).

However, critics such as Janet Adelman (1999), Laura Levine (1995), Patricia Parker (1993), and Gail Kern Paster (1998) share a concern for the ways in which the discourses of medicine are *not* the primary sites through which gendered representations are constructed:

[I]t's by no means clear in the twentieth century, let alone the sixteenth, that our notions of our bodies are more indebted to medicine and science than, say, to religious doctrine or to all the cultural and individual practices—and accompanying psychic fantasies— that teach us who we are in a bodily sense from birth onward (Adelman, 1999, p.25).

Again privileging medical discourse, Peter Stallybrass and Ann Rosalind Jones suggest:

We even have to reconsider menstruation in a world where it was believed that men as well as women should have their periods—hence, the medical significance of purgation or letting blood through incision, cupping or leeching (Stallybrass and Jones, 1991, p.81).

However, the work of Paster (1993) suggests that whilst it is true that both men and women underwent bloodletting, this is not necessarily a signifier of sameness. Laqueur registers only a difference in the fluid *balance* of the body. Paster also produces an argument, through readings of various Renaissance plays, for the difference between male and female blood as pivoting on the *quality* of fluids, particularly whether blood is shed by choice (as a badge of male heroism) or involuntarily (as menstruation):

Menstruation comes to resemble other varieties of female incontinence—sexual, urinary, linguistic—that served as powerful signs of woman's inability to control the workings of her own body (Paster, 1993, p.83).

Adelman notes that in the teleology of gender perfection proposed by Greenblatt and Laqueur, women move up the hierarchy to become male. It works in terms of 'female's failed maleness, not in terms of male's originary femaleness' (Adelman, 1999, p.40). The model cannot account for the possibility that men will move *down* the hierarchy, even as it persists as a possibility for critics such as Orgel who otherwise embrace the one-sex model:

> The frightening part of the teleology for the Renaissance mind, however, is precisely the fantasy of its reversal, the conviction that men can turn into—or be turned into—women; or perhaps more exactly, can be turned *back* into women, losing the strength that enabled the male potential to be realized in the first place (Orgel, 1989, p.14).

Parker criticizes Laqueur for overlooking counterexamples, which overturn the idea that women turn into men but never the contrary. She points to accounts of male lack, stories of sixteenth-century penises that stop working, rendering their owners symbolically feminine. In the 'thematics of impotence', she suggests, Galenic teleologies in which women arrive at a biological ideal by becoming male fail to preserve men from the spectre of feminization (Parker, 1993).

From Laqueur's epigrammatic use of *Twelfth Night* on, Shakespeare's cross-dressing comedies have proved a productive site for playing with this sex that is one. It is in the reading of a tragedy, however, that Adelman finds evidence of 'the beginnings of a shift from definition by *telos* to definition by *origin*...(Adelman, 1999, p.42). Adelman (1999) reads a passage from *Antony and Cleopatra* as foregrounding a difference between a 'real woman' and the boy actor, in the process making a claim for a binary model of sexual difference quite different from the playful ambiguity of Viola-as-Cesario in *Twelfth Night*. Partly, this is enabled by the significant shift in representation of female sexuality from Elizabethan comedy to Jacobean tragedy, as pointed out by Leonard Tennenhouse (1989). However, Paster also finds a discourse of binary sexual difference in *Twelfth Night*, offering a corrective to Greenblatt by arguing that the different levels of heat in the humoural body create a pervasive sexual difference:

> What the circular argument about heat offers, finally, is a theory of sexual difference in which femaleness is not a matter of genital difference alone but a form of difference thoroughly saturating female flesh and the subject within it (Paster, 1998, p.430).

These readings suggest that there are limits to the cultural claims that can be made for the gender play often celebrated in readings of the transvestite comedies. Mark Breitenberg (1996) points out that on the Renaissance stage the performance of gender was only available to males. The license to play the woman thus belonged to male bodies. The play of gender remained a male privilege.

Adelman (1999) is suspicious of the sudden popularity of the one-sex body in Renaissance studies, speculating that it arises from an unconscious desire on the part of critics to efface the category of woman. She warns that what is lost in the freedom from gender fixity offered by the one-sex model is the specificity of the female body. Lorna Hutson (1996) argues that a legacy of Greenblatt's interpretation is its masking of the necessity of accounting, in feminist terms, for the historical reality of the non-appearance of women's bodies on the Renaissance stage. Further, she associates Greenblatt's position with the work of Judith Butler, suggesting a dangerous slippage into free play:

> 'Self-fashioning' thereby becomes synonymous with a quite unspecific notion of 'theatricality', which in turn is easily assimilated to the concept of 'performativity' articulated by Judith Butler in relation to the category of gender (Hutson, 1996, p.157).

Unfortunately, Hutson goes no further with her discussion of Judith Butler, and indeed this is typical of Butler's status in Renaissance studies: often footnoted, rarely put to use. Butler's argument that understandings of gender are reified through performance and repetition seems particularly relevant to the critically contested understandings of Renaissance gender. Rather than being the expression of essence, gender, Butler suggests, is constructed on the surface of the body through behaviours and appearances that create the effect of a private gendered centre:

> Because there is neither an 'essence' that gender expresses or externalizes nor an objective ideal to which gender aspires, and because gender is not a fact, the various acts of gender create the idea of gender, and without those acts, there would be no gender at all (Butler, 1990, p.140).

These are *performative* in the sense that the nature or selfhood they claim is not a manifestation of essence, but rather is produced and sustained through discourse.

To associate Butler's work simply with a celebration of the free play of gender, however, is a misappropriation. On the contrary, Butler's approach provides the means for a politicized invocation of the categories of 'gender' and of 'woman', even as it questions the categories of identity politics. While it may be tempting to call on a 'lost' female specificity to critique Laqueur's one-sex body, it is conceptually and politically vital for feminist readers of the Renaissance to avoid a reading of the body that treats it as biologically, rather than discursively, determined. As the work of Butler, amongst others, has pointed out, the sex/gender system, where sex is biology and gender its social construction, is in complicity with the heterosexual matrix:

> I use the term *heterosexual matrix*...to designate that grid of cultural intelligibility through which bodies, genders, and desires are naturalized. I am drawing from Monique Wittig's notion of the 'heterosexual contract' and, to a lesser extent, on Adrienne Rich's notion of 'compulsory heterosexuality' to characterize a hegemonic discursive/epistemic model of gender intelligibility that assumes that for bodies to cohere and make sense

there must be a stable sex expressed through a stable gender...that is oppositionally and hierarchically defined through the compulsory practice of heterosexuality (Butler, 1990, p.151).

The operation of the heterosexual matrix produces gendered notions of biological sex through the binary 'complementarity' necessary to a heterosexual economy.

If bodies are only known and produced discursively, then it becomes far more difficult to divorce (social) gender from material (biological) sex, for the body is not simply a blank sheet awaiting the inscription of masculinity or femininity. From *Gender Trouble* (1990) to *Bodies That Matter* (1993), Butler's work carries a warning about the dangers of separating the body from representation, a warning informed by a political commitment to the denaturalization of the gender categories normatively produced by the regime of compulsory heterosexuality.

Witchcraft, Maternity, Materialization

In my own work on female witches in Jacobean England, I have met similar limits to those faced by critics of the one-sex model. Whether implicitly or explicitly, the study of witchcraft in Early Modern England demands that one take a position (in the spirit of engagement or dismissal) on the question of why many more witches were women than men. Judicial records show that accused witches in England were nearly always poor and nearly always women. Contemporary witchcraft treatises used this fact to back up broader misogynist claims: King James I calculated the ratio of female witches to male as twenty to one (James I, [1597] 1982, p.30) and Alexander Roberts (1616) suggested the ratio was as high as one hundred to one:

> More women in a farre different proportion prooue Witches then men, by a hundred to one; therefor the Lawe of God noteth that Sex, as more subiect to that sinne, Exodus 22.18. It is a common speach amongst the Iewish Rabbins, many women, many witches (Roberts, 1616, p.40).

Of the one hundred and one persons whom C. L'Estrange Ewen (1929) showed to have been executed on the Home Circuit, only seven were men. They were also predominantly from the lower classes: of the six hundred 'charged' on the Home Circuit, Ewen (1929) calculated that all but four were trades-people, farmers, labourers, and the wives and widows thereof.

In choosing to tackle the question of why English witches were so often women, my work on witches has been shaped in response to the 'maternalist' readings of witchcraft offered by Adelman (1991) and by Deborah Willis (1995), who base their analyses on object-relations psychoanalysis. Both foreground the links between English witch accusations and ambivalent relationships to the maternal body: Willis's project, for instance, is clear in her statement that 'witches were women, I believe, because women are mothers' (Willis, 1995, p.6). She notes that altercations leading to complaints of witchcraft often centered on the business of feeding and child care, and offers an analysis of the processes of subject formation entailed in the fear of witches. If such accounts are gratifying for a feminist reader alarmed at the sizeable statistical over-representation of women in English witch annals, they can also be problematic. Karen Newman (1991) notes that the danger of such a reading is that it 'naturalizes hostility toward women' by locating misogyny in a universal mother-child conflict, rather than in specific cultural formations (Newman, 1991, p.62).

If statistical proofs are a sufficient indication of the *gender* of the victims of witch accusations in England, they are, nevertheless, insufficient in themselves to account for the *gendering* of witchcraft: in particular, the process whereby witchcraft becomes a crime intricately linked to the female body itself. What I suggest in the following pages is that Judith Butler's work offers a useful framework for thinking through the gendering that operates in the representation of female witches, and a framework that avoids the naturalizing tendencies of which Newman warns. The answer clearly does not lie in a wholesale rejection of performativity in favour of some essentialist 'real' women, even if that can seem politically attractive. Butler's work enables a discussion of 'modes of embodiment', which treats the body not as irreducible fact but rather as interwoven with and composed of representational systems. The body, signified as preceding representation, is an *effect* of systems of representation and hence of power:

> [T]he mimetic or representational status of language, which claims that signs follow bodies as their necessary mirrors, is not mimetic at all. On the contrary, it is productive, constitutive, one might even argue *performative*, inasmuch as this signifying act delimits and contours the body that it then claims to find prior to any and all signification (Butler, 1993, p.30).

Butler is not here reducing the materiality of bodies to a linguistic effect, but rather arguing that language is the condition under which materiality *can be said* to appear; the process of signification effects the very sense of the corporeal body, a process that operates differentially, by projecting a realm of inconceivable abject anti-bodies.

Jacobean witchcraft offers a productive intersection between concerns about theatre and concerns about gender—both in the way treatises and accounts of trials articulate those concerns, and in the play texts that represent witches. English witch trials revolve particularly around the spectacle of the body on trial, a body that is stereotypically female, old, and 'unattractive'. Homi Bhabha has described the logic of the colonial stereotype as registering difference within a certain system of knowledge, while at the same time masking the more radical difference that might contest the ideological underpinnings of the dominant system. Similarly, the stereotype of the female witch—the old ugly malicious sterile woman—depends on a production of the body and of difference, which establishes fixity through 'sight' and 'knowledge' (Bhabha, 1983). A scene of being seen establishes a woman as a witch; moments frequently occur in the pamphlet accounts that recall

Frantz Fanon's 'primal scene': 'Look, a Negro...Mama, see the Negro! I'm frightened. Frightened! Frightened!' (Fanon, 1967, p.112):

> [T]he Infante cryed to the mother, wo, wo, and poynted with the finger to the wyndowe wardes (W., 1582, B1).

> [L]ooke where the old witch setteth...did you euer see...one more like a witch than she is? (Anon., *Most Strange* 1593, B1).

Sight here establishes the recognition and interpretation of difference. A woman's witchcraft could be read off the visible signs of her body, like a map. In this sense, then, the witch body is similar to other forms of monstrous body in the Early Modern period. Helaine Razovsky's study of the monstrous births in fifteen broadsides from 1562-1687 points out the way in which the child's body is imagined both as visual spectacle and as text to be interpreted:

> [W]riters of these broadsides assumed that anything is a potential text for exegesis using standard hermeneutic principles; therefore, the comparison of texts that is one step in the practice of hermeneutics means not simply comparison of Bible verses and/or of other graphic texts, but also of graphic texts and other objects (Razovsky, 1996, p.30).

Where the monstrous birth, however, was often read to signify a divine judgement on either the child's mother or even humanity in general, the witch body was of the witch's own doing, a sign of her own guilt.

The witch body is thus the outcome of an intersection of visual spectacle and discursive process. This discursive process is part of what Butler terms a 'regulatory schema', criteria of intelligibility that yield what she describes as 'Bodies That Matter' (Butler, 1993). The pun on matter is double: it describes both bodies that count, or are important, and bodies that are produced as a recognizable materiality. Butler draws on Michel Foucault to argue that power operates in the structure of the very materiality of the subject. The fantasy of the female witch is one such mode of materialization, which operates both as a public mode, and is also bound up in the production of the private subject. Not only is the figure of the female witch a cultural fantasy in the public space of the courtroom, scaffold, or theatre, it is also a figure in which the subject invests, and against which the subject defines itself. In the context of English witchcraft, the body that matters is also *mater*, it is a maternal(ized) body. However, a Butlerian reading offers a means of escape from the positing of a normative maternal body, into which 'maternalist' readings of witchcraft can fall, by calling for an examination of the ways in which particular historical discourses produce the maternal body (Butler, 1990, p.81). The witch body is not simply a surface awaiting the inscription of meaning but rather the product of a series of historically located personal and social limits. What Butler (1993) proposes in place of a constructivist model is the idea of matter not as surface, but rather as a *process* of materialization that stabilizes over time to produce the *effect* of matter. The body is not simply invested by external power relations, but is a nodal point at which corporeality and the investiture of meaning are coextensive. Further, matter-as-process must be veiled by matter-as-'thereness'. Where materiality is seen as primary data, as an ontological given, the regulatory schema that produce that effect remain intact.

This body-as-process is particularly useful for theorizing the materiality of the witch-body. Material features such as warts, moles, a tendency to curse and the capacity to float were presumably not particularly unusual phenomena, but the production of the witch's body through a *discursive process* transformed these bodily features and behaviours into 'witch marks'. As Paster (1993) notes, the examination of the witch for 'marks' produces involuntary significations of her body. The purpose of torture and of examination was to force the body to betray, to make visible, the truth about a woman's status as a witch. The term 'witch' is what Butler describes as an 'injurious name', a name that interpolates its object as a certain type of subject, through which they are scorned and degraded (Butler, 1997, p.2). The stereotype of the female witch is an ideological figure which produces the recognition, and hence the category, of social deviance. Further, this process of visual stereotyping produces witchcraft as a feminine mode of embodiment, and, by implication, produces femininity as an embodied mode of witchcraft. The production of witchcraft as a demonic potential of the female body suggests a more polarized version of gender in circulation than Laqueur's one-sex model acknowledges. The Jacobean pamphlets and treatises on witchcraft regularly represent the maternal body as a source of disruption to the state. Contra Laqueur, and via Butler's (1990) use of materialization and abjection, I suggest that, in this particular instance, the association of witchcraft with an imagined maternal body operates through a *biologizing of gender*, which anticipates the production of sexual difference that Laqueur locates in the eighteenth century.

Pamphlets and academic treatises on female witches construct the witch through what Newman describes as 'maternal inversion' (Newman, 1991, p.58). Where a mother nourishes her child, the witch cooks it; the kitchen becomes the coven and cauldron that issues food that kills rather than nurtures, and the breasts nourish spirits and animals rather than humans, yielding blood instead of milk. The notion of suckling familiars, a feature particular to English witchcraft, appears frequently. Witches were said to suckle a veritable menagerie of dogs, cats, ferrets, and other creatures. Many confessed that they permitted their familiars to drain blood from them through teats, usually located in or around their genitals:

> ...haue some honest and discreete women neare which presently search her for the secret marke of witches, as Teates, blond moales, moist warts, and the like... (Anon., *Wonderfull Discoverie*, 1618, D3).

While this might appear a kind of phallic displacement, it must also be noted that more often than not these marks are characterized through a language of lactation and breast-feeding. Elizabeth Sawyer, the 'witch of Edmonton', had a witch mark just above her 'fundament':

[a] thing like a teat the bigness of the little finger, and the length of half a finger which was branched at the top like a teat, and seemed as though one had sucked it, and that the bottom thereof was blue, and the top of it was red (Goodcole, [1621] 1980, pp.387-388).

Her familiar, alleged to be a dog called Tom, was believed to have suckled at this teat. In another of the more graphic accounts of the witch's teat, a jailer reported the following 'find' on the body of Alice Samuell after her execution:

...adioyning so secrete a place which was not to be seene...a little lump of flesh, in manner sticking out....The Jaylors wife tooke the same teate in her hand, and seeming to straine it, there issued out at the first, as if it had beene beefenings (to use the Jaylers word) which is a mixture of yellowe milke and water. At the second time, there come out, in similitude as cleer Mylke, and in the end verie bloud it self (Anon., *Most Strange and* Admirable, 1593, P3).

Whatever the suspiciously pustular sounding substance might have been, it is described in terms of its likeness to breast milk, one of the 'natural' flows of the female body. Incidentally, the excessive perverse milk has its complement in the perverse *lack* of tears that was also believed to characterize the witch—in this sense, she becomes a perverse parody of the ultimate mother, the Mater Dolorosa, whose 'privileged signs' are milk and tears (Weir, 1993, p.82).

The witch's teat is a sign that the witch's body is a *maternal* body turned upside down, where a natural function is displaced onto another site and used for another purpose. In its obsession with the reproductive body, the discourse of female witchcraft worked to promote appropriate maternity and to suggest the radical difference of maternity itself. It plays a constitutive role in the production of the materiality of the female maternal body, one that, nonetheless, erases its own discursivity and claims instead to read only what is materially already there. As Butler suggests:

Discourse designates the site at which power is installed as the historically contingent formative power of things within a given epistemic field...'Materiality' appears only when its status as contingently constituted through discourse is erased, concealed, covered over (Butler, 1993, p.251).

The search for the teat, as evidence of a carnal relationship with a representative of the devil, suggests that witches are not witches simply because of the devil but because of the female body, a body that requires examination and control. The devil preys on women, on aging lower-class women, precisely because they are hierarchically inferior and, therefore, easier targets. What representations of witchcraft seem to suggest is not just that witchcraft is a susceptibility of flesh, but a susceptibility of *female flesh*.

Such morphological representations imagine femininity not just as a social position, but as a specific mode of embodiment. This is achieved through a process that Butler describes as 'social abjection' (Butler, 1990, p.133). In the humoural model, all bodies were indeed fluid, but *female* bodies had the added feature of viscosity—they were cooler, more clogged. These thicker fluids do not make the female body more solid but rather more liminal. As Mary Douglas rather dramatically describes it:

> The viscous is a state half-way between solid and liquid....It is unstable, but it does not flow....Its stickiness is a trap, it clings like a leech; it attacks the boundary between myself and it. Long columns falling off my fingers suggest my own substance flowing into the pool of stickiness...to touch stickiness is to risk diluting myself into viscosity (Douglas, 1966, p.38).

Jacobean medicine and witch hunting both produce a female body that is characterized by this viscosity, a tendency to breach the clean and proper, which Paster (1993) describes as a feature of the 'leaky body'. If, in the humoural model, the male body is also fluid, it is not *viscous*. It is this vision of an abject body that underpins the production of sexual difference in the humoural model. As Adelman (1999) argues:

> If humoural theory might, for example, explain the failure of a woman to extrude a set of genitals in every way homologous with man's and so might be understood as the basis for the Galenic model, it might equally well be understood as the basis for a theory of sexual difference (Adelman, 1999, p.30).

The abject is here a useful category of analysis: Butler argues that it is abjection that produces the 'internal' and the 'external' as spatial metaphors (Butler, 1990, pp.133-134). Butler describes abjection as a process that 'founds and consolidates culturally hegemonic identities along sex/race axes of differentiation.... In effect, this is the mode by which Others become shit' (Butler, 1990, pp.133–134). This reading of abjection as the founding and consolidating of culturally hegemonic identities makes clear the possibility of the historical variability of the abject. In Butlerian terms, it does not describe some fundamental transhistorical or transcultural mechanism as it often seems to in Julia Kristeva's work, 'passing through the memories of a thousand years' (Kristeva, 1982, p.207). It rather describes a particular process that is a function of a certain regime of gender differentiation within a particular historical location.

Representations of female witches in Jacobean England deploy this abject female body as difference, as both inside and outside, and therefore threatening the social order. They rally particularly around the maternal body, functioning as a site of social differentiation where woman is more than just the imperfect man of Laqueur's one-sex model, but is rather entirely *other*. Paster (1993) argues that in the seventeenth century, the humoural conception of the uncontrollable body was shifting towards new modalities of physical self-discipline. The gendering of bodily fluids, if already in place, was increasingly useful as a way of policing a new kind of body, divided along lines of rigid sexual difference that rendered only female bodies uncontrollable. The relegation of the 'fluid' body to the feminine is part of the project of formulating masculine identity as 'solid' or self-identical. The witch body is a feminine one imagined through the fluid, humoural model of the body and in terms of that emergent regime of the sexed body whereby:

> ...in the West...the female body has been constructed not only as a lack or absence but with more complexity, as a leaking, uncontrollable, seeping liquid; as formless flow; as viscosity, entrapping, secreting; as lacking not so much or simply the phallus but self-containment—not a cracked or porous vessel, like a leaking ship, but a formlessness that engulfs all form, a disorder that threatens all order... (Grosz, 1994, p.203).

As a fantasy of the excessive, fluid, female body, witchcraft is a productive category: it is produced by and produces categories of sexual difference that hinge on a model of feminine embodiment as uncontrollable viscosity. This uncontrollable feminine viscosity is what Butler would describe as a 'constitutive outside' (Butler, 1993, p.3).

From the Theatricality to Performativity: Reiteration and Resistance

The biologizing of gender that I have described as being effected through witchcraft discourse was not a finished project in the Early Modern period. In so far as gender was contingent upon the performance of appropriate behaviours, it was, in effect, a theatrical mode in which the performance of 'natural role' was crucial. While the witch is produced through a materializing logic, it is also inscribed by the language of theatre. Thomas Potts's account of the Pendle witches consistently imagines their trial through the rhetoric of the theatre. He describes the whole case as 'this late woefull and lamentable Tragedie' (Potts, 1613, B). One of the men on trial is described as having been 'brought to act his part in this woefull Tragedie' by two of the women accused (Potts, 1613, G3). Isabel Robey, not connected with the other witches but tried at the same assize, is 'the last that came to act her part in this lamentable and wofull Tragedie' (Potts, 1613, T2). By imagining the trial as a tragedy, the accused as actors, Potts foregrounds the trial as a public staging of the workings of justice. Other pamphlet accounts similarly treat towns as stages, women as actresses:

> there are dyvers Gentlemen, of honest report, ready to confyrme the same uppon their oathes, if neede should require, that were present, some at one tyme, and some at another, at all these seuerall Tragedies (as they might be tearmed) (Anon., *Most Strange*, 1593, G2).

> to come unto the daughter Agnes Samuel, who now commeth upon the stage with her part in this tragedie (Anon., *Most Strange*, 1593, J5).

> At last this Tragicke-Comedie drawing to an end... (Anon., *Witches Apprehended*, 1613, B).

I haue presumed to present on the stage of verity for the good of my country and the loue of truth, the late wofull Tragedy of the destruction of the Right Honourable the Earle of Rutland's Children (Anon., *Wonderfull Discoverie*, 1618, B3).

If pamphlet accounts often claim to tell the truth about witches on the 'stage of verity', they are nevertheless bound by the logic of that most duplicitous of spaces, the theatre. As such a space, the theatre should be in contradiction with the 'truth' that the courtroom represents. Yet the trials themselves are consistently imagined as theatrical spectacles, as performances. Compelled by the logic of performance, the trial cannot produce a stable truth. The witch it produces must be reiterated—as in the case of the story of Sawyer, where the pattern of iterations moves from village gossip to trial to ballad to pamphlet to play. In Butler's (1990) terms, it is the very necessity for reiteration that produces instability in a regulatory schema. In the case of Sawyer, the stage production sabotages the homiletic project of the pamphlet writer, Henry Goodcole ([1621] 1980). The front page of the first printed edition of the play *The Witch of Edmonton* inserts the story into the theatrical:

The Witch of Edmonton:
A known true STORY
Composed into
A TRAGICOMEDY.

The prologue describes Edmonton as having 'lent the stage/A Devil and a Witch'. In doing so it refigures Sawyer in the spectacular terms that Goodcole earnestly denies. Describing his account as having been 'extorted' from him, 'who would have been content to have concealed it' (Goodcole, [1621] 1980, p.381), Goodcole claims to have been forced to make a private confession public. He writes this not for pleasure, but in the name of a truth obscured by 'base and false ballads' about the case (Goodcole, [1621] 1980, p.382).

As critics have pointed out, Renaissance theatre as a cultural practice could produce deontologizing effects, a denaturing of sex and class roles. Men become women, women become men, and commoners become kings. In anti-theatrical discourse, the theatre itself is often troped as a duplicitous woman who destabilizes sight, knowledge, and identity. Theatre thus becomes a site at which a Butlerian reading can be produced: a site where subversive reiterations can occur. If, as I have argued elsewhere, gender was being increasingly naturalized, read off the bodies of witches, in the theatre gender was not nearly so stable. The stereotype of the female witch is supposed to produce a readable materiality, a body that is recognizably female and maternal, the significations of which are agreed upon. Yet in theatrical representations, the nature of this body and its powers are variously questioned and caricatured in plays such as William Shakespeare's *Macbeth* ([1603-1606] 1984), Thomas Middleton's *The Witch* ([1613-1627] 1986), and the collaboratively written *The Witch of Edmonton* (by William Rowley and Thomas Dekker, among others, 1621).

The theatrical staging of witchcraft intersects with and problematizes its status elsewhere. The demonization of the female body that the representation of female witches achieves is necessary precisely because the patriarchal project is neither self-sufficient nor natural, but reliant on a binary opposition which must be reiterated to be real-ized. Female witchcraft 'originates internally to just those things it threatens' (Dollimore, 1990, p.4). Whilst the alterity of the inverted mother, through which the witch is constructed, serves to reinforce what is maternal, it must also at the very least give voice or representative reality to the inverted mother. It projects the possibility of a maternal subject who reverses the structure of the supposedly essential order, and refuses socially sanctioned roles.

Female witchcraft can thus be seen as a mechanism of power, but also as a site of conflict:

> [T]he ideological production of domesticated, privatized woman in the Renaissance is one of the prime (and, it hardly needs to be said, dubious) accomplishments of the humanism that Montrose celebrates. Legal disenfranchisements of women in the period are real. Nonetheless, not even these massive closures are effective everywhere, and within the repressions and exclusions of women are also mechanisms that are productive—sites of resistance or of failure within the system, excesses or lacks (Goldberg, 1992, p.8).

The task of accounting for the diversity of Jacobean treatments of witchcraft is not helped by searching *either* for containment or for subversion, for, as John Michael Archer and Richard Burt argue, there is a complex relationship between subversion and containment: 'Boundaries are made possible by the very things they exclude; what we retrospectively call subversion founds a fragile process of containment' (Archer and Burt, 1994, p.4). Butler suggests that such formulations are the productive possibility of Foucault's formulation of power:

> [The] insistence on the dual possibility of being both *constituted* by the law and *an effect of resistance* to the law marks a departure from the Lacanian framework, for where Lacan restricts the notions of social power to that of the symbolic domain, and delegates resistance to the imaginary, Foucault will recast the symbolic as relations of power, and understand resistance as an effect of power itself (Butler, 1995, p.241).

The symbolic produces the potentiality for its own subversions. Female witches exist at a limit between an understanding of gender as performance and an understanding of gender as biology. On the one hand, their inappropriate performances suggest the instability of gender; on the other, their perversity suggests a deviation from the 'natural' state of being woman. Thus, witchcraft emerges not as a seamless technology of the body, but rather as a site of opposition or of *failure*. As Butler points out, correct repetitions of gendered norms are crucial to the coherence of gender, and to the veiling of its performativity. Butler sees this as a liberating possibility, because it is in the failure to repeat these acts, or their over-repetition through parody, that the possibility for transformation exists. Of course, some wariness is in order here. Even if the witch acts as a kind of parody, this is not to suggest intention, nor is there any guarantee that the witch-as-mimic is *effectively* subversive:

> Parody by itself is not subversive, and there must be a way to understand what makes certain kinds of parodic repetitions effectively disruptive, truly troubling, and which repetitions become domesticated and recirculated as instruments of cultural hegemony (Butler, 1990, p.139).

This is a warning also sounded by Diane Purkiss:

> The fact that witchcraft was a role did not always make it an interesting subversion of gender boundaries. Once convicted and hanged, the witch's opportunities for exciting unfixings of the assumptions of others were rather limited (Purkiss, 1996, p.208).

Butler is aware of such constraints. In *Gender Trouble* she does not hesitate to name these constraints through the language of violence:

> The historical possibilities materialized through various corporeal styles are nothing other than those punitively regulated cultural fictions alternately embodied and deflected under duress (Butler, 1990, p.140).

Further, throughout *Bodies That Matter*, Butler recognizes the relationship between performativity and constraint:

> Performativity is neither free play nor theatrical self-representation; nor can it be simply equated with performance...Moreover, constraint is not necessarily that which sets a limit to performativity; constraint is, rather, that which impels and sustains performativity (Butler, 1993, p.95).

Female witchcraft as an abject unintelligible possibility is 'punitively regulated' through trials and transformed into a knowable entity. However, this knowability is in the terms of the discourse for which it constitutes the limit, and hence excess is always produced: the witch is never completely known because she is located at the limits of intelligibility. In the very act of representing the witch, the limits of control over gender are acknowledged: all women are possible witches. Epistemic and corporeal violence largely recuperate the subversive possibilities of that realization. It is because of this violent recuperation that the language of agency cannot capture the subversive possibilities of the witch. However, because the category 'witch' is haunted by the instabilities that it produces, it is possible to trace a subversive effect based neither on a voluntarist subject nor on a notion of confinement. Rather one can argue that because the hegemonic project must always aim, and fail, to flatten contradictions, it is always unstable:

> [T]he repression of the feminine does not require that the agency of repression and the object of repression be ontologically distinct. Indeed, repression may be understood to

produce the object that it comes to deny. That production may well be an elaboration of the agency of repression itself. As Foucault makes clear, the culturally contradictory enterprise of the mechanism of repression is prohibitive and generative at once and makes the problematic of 'liberation' especially acute (Butler, 1990, p.93).

That the effort in practice to repress witches, through the erasure of their material existence, coincides with, even requires, a reversal of that repression in discourse is a symptom of this contradictory structure: they must be continually talked about and brought into existence at a textual and material level.

Without recourse to a notion of an 'individual' who escapes the discursive relations that produce it, Butler suggests that a displacement can occur within the terms of a constructed subject position and that this can be theorized without recourse to the notion of an 'individual' who escapes the discursive relations by which she/he is produced. This opens up a series of possible reading strategies, based on Butler's contention that 'possibilities exist *by virtue of* the constructed character of sex and gender' (Butler, 1990, p.32, emphasis in original). The destabilizing possibilities for female witchcraft hinge on the fact that it is controlled through the deployment of the maternal body. Deploying the witch as the signifier of defective maternal practices in turn controls maternity. The process of this deployment, however, repeats and relocates maternity as unstable: the maternal body itself is prone to witchcraft. Reinscription of this kind results in an exacerbation of the instabilities intrinsic to the oppressive norm of the 'good' mother. Witchcraft, of course, is nothing like the conscious practice of reinscription suggested by Butler's description of drag in *Gender Trouble*. Butler herself acknowledges the limits of her use of drag as a paradigm of performative reinscription, both in *Bodies That Matter* and elsewhere:

> The problem with drag is that I offered it as an example of performativity, but it has been taken up as the paradigm for performativity. One ought always to be wary of one's examples. What's interesting is that this voluntarist interpretation, this desire for a kind of radical theatrical remaking of the body, is obviously out there in the public sphere. There's a desire for a fully phantasmatic transfiguration of the body. But no, I don't think that drag is a paradigm for the subversion of gender. I don't think that if we were all more dragged out gender life would become more expansive and less restrictive (Butler, 1996, p.111).

It is not possible to trace such subversive intent without eliding the historical constraints on women. Nevertheless, there is a disruption at work, which is internal to witchcraft, a disruption that leaves a trace. From such a reading, Jacobean witchcraft emerges as a key site in the struggle to *materialize* gender, to split the one-sex body in two, inaugurating binary sexual difference.

Butler's ability to work aporetically, in the space between constructivism and essentialism, has important implications for debates about the female body in Renaissance studies. In her recasting of performativity as citationality/iterability, as the repetition of social norms that are always constrained, never entirely voluntary, but nonetheless contradictory and, therefore, space for resistance or instability, she offers a corrective to the impulse to counter examples of gender play with examples of gender policing, suggesting a space beyond the logic of the and/or.

[T]he inquiry into the kinds of erasures and exclusions by which the construction of the subject operates is no longer constructivism, but neither is it essentialism. For there is an 'outside' to what is constructed by discourse, but this is not an absolute 'outside', an ontological thereness that exceeds or counters the boundaries of discourse (Butler, 1993, p.8).

While recognizing the political importance that the 'presumption of the material irreducibility of sex' (Butler, 1993, p.28) has held for feminism, Butler offers a reading strategy that can also recognize the irreducibility of materiality and hence the potential for its revisability. Such a reading strategy has the capacity to open the debates within Renaissance studies about the 'location' of sexual difference, towards a recognition of both its discursivity and its materiality.

References

Adelman, Janet (1991), *Suffocating Mothers: Fantasies of Maternal Origin in Shakespeare's Plays*, Routledge, Routledge.
———— (1999), 'Making Defect Perfection: Shakespeare and the One-Sex Model', in V. Comensoli and A. Russell (eds), *Enacting Gender on the English Renaissance Stage*, University of Illinois Press, Urbana, pp.23-52.
Anon. (1593), *The Most Strange and Admirable Discouerie of the Three Witches of Warboys*, London.
Anon. (1613), *Witches Apprehended, Examined, and Executed, for Notable Villanies by Them Committed Both by Land and Water*, London
Anon., (1618), *The Wonderfull Discoverie of the Witchcrafts of Margaret and Phillip Flower*, London.
Archer, John M. and Burt, Richard (1994), 'Introduction' in J.M. Archer and R. Burt (eds), *Enclosure Acts: Sexuality, Property and Culture in Early Modern England*, Cornell University Press, Ithaca.
Bakhtin, Mikhail (1984), *Rabelais and His World*, H. Iswolsky (trans.), Indiana University Press, Bloomington.
Bhabha, Homi K. (1983), 'The Other Question—The Stereotype and Colonial Discourse', *Screen*, vol. 24, no. 6, pp.18-36.
Breitenberg, Mark (1996), *Anxious Masculinity in Early Modern England*, Cambridge University Press, Cambridge.
Butler, Judith (1990), *Gender Trouble: Feminism and the Subversion of Identity*, Routledge, London.
———— (1993), *Bodies That Matter: On the Discursive Limits of 'Sex'*, Routledge, London.
———— (1995), 'Subjection, Resistance, Resignification: Between Freud and Foucault', in J. Rajchman (ed.), *The identity in Question*, Routledge, London, pp.229-49.
———— (1996), 'Gender as Performance', in P. Osborne (ed.), *A Critical Sense: Interviews with Intellectuals*, Routledge, London, pp.109-126.
———— (1997), *Excitable Speech: A Politics of the Performative*, Routledge, New York.
Dollimore, J. (1990), 'The Cultural Politics of Perversion', *Genders*, vol. 8, pp.1-16.

Douglas, Mary (1966), *Purity and Danger: An Analysis of Conceptions of Pollution*, Routledge and Kegan Paul, London.

Ewen, C.L'Estrange (1929), *Witch Hunting and Witch Trials*, Kegan Paul, London.

Fanon, Frantz (1967), *Black Skin, White Masks*, C.L. Markmann (trans.), Grove, New York.

Fausto-Sterling, Anne (1992), *Myths of Gender: Biological Theories about Women and Men*, revised edition, Basic Books, New York.

———— (2000), *Sexing the Body: Gender Politics and the Construction of Sexuality*, Basic Books, New York.

Foucault, Michel (1977), *Discipline and Punish*, A. Sheridan (trans.), Penguin, London.

Goldberg, Jonathan (1992), *Sodometries: Renaissance Texts, Modern Sexualities*, Stanford University Press, Stanford.

Goodcole, Henry ([1621] 1980), *The Wonderful Discoverie of Elizabeth Sawyer A Witch*, in E.S. Onat (ed.), *The Witch of Edmonton: A Critical Edition*, Garland, London, pp.381-400.

Greenblatt, Stephen (1988), *Shakespearean Negotiations: The Circulation of Social Energy in Renaissance England*, Oxford University Press, Oxford.

Grosz, Elizabeth (1994), *Volatile Bodies: Toward a Corporeal Feminism*, Allen and Unwin, St Leonards.

Harvey, Elizabeth (1992), *Ventriloquized Voices: Feminist Theory and English Renaissance Texts*, Routledge, London.

Hutson, Lorna (1996), 'On Not Being Deceived: Rhetoric and the Body in *Twelfth Night*', *Texas Studies in Language and Literature*, vol. 38, no. 1, pp.140-174.

James I. ([1597] 1982), 'Daemonologie', in J. Craigie (ed.), *Minor Prose Works of King James VI and I*, Scottish Text Society, Edinburgh, pp.1-58.

Kristeva, Julia (1982), *Powers of Horror*, L.S. Roudiez (trans.), Columbia University Press, New York.

Laqueur, Thomas (1990), *Making Sex*, Harvard University Press, Cambridge.

Levine, Laura (1995), *Men in Women's Clothing: Antitheatricality and Effeminization, 1579-1642*, Cambridge University Press, Cambridge.

Middleton, Thomas ([1613-1627] 1986), *The Witch*, in P. Corbin and D. Sedge (eds), *Three Jacobean Witchcraft Plays*, Manchester University Press, Manchester, pp.85-142.

Montaigne, Michel (1983), *Montaigne's Travel Journal*, D. Frame (trans.), North Point Press, San Francisco.

Newman, Karen (1991), *Fashioning Femininity and English Renaissance Drama*, University of Chicago Press, Chicago.

Orgel, Stephen (1989), 'Nobody's Perfect; Or, Why Did the English Stage Take Boys for Women?', *South Atlantic Quarterly*, vol. 88, pp.7-29.

Paré, Ambrose (1968), *The Collected Works of Ambrose Paré*, T. Johnson (trans.), Milford House, Round Ridge.

Parker, Patricia (1993), 'Gender Ideology, Gender Change: The Case of Marie Germain', *Critical Inquiry*, vol. 19, no. 2, pp.337-364.

Paster, Gail K. (1993), *The Body Embarrassed: Drama and the Disciplines of Shame in Early Modern England*, Cornell University Press, Ithaca.

———— (1998), 'The Unbearable Coldness of Female Being: Women's Imperfection and the Humoral Economy', *English Literary Renaissance*, vol. 28, no. 3, pp.416-40.

Potts, Thomas (1613), *The Wonderful Discouerie of Witches in the Countie of Lancaster*, London.

Purkiss, Diane (1996), *The Witch in History: Early Modern and Twentieth-Century Representations*, Routledge, London.

Razovksy, Helaine (1996), 'Popular Hermeneutics: Monstrous Children in English Renaissance Broadside Ballads', *EMLS: Early Modern Literary Studies*, vol. 2, no. 3, pp. 1-34, http://www.shu.ac.uk/schools/cs/emls/02-3/razoball.html.

Roberts, Alexander (1616), *A Treatise of Witchcraft*, London.

Rowley, William et al. ([1621] 1986), 'The Witch of Edmonton', in P. Corbin and D. Sedge (eds), *Three Jacobean Witchcraft Plays*, Manchester University Press, Manchester, pp.143-209.

Sedgwick, Eve K. (1985), *Between Men: English Literature and Male Homosocial Desire*, Columbia University Press, New York.

Shakespeare, William, ([1603-1606] 1984), *Macbeth*, K. Muir (ed.), *The Arden Shakespeare*, Routledge, London.

Sinfield, Alan (1992), *Faultlines: Cultural Materialism and the Politics of Dissident Reading*, Clarendon Press, Oxford.

Stallybrass, Peter (1991), 'Reading the Body and the Jacobean Theatre of Consumption' in D.S. Kasten and P. Stallybrass (eds), *Staging the Renaissance: Reinterpretation of Elizabethan and Jacobean Drama*, Routledge, London, pp.210-220.

Stallybrass, Peter and Jones, Ann R. (1991), 'Fetishizing Gender: Constructing the Hermaphrodite in Renaissance Europe', in J. Epstein and K. Straub (eds), *BodyGuards: The Cultural Politics of Gender Ambiguity*, Routledge, New York.

Tennenhouse, Leonard (1989), *Power on Display*, Methuen, London.

W., W. (1582), *A True and Iust Recorde, of the Information, Examination and Confession of Al the Witches, Taken at S. Oses in the Countie of Essex: Whereof Some Were Executed, and Other Some Entreated According to the Determination of the Lawe*, London.

Weir, A. (1993), 'Identification with the Divided Mother: Kristeva's ambivalence', in K. Oliver (ed.), *Ethics, Politics, and Difference in Julia Kristeva's Writing*, Routledge, New York, pp.79-91.

Willis, Deborah (1995), *Malevolent Nurture*, Cornell University Press, Ithaca.

Chapter 10

Gender Trouble in the Literature Classroom: Unintelligible Genders in *The Metamorphosis* and *The Well of Loneliness*

Margaret Sönser Breen

Introduction

In her preface to the 1999 edition of *Gender Trouble: Feminism and the Subversion of Identity*, Judith Butler asks a series of questions that reveal how gender, particularly the idea of a normative gender, functions as a vehicle for social control.[1] She writes:

> What continues to concern me most is the following kinds of questions: what will and will not constitute an intelligible life, and how do presumptions about normative gender and sexuality determine in advance what will qualify as the 'human' and the 'livable'? In other words, how do normative gender presumptions work to delimit the very field of description that we have for the human? (Butler, 1999, p.xxii.)

Butler's questions articulate the importance, indeed the urgency, of studying and teaching gender. Certain genders are 'intelligible', 'human' and 'livable'; they are real and legitimate. Others are not. Certain genders may be thought and articulated. Others cannot. These distinctions suggest the powerful political ways in which gender may be invoked and deployed in order to naturalize and so dismiss the oppression of various gender and sexual minorities. Throughout, *Gender Trouble* provides a theoretical framework for understanding the punitive social consequences of gender and sexual transgression.

    Gender Trouble thus proves an invaluable text for any course engaged in the study of non-normative genders and sexualities. Within the classroom, as people struggle to formulate their understanding of gender, *Gender Trouble* offers them an awareness that the struggle, the difficulty, at times the seeming impossibility, of

---

[1] *Gender Trouble: Feminism and the Subversion of Identity* was originally published in 1990. This chapter makes use of both editions: the 1990 edition when quoting the body of the text; the 1999 edition when quoting the 1999 preface.

articulating gender is at least in part an expression of the social value placed on intolerance for various gender and sexual minorities, and that awareness comes as an empowering relief to teachers and students alike. That relief speaks to what Butler calls 'the reading public['s] capacity and desire for reading complicated and challenging texts, when the complication is not gratuitous, when the challenge is in the service of calling taken-for-granted truths into question, when the taken for grantedness of those truths is, indeed, oppressive' (Butler, 1999, p.xviii). The difficulty of reading gender, specifically reading gender through reading *Gender Trouble*, is largely a measure of the epistemological entrenchment of various forms of gender prejudice.

The particular test case that this article offers for understanding the pedagogical importance of Butler's work focuses on this struggle to articulate gender within the literature classroom, especially when the gender in question is constructed as unthinkable and unspeakable. Employing *Gender Trouble* as its critical lens, this article examines gender and sexual transgression in late nineteenth- and early twentieth-century fiction. Specifically, this article focuses on two early twentieth-century texts, Franz Kafka's *The Metamorphosis* ([1915] 1972) – (*Die Verwandlung* (1999)) – and Radclyffe Hall's *The Well of Loneliness* ([1928] 1981).[2] Both of these texts, turning on the trope of gender metamorphosis, draw on *fin-de-siècle* sexological discussions as well as late nineteenth- and early twentieth-century literary representations of non-normative genders and sexualities. This article considers Kafka and Hall's work and their source texts, particularly in light of Butler's *Gender Trouble*.

My reading of Kafka's *The Metamorphosis* specifically looks at the work's relation to Krafft-Ebing's *Psychopathia Sexualis*, which, first published in 1886, is perhaps the most important sexological text of the *fin-de-siècle*.[3] Drawing on Krafft-Ebing's discussions of fetishism, masturbation, and homosexuality, as well as Sacher-Masoch's narrative of masochism, the novella *Venus in Furs* (*Venus im Pelz*) ([1870] 2000), Kafka not only represents metamorphosed protagonist Gregor Samsa as engaged in deviant sexual behaviors. Examining these behaviors via the critical lens of *Gender Trouble*, one recognizes how Gregor resists and in so doing destabilizes normative bourgeois constructions of masculinity and heterosexuality.

The second part of my article considers *The Well of Loneliness*, a novel that has been both praised and condemned as a 'lesbian Bible' and, more recently, been discussed as a transgender narrative. The novel's representation of hero Stephen Gordon owes much to Krafft-Ebing's work on inversion, particularly his account of Count Sandor in Case 166 of *Psychopathia*.[4] I argue that in functioning as an

---

[2] Though I have not cited any of the page numbers from it, the particular edition of Kafka's *Die Verwandlung* with which I have been working is the 1999 Suhrkamp edition.

[3] For a discussion of the importance of turn-of-the-century sexologists for Kafka's work, see Mark Anderson, 1996.

[4] In the 13th German edition of *Psychopathia Sexualis* (published in 1907) this case is number 173. In the [1902] 1998 English-language edition in use in this article, the number is 166.

apologia for inversion, *The Well* does not simply offer descriptions or characterizations of the invert that are faithful to the earlier sexological discussions; the novel participates in a Butlerian destabilization of gender and sexual norms. Further, I argue that *The Well*, particularly with regard to its representations of gender variability, offers a heretofore unexplored reworking of Bram Stoker's little discussed New Woman novel *The Man* ([1905] 2001).

Early in her landmark study, Judith Butler writes:

> 'Intelligible' genders are those which in some sense institute and maintain relations of coherence and continuity among sex, gender, sexual practice, and desire. In other words, the spectres of discontinuity and incoherence, themselves thinkable only in relation to existing norms of continuity and coherence, are constantly prohibited and produced by the very laws that seek to establish causal or expressive lines of connection among biological sex, culturally constituted genders, and the 'expression' or 'effect' of both in the manifestation of sexual desire through sexual practice (Butler, 1990, p.17).

This passage illuminates classroom discussions of Gregor Samsa and Stephen Gordon. In this article I argue that both protagonists prove unintelligible genders. It is their monstrosity, where monstrosity extends to desire, behavior, and body, that simultaneously discloses and maintains the boundaries of normative social behavior from which they are themselves excluded.

Kafka's *The Metamorphosis*, Krafft-Ebing's *Psychopathia Sexualis*, and Sacher-Masoch's *Venus in Furs*

In the first part of Kafka's *Metamorphosis* there is a description of a photograph that hangs in the front room of the Samsa apartment: 'On the wall...hung a photograph of Gregor from his army days, in a lieutenant's uniform, his hand on his sword, a carefree smile on his lips, demanding respect for his bearing and his rank' (Kafka, [1915] 1972, p.15). In this novella, which immerses the reader in the horrors of gender and sexual policing, the picture is significant. It functions as an image of gender and spatial intelligibility. Gregor the officer is a prototype of Habsburgian male authority. Hand on sword, he exacts the viewer's respect. From its vantage point, Gregor's picture overlooks the comings and goings of the Samsa family and their visitors. So, Kafka moves from this description of the photograph to the doorway connecting the front room to the foyer and, beyond that, to the outside: 'The door to the foyer was *open*, and since the front door was *open* too, it was possible to see out onto the landing and the top of the stairs going down' (Kafka, [1915] 1972, p.15, emphasis added). Seemingly, an exchange between inside and outside, between family and society, is possible because Gregor's photograph presides over that exchange.

Tellingly, aside from this description of the photograph, the reader never encounters Gregor as either an embodiment of gender normativity or a sign of social access or mobility. From the outset, Gregor proves a social cipher: an unintelligible gender and a sign of spatial confinement. He is 'a monstrous vermin' (Kafka, [1915] 1972, p.3), ('ein ungeheures Ungeziefer'), an 'it' or 'es', gendered neither male nor female. For much of the story he is locked within his room, where eventually he dies; his movement from space to space is often figured as transgression, as in 'he broke out' (Kafka, [1915] 1972, cf. pp.35, 37), and it is met by his family with violence. Gregor, then, is a figure of abjection. As Judith Butler explains, 'Those bodily figures who do not fit into either gender fall outside the human, indeed, constitute the domain of the dehumanized and the abject against which the human itself is constituted' (Butler, 1999, p.142). In contrast to the image that regulates the Samsa household, the image of the young self-possessed lieutenant grasping his sword, Gregor in his metamorphosis appears as an image of vulnerability and even sexual lack. Kafka describes how Gregor, with his 'vaulted brown belly...arch-shaped ribs...[and] many legs, pitifully thin...waving helplessly' (Kafka, [1915] 1972, p.3), is unable to lift himself out of bed; unable even to see that 'lower part of his body...his most sensitive' part (Kafka, [1915] 1972, p.7). How is one to understand Gregor's metamorphosis? Interestingly, as Gregor, contemplating his bug-like body, asks himself the same question ('What's happened to me?' (Kafka, [1915] 1972, p.3)), his attention turns toward the picture hanging over his desk. 'It showed a lady done up in a fur hat and a fur boa, sitting upright and raising up against the viewer a heavy fur muff in which her whole forearm had disappeared' (Kafka, [1915] 1972, p.3). As critics, most notably Mark Anderson, have suggested, the answer that this picture holds is an intertextual one.[5] The picture recalls the title of Leopold von Sacher-Masoch's literary exploration of sexual dominance and submission, *Venus in Furs*, the novel that forms the basis for Krafft-Ebing's discussion of masochism in *Psychopathia*. In the novel, protagonist Severin is renamed 'Gregor' once he undertakes the masochistic role of his lover's slave. Thus, in Kafka's text the picture of the woman in furs suggests that Gregor's metamorphosis is bound up with his own sexual desires.

A key scene at the end of the second part of *The Metamorphosis* makes that connection between Gregor's desire and his unintelligible gender clear. In this scene Gregor climbs atop the picture of the woman in furs in order to prevent his mother and sister from removing it along with all of his furniture. The picture is his prized possession; before his metamorphosis, the carving of its gilt frame was, as his mother comments early in the text, his one recent evening 'distraction' (Kafka, [1915] 1972, p.10). Atop the woman in furs, Gregor himself becomes framed, in effect creating a new image:

> ...he broke out...then he saw hanging conspicuously on the wall...the picture of the lady all dressed in furs, hurriedly crawled up on it and pressed himself against the glass, which gave a *good surface to stick to* and soothed his *hot belly*. At least no one would take away this picture, while *Gregor completely covered it up*.
> ...He *squatted* on his picture and would not give it up (Kafka, [1915] 1972, p.35, emphasis added).

---

[5] See Mark Anderson, 1983. See also Ruth Angress, 1970 and Larry Wolff, 2000.

The image directs one's attention to the lower part of Gregor's body, the 'hot belly', at the story's outset that unseen part (blind spot?). Squatting on the picture of the woman in furs, 'completely cover[ing] it up', Gregor, specifically his hot sticky belly, becomes the locus of unintelligible desire(s).

That is, read through a Butlerian lens, the image of Gregor ruptures the notion of a fixed gender binary. Butler writes:

> The internal coherence or unity of either gender, man or woman...requires both a stable and oppositional heterosexuality. That institutionally heterosexuality both requires and produces the univocity of each of the gendered terms that constitute the limit of gendered possibilities within an oppositional, binary gender system. This conception of gender presupposes not only a causal relation among sex, gender, and desire, but suggests as well that desire reflects or expresses gender and that gender reflects or expresses desire. The metaphysical unity of the three is assumed to be truly known and expressed in a differentiating desire for an oppositional gender—that is, in a form of oppositional heterosexuality (Butler, 1990, p.22).

The image of Gregor atop the picture of the woman in furs disrupts that 'metaphysical unity'. He challenges paradigms of male dominance and of heterosexuality.

Most immediately, that image is of a masturbator. Sticking to the picture of the woman in furs, where fur, particularly the muff, constitutes a conventional sign for female genitalia,[6] Gregor 'soothe[s] his hot belly'. More broadly, the stickiness of Gregor's body attests to the semiotic stickiness of the scene itself, which, read from the vantage point of *Psychopathia*, invites comparisons with and indeed compounds any number of sexual perversions, including fetishism, homosexuality, and masochism, the first two of which I will discuss.[7]

Thus, the image constituted by Gregor's position atop the magazine picture of the woman in furs may be read in terms of *Psychopathia*'s discussion of fetishism, a perversion in which, according to Krafft-Ebing, 'lie conditions favouring psychical and physical onanism' (Krafft-Ebing, [1902] 1998, p.146). Krafft-Ebing writes:

> *Fetishism of inanimate objects or articles of dress*...in all cases, may well be regarded as a pathological phenomenon, since its object falls without the circle of normal sexual

---

[6] See Elizabeth Boa, 1996, p.128.

[7] For a discussion of this scene in terms of masochism, see Mark Anderson, 1983. Anderson reads this scene, as well as the novella as a whole, in terms of its masochistic potential. For him 'what in Sacher-Masoch's novel is fundamentally a dialectic of submission between a male slave and a female mistress operates, in Kafka's novella, on two levels. The opening scene depicts Gregor, like Gregor-Severin...as dominated by the woman in furs. But as the story develops this domination is increasingly exercised by Gregor's family' (pp.9-10). So, for Anderson, 'Gregor's obscene coupling with the picture of his "Venus in furs"...causes his mother to faint and his father to lose all patience'. Gregor then readily 'submit[s] to corporal punishment. The beating delivered by the father comes as a secretly desired judgment' (p.12).

stimuli. But even here, in the phenomena, there is a certain outward correspondence with processes of the normal psychical sexual life; the inner connection and meaning of pathological fetichism, however, are entirely different. In the ecstatic love of a man mentally normal, a handkerchief or shoe, a love letter, the flower 'she gave', or a lock of hair, etc., may become the object of worship, but only because they represent a mnemonic symbol of the beloved person—absent or dead—whose whole personality is reproduced by them. The pathological fetichist has no such relations. The fetich constitutes the entire content of his idea. When he becomes aware of its presence, sexual excitement occurs, and the fetich makes itself felt (Krafft-Ebing, [1902] 1998, pp.144-145).

From this discussion, one may understand Gregor as a pathological fetishist. Ground and goal for his sexual pleasure, the picture of the woman replaces not simply a woman in his life but a woman *who was never really there except as a sign*.

Krafft-Ebing continues, '[n]ot infrequently fetishism occurs in the most various forms in combination with inverted sexuality...' (Krafft-Ebing, [1902] 1998, p.145), and, indeed, his discussion of homosexuality seems particularly relevant to an analysis of Kafka's woman-in-furs scene. In the section of *Psychopathia* titled 'Homo-sexual Feeling as an Acquired Manifestation in Both Sexes', Krafft-Ebing discusses the physical and mental transformation that homosexuality threatens. This danger of 'metamorphosis' is particularly acute for the masturbator, for whom homosexuality potentially functions as a latent identity category. Krafft-Ebing writes:

> Nothing is so prone to contaminate—under certain circumstances even to exhaust—the source of all noble and ideal sentiments, which arise of themselves from a normally developing sexual instinct, as the practice of masturbation in early years...If an individual, thus depraved, reaches the age of maturity, there is wanting in him that aesthetic, ideal, pure and free impulse which draws the opposite sexes together...This defect influences the morals, the character, fancy, feeling and instinct of the youthful masturbator, male or female, in an unfavourable manner, even causing, under certain circumstances, the desire for the opposite sex to sink to *nil*; so that masturbation is preferred to the natural mode of satisfaction...
>
> With *tainted* individuals, the matter is quite different.[8] The latent perverse sexuality is developed under the influence of neurasthenia induced by masturbation, abstinence, or otherwise.

---

[8] This sentence, in the 1907 German edition of *Psychopathia*, includes a qualification missing from the [1902] 1998 English edition. In the 1907 edition, the sentence in its entirety reads, 'Anders liegt die Sache beim *belasteten*, wahrscheinlich bisexual veranlagt gebliebenen, d. h. nicht zu ausschliesslich heterosexualer Empfindung ausgebildeten Individuum' (Krafft-Ebing, 1907, p.224). The second part of the sentence—'wahrscheinlich bisexual veranlagt gebliebenen, d. h. nicht zu ausschliesslich heterosexualer Empfindung ausgebildeten Individuum'—is what is missing. My translation of the whole sentence is as follows: 'With tainted individuals, who have probably remained bisexually oriented, that is, individuals who have not developed exclusively heterosexual feelings, the matter is quite different'.

Gradually, in contact with persons of the same sex, sexual excitation by them is induced. Related ideas are coloured with lustful feelings, and awaken corresponding desires. This decidedly degenerate reaction is the beginning of a process of physical and mental transformation...This *metamorphosis* presents different stages, or degrees (Krafft-Ebing, [1902] 1998, pp.188-190, first two emphases in original, third emphasis added).

For Krafft-Ebing, masturbation must be understood as something more than a non-normative sexual behavior capable of thwarting healthy heterosexual relations; masturbation potentially engenders homosexuality. As all of the excerpts from *Psychopathia* underscore, sexual perversions compound one another. Fetishism, masturbation, and homosexuality all call one another forth and all threaten mental and physical degeneration or, again, 'metamorphosis'.

Reading the discussions of fetishism, masturbation, and homosexuality along side Kafka's woman-in-furs scene, Gregor's *Verwandlung* (transfiguration) or 'Metamorphose' (metamorphosis),[9] as Krafft-Ebing terms it, seems all but inevitable. Indeed, as the above discussion of the metonymic proliferation of illicit desires suggests, metamorphosis itself functions as a trope for gender and sexual transgression. Atop the picture of the woman Gregor functions as a sign of perversion, if not perversions. He is a far cry from the self-assured lieutenant whose gender normative image presides over the Samsa household, and when his mother and sister see him, they scream.

Judith Butler helps one understand this inarticulate reaction to the 'verwandelte' Gregor. In this moment, *being* and sexual act collapse together. He becomes a 'spectre[ ] of discontinuity and incoherence' (Butler, 1990, p.17), whose desire disrupts his family's understanding of the natural and the human. She writes:

> The strategy of desire is in part the *transfiguration* of the desiring body itself. Indeed, in order to desire at all it may be necessary to believe in an altered bodily ego which, within the gendered rules of the imaginary, might fit the requirements of a body capable of desire. This imaginary condition of desire always exceeds the physical body through or on which it works (Butler, 1990, p.71, emphasis added).

Within the 'gendered rules' of the Samsa family's 'imaginary', Gregor necessarily appears as a 'monster' (Kafka, [1915] 1972, p.51), an 'Untier'—an unintelligible gender. As his sister remarks after seeing him atop the picture, 'I won't pronounce the name of my brother in front of this monster, and so all I can say is: we have to

---

[9] See p.224 of the 1907 German edition. Krafft-Ebing's discussion of perverse metamorphosis (*metamorphosis sexualis*) finds resonance in this moment in Kafka's *Metamorphosis* in which Gregor presses himself against the picture. In the German, while Krafft-Ebing uses the term '*Metamorphose*', Kafka chooses '*Verwandlung*', that is, 'transfiguration'. Kafka's word choice in effect allows him to keep the reference to Krafft-Ebing in play, even as '*Verwandlung*' foregrounds the tension between sexuality and conventional Christian morality within Gregor's world. For a discussion on the interconnections between the sacred and the monstrous, see Edward J. Ingebretsen, 2001.

try to get rid of *it*' (Kafka, [1915] 1972, p.51; emphasis added). And again: '…how can it be Gregor? If it were Gregor, he would have realized long ago that it isn't possible for human beings to live with such a creature, and he would have gone away of his own free will' (Kafka, [1915] 1972, p.52). Confined to his room, Gregor exists (and ultimately dies) apart from the family and, in so doing, in effect solidifies their understanding of themselves *as family*.

Gregor is a 'monstrous vermin'.[10] His story offers students and teachers alike a powerful example of how society polices its members through the 'regulatory fiction' of gender normativity (Butler, 1990, p.141).

Hall's *The Well of Loneliness*, Krafft-Ebing's *Psychopathia Sexualis*, and Bram Stoker's *The Man*

The Well of Loneliness provides another such example of gender policing. Like Kafka's text Hall's turns on the trope of metamorphosis. Stephen Gordon is an invert, whose gender dysphoria, like Gregor Samsa's monstrous vermin status, ruptures the conventionally naturalized relations between body, gender, and desire. Stephen's challenge, one might say, is the issue of how to *be* a masculine woman who can love a woman (or, perhaps, how to *become* a man within a society that refuses to understand ontology, and so gender, as the effect of that society's heterosexist injunctions). Within this context, Stephen Gordon, like Gregor Samsa, necessarily proves an unintelligible gender.

Early in *Gender Trouble*, Judith Butler, drawing on Monique Wittig, asks the question, 'To what extent does the category of women achieve stability and coherence only in the context of the heterosexual matrix?' (Butler, 1990, p.5). In some sense, this question proves the point of departure for Radclyffe Hall's 1928 lesbian classic *The Well of Loneliness*.

Indeed, this question functions as the framing question of the novel, at least in part because it so clearly articulates the anxiety at work in both Krafft-Ebing's discussions of gender and sexual variability in *Psychopathia* and the New Woman novels of the early twentieth century, against both of which *The Well* defines itself. Krafft-Ebing's account of Count Sandor, Case 166 or the case of hermaphroditism in *Psychopathia*, has been duly noted as a key source text for *The Well*. Count Sandor, Jay Prosser writes, 'with his aristocratic upbringing, the father who raises her a boy, with a love of riding and fencing, seems of all sexological case histories closest to Stephen's plot' (Prosser, 2001, p.133). By contrast, another likely source, the New Woman novel *The Man* by Bram Stoker has not yet been linked to *The Well*. Even as it is not within the scope of this article to discuss the many parallels between the two novels, I will spend a bit of time commenting on some of

---

[10] Gregor is 'das ungeheure Ungeziefer', where, according to Stanley Corngold, '"*Ungeheuer*" connotes the creature who has no place in the family; [and] "*Ungeziefer*", the unclean animal unsuited for sacrifice, the creature without a place in God's order' (Corngold, 1972, p.xix).

the intertextual connections before then addressing Krafft-Ebing's impo,
The Well.

To begin with, one considers the following summary, which applie
well to Stoker's and Hall's novels. The protagonist Stephen is a wom   ....u,
beginning with her name (Stephen Norman in the first case; Stephen Gordon in the
second case), is at least in part raised to be the son of an adoring father. (This
father dies suddenly in an accident when Stephen is on the threshold of adulthood.)
Aside from her name, Stephen is gendered male in terms of her body: she is tall,
firm of jaw, and lanky. As an adult Stephen challenges gender conventions by
desiring the wrong person and, what is more transgressive, insisting on the *right* to
the voicing of her desire. Finally, Stephen, battling her own loneliness and sense of
shame, calls upon God to reassert a gender order that allows for her own
happiness.

This is the basic outline for both novels; here, though, the similarity ends. 'The
Man' referred to in Stoker's novel's subversion-promising title is not Stephen
Norman at all, but rather the man whom she realizes she, her investment in non-
normative gender behavior notwithstanding, has always been in love with, Harold
An Wolf. In contrast to *The Well*, then, Stoker's novel is a cautionary tale of
gender transgression that, in the end, celebrates the triumph of gender norms. In
other words, Stephen, a character who at the novel's beginning, flouts gender
conventions in her mannerisms, thoughts, and her very body, is by the novel's end
a character whose various affects (including her body) uphold gender norms.

Significantly, the reestablishment of these conventions of gender and
heterosexual romance depends upon the novel's drastic alteration of the discursive
imagining of Stephen's gender. Here Judith Butler's rhetorical question comes to
mind: 'To what extent does the body *come into being* in and through the mark(s) of
gender?' (Butler, 1990, p.8). Stephen Norman's body (or rather the discursive
imagining of it) undergoes a metamorphosis between the novel's beginning and
end—a metamorphosis that serves ultimately to uphold the gender conventions
that Stephen's *being*—where that *being* exposes that 'ontology is…not a
foundation, but a normative injunction that operates insidiously by installing itself
into political discourse as its necessary ground' (Butler, 1990, p.148)—initially
challenges. So, for example, Stephen's initial gender transgression may be
understood in terms of the name that inscribes her gender:

> When in the fullness of time it was known that an heir was expected, Squire Norman
> took for granted that the child would be a boy, and held the idea so tenaciously that his
> wife, who loved him deeply, gave up warning and remonstrance after she had once tried
> to caution him against too fond a hope. She saw how bitterly he would be disappointed
> in case it should prove to be a girl. He was, however, so fixed on the point that she
> determined to say no more. After all, it might be a boy; the chances were equal. The
> Squire would not listen to any one else at all; so as the time went on his idea was more
> firmly fixed than ever. His arrangements were made on the base that he would have a
> son. The name was of course decided. Stephen had been the name of all the Squires of
> Normanstand for ages—as far back as the records went; and Stephen the new heir of
> course would be (Stoker, [1905] 2001, pp.10-11).

It is this gender plot that in turn determines Stoker's representation of Stephen's body. By age 14, Stephen has:

> [t]he firm-set jaw, with chin broader and more square than is usual in a woman, and the wide fine forehead and aquiline nose marked the high descent from Saxon through Norman....Already she was tall for her age, with something of that lankiness which marks the early development of a really fine figure. [She was] [l]ong-legged, long-necked, as straight as a lance... (Stoker, [1905] 2001, p.6).

Finally, what with her name and body gendered masculine, Stephen proves her father's son:

> [Squire Norman] never, not then nor afterwards, quite lost the old belief that Stephen was indeed a son....This belief tinged all his after-life and molded his policy with regard to his girl's upbringing. If she was to be indeed his son as well as his daughter, she must from the first be accustomed to boyish as well as girlish ways (Stoker, [1905] 2001, p.16).

Yet, Stephen soon discovers that the price for her gender transgression is 'shame': '"Shame" was the generic word which now summarized to herself her thought of her conduct' (Stoker, [1905] 2001, p.92). Her behavior proves 'an outrage on convention' (Stoker, [1905] 2001, p.129).

Only at the novel's end when Stephen aligns herself with gender conventions can she relinquish her sense of shame and her loneliness.[11] Only then can this 'queer girl' (Stoker, [1905] 2001, p.140) begin 'to take herself to task more seriously than she had ever done with regard to social and conventional duties' (Stoker, [1905] 2001, p.214). At the novel's end Stoker reinscribes Stephen within gender norms. So, for example, her union with Harold is prefigured by her alignment with a little girl named Pearl. By novel's end it is not Stephen's manliness but rather her womanliness that Stoker underscores:

> The two faces so different, and yet with so much in common. The red hair and the flaxen, both tints of gold. The fine color of each heightened to a bright flush in their eagerness. Stephen was so little used to children, and yet loved them so, that *all the womanhood* in her, which is possible motherhood, went out in an instant to the lovely eager child (Stoker, [1905] 2001, p.216, emphasis added).

It is this moment of physical likeness that marks 'all the womanhood' in Stephen. In the end, Stephen proves 'a woman! A woman who waited the coming of a man! ...She was all woman now; all-patient, and all-submissive. She waited the man; and the man was coming!' (Stoker, [1905] 2001, pp.235-236). In the end Stephen Norman performs an intelligible gender.

This is not the case of Count Sandor, however, the other crucial and the obvious historical figure behind Hall's Stephen Gordon. Krafft-Ebing describes

---

[11] See, for example, *The Man*, pp.54, 175, 176, and 230.

Sandor as 'this ostensible Count [who]...was no man at all, but a woman in male attire—Sarolta (Charlotte), Countess V.' (Krafft-Ebing, [1902] 1998, p.284).[12] Krafft-Ebing's account includes a passage that records the excerpts from the Count's letters and writings. One of these writings, bearing remarkable similarity to the final passage of *The Well*, is addressed to the various legal and medical authorities involved in his prosecution for deception and forgery of public documents. The Count writes:

> Gentlemen, you learned in the law, psychologists and pathologists, do me justice! Love led me to take the step I took; all my deeds were conditioned by it. God put it in my heart.
>
> If he created me so, and not otherwise, am I then guilty; or is it the eternal, incomprehensible way of fate? I relied on God, that one day my emancipation would come; for my thought was only love itself, which is the foundation, the guiding principle, of His teaching and His kingdom.
>
> O God, Though All-pitying, Almighty One! Though seest my distress; Thou knowest how I suffer. Incline Thyself to me; extend Thy helping hand to me, deserted by all the world. Only God is just (Krafft-Ebing, [1902] 1998, p.288).

Telling here is the Count's address of juridical experts, 'you learned in the law, psychologists and pathologists'. Even as the Count claims at passage's end that 'only God is just', he understands that his gender—and not simply the case of deception and forgery—is subject to the court's juridical authority.

Interestingly, the court pardoned the Count:

> The opinion given showed that in S. there was a congenitally abnormal inversion of the sexual instinct, which expressed itself, anthropologically, in anomalies of development of the body, depending upon great hereditary taint; further, that the criminal acts of S. had their foundation in her abnormal and irresistible sexuality.
>
> S.'s characteristic expressions—'God put love in my heart. If He created me so, and not otherwise, am I, then, guilty; or is it the eternal *incomprehensible* way of fate?' are really justified.
>
> The court granted pardon... (Krafft-Ebing, [1902] 1998, p.291, emphasis added).

In effect, the court releases the Count because he is determined *to be* 'a congentially abnormal inver[t]'. That is, he is the very gender monstrosity, discursively marked and sustained in *Psychopathia* with the use of the female pronoun to describe him, that proves the rule of normative gendered bodies, behaviors, and desires. Juridically speaking, the Count functions as one of those 'spectres of discontinuity and incoherence, themselves thinkable only in relation to existing norms of continuity and coherence' (Butler, 1990, p.17), which, Butler explains, serve to naturalize heteronormative gendered behavior. In *Psychopathia*'s account of Sandor, '[w]hat emerges is a split between bodily

---

[12] In the 1907 German edition, the case of Count Sandor (case 173) may be found on pp.315-321.

feeling and body, gender, and sex that cannot be compensated by love for the other' (Prosser, 2001, p.133). Sandor proves an unintelligible gender.

The same may of course be said of *The Well*'s protagonist. In the final passage of the novel, Stephen Gordon, whose language paraphrases Count Sandor's, undergoes a gender metamorphosis. This metamorphosis, in contrast to Stephen Norman's in *The Man*, which asserts the propriety and value of gender norms, works to underscore her gender dissonance. With *The Well*'s ending, as in *The Metamorphosis*, one is reminded of Butler's point:

> The strategy of desire is in part the *transfiguration* of the desiring body itself. Indeed, in order to desire at all it may be necessary to believe in an altered bodily ego which, within the gendered rules of the imaginary, might fit the requirements of a body capable of desire. This imaginary condition of desire always exceeds the physical body through or on which it works (Butler, 1990, p.71, emphasis added).

Much like Gregor Samsa's sticky body atop the framed magazine picture, Stephen Gordon at the novel's end proves a figure that exceeds normative injunctions of sex, body, and desire. Stephen's body and desire signal different genders and, in so doing, rupture the category of woman. (For Jay Prosser this split is so marked that he terms *The Well* a transgendered narrative rather than a lesbian text, with Stephen a female-to-male transsexual.)[13] In the novel's final passage, Stephen Gordon's own 'strategy of desire' performs a remarkable transfiguration. Stephen's desire performs a paradoxically inexpressible annunciation that necessarily exceeds her body, sexed female:

> Her barren womb became fruitful—it ached with its fearful and sterile burden. It ached with the fierce yet helpless children who would clamour in vain for their right to salvation. They would turn first to God, and then to the world, and then to her. They would cry out accusing...
>
> And now there was only one voice, one demand; her own voice into which those millions had entered....A terrifying voice that made her ears throb...that shook her very entrails, until she must stagger and all but fall beneath this appalling burden of sound that strangled her in its will to be uttered.
>
> 'God', she gasped, 'we believe; we have told You we believe...We have not denied You, then rise up and defend us. Acknowledge us, oh God, before the whole world. Give us also the right to our existence!' (Hall, [1928] 1981, p.437).

Notwithstanding normative gender injunctions, Stephen's body is impregnated by a discourse of inverted desire. Her strangled prayer, 'God...Give us also the right to our existence', echoing both Stephen Norman's wish 'To be God, and able to do things' (Stoker, [1905] 2001, pp.187, 189) and Count Sandor's cry, 'O God... Incline Thyself to me' (Krafft-Ebing, [1902] 1998, p.288), discloses ontology's

---

[13] Jay Prosser writes, Stephen Gordon's understanding of her body shapes 'a body narrative that shows Stephen as a female-to-male transsexual, not woman or lesbian, undergoing progressive realization of her wrong embodiment' (Prosser, 2001, p.135).

function as a political construct that deems inverted desire inexpressible and Stephen Gordon's gender unintelligible.

Conclusion

What is to be gained from reading through a Butlerian lens Kafka's *Metamorphosis* along side of Hall's *The Well*? I believe that this article suggests a few answers. First, both texts attest to the importance not only of Krafft-Ebing's *Psychopathia* but also of earlier *fin-de-siècle* literary texts for early twentieth-century literary explorations of gender variability. Second, taken together, the novella and novel underscore the importance of the trope of metamorphosis/ transfiguration for both literary and sexological treatments of gender normativity. Indeed, looking ahead to texts as diverse as Jane Rule's *Desert of the Heart* (1964), Jeanette Winterson's *Oranges Are Not the Only Fruit* (1985), Leslie Feinberg's *Stone Butch Blues* (1993), and Cherríe Moraga's *Loving in the War Years* (1983, 2000), to the poems of Audre Lorde, Adrienne Rich, and Mark Doty—to name just a few—one might argue that metamorphosis proves itself a key trope for twentieth-century literary interrogations of gender. Above all, one recognizes the value of teaching *The Metamorphosis* and *The Well* through a Butlerian lens. Judith Butler's *Gender Trouble* allows one to recognize not only the subversive political potential of Kafka's and Hall's work but also, more generally, the potentially violent and dehumanizing consequences of a widespread cultural insistence on the institution and regulation of gender norms. Finally, *Gender Trouble* attests to the critical importance of engaging gender in the classroom, where the struggle to articulate gender itself may serve as a means of social empowerment.

References

Anderson, Mark (December 1983), 'Kafka and Sacher-Masoch', *Journal of the Kafka Society of America*, vol. 7, no. 2, pp.4-19.

—— (1996), 'Kafka, Homosexuality, and the Aesthetics of "Male" Culture', in R. Robertson and E. Timms (eds), *Gender and Politics in Austrian Fiction. Austrian Studies VII*, Edinburgh University Press, Edinburgh, pp.79-99.

Angress, Ruth K., (1970), 'Kafka and Sacher-Masoch: A Note on *The Metamorphosis*', *Modern Language Notes*, vol. 85, pp.745-746.

Boa, Elizabeth (1996), *Kafka, Gender, Class, and Race in the Letters and Fictions*, Clarendon, Oxford.

Butler, Judith (1990, 1999), *Gender Trouble: Feminism and the Subversion of Identity*, Routledge, New York.

Corngold, Stanley (1972), 'Introduction', in Franz Kafka, *The Metamorphosis*, S. Corngold (trans. and ed.) ([1915] 1972), Bantam, New York, pp.xi-xxii.

Feinberg, Leslie (1993), *Stone Butch Blues*, Firebrand, Ithaca, New York.

Hall, Radclyffe ([1928] 1981), *The Well of Loneliness*, Doubleday and Co., New York.

Ingebretsen, Edward J. (2001), *At Stake: Monsters and the Rhetoric of Fear in Public Culture*, University of Chicago Press, Chicago.

Kafka, Franz ([1915] 1972), *The Metamorphosis*, S. Corngold (trans. and ed.), Bantam, New York.

––––––– ([1915] 1999), *Die Verwandlung*, Suhrkamp, Frankfurt am Main.

Krafft-Ebing, Richard von (1907), *Psychopathia Sexualis*, 13th edition, Ferdinand Enke, Stuttgart.

––––––– ([1902] 1998), *Psychopathia Sexualis*, Franklin S. Klaf (trans.), translation of the 12th edition, Arcade, New York.

Moraga, Cherríe (1983, 2000), *Loving in the War Years: Lo Que Nunca Pasó Por Sus Labios*, South End Press, Cambridge, MA.

Prosser, Jay (2001), '"Some Primitive Thing Conceived in a Turbulent Age of Transition": The Transsexual Emerging from *The Well*', in Laura Doan and Jay Prosser (eds), *Palatable Poison: Critical Perspectives on* The Well of Loneliness, Columbia University Press, New York.

Rule, Jane (1964), *Desert of the Heart*, Macmillan, Toronto.

Sacher-Masoch, Leopold von ([1870] 2000), *Venus in Furs (Venus im Pelz)*, Joachim Neugroschel (trans.), Penguin, Harmondsworth.

Stoker, Bram ([1905] 2001), *The Man*, Wildside Press, Doylestown, PA.

Winterson, Jeanette (1985), *Oranges Are Not the Only Fruit*, Pandora Press, London.

Wolff, Larry (2000), 'Introduction', Leopold von Sacher-Masoch, *Venus in Furs*, Joachim Neugroschel (trans.), Penguin, Harmondsworth, pp.vii-xxviii.

Chapter 11

Butler's Corporeal Politics: Matters of Politicized Abjection

Natalie Wilson[1]

In her preface to *Bodies That Matter: On the Discursive Limits of 'Sex'* (1993), Judith Butler refers to philosophy as 'always at some distance from corporeal matters (Butler, 1993, p.ix). In this paper, I examine Butler's own distance from corporeal matters in order to posit that her work is not as distanced from the actual materiality of the body as critics have claimed. That, in fact, her analysis of the abject body serves as a sustained consideration of a political subversion grounded in materiality—a subversion that endorses the individual body as potentially disruptive to the symbolic domain of viable bodies. Focussing on *Bodies That Matter*, I discuss Butler's analysis of matter in relation to signification and how, in our culture, certain bodies come to *matter* more than others. Through a consideration of the novels *Mister Sandman* (1996), by Barbara Gowdy, and *Geek Love* (1989), by Katherine Dunn, novels largely concerned with bodily abnormality, I consider the ramifications of Butler's theories on bodily identity for the various abject bodies that populate these texts. In particular, I argue that while Butler's work revolving around abject materiality is overshadowed by a theoretical focus on gender and performativity, this aspect of her work actually constitutes the most sustained analysis of bodily materiality as politically constituted. While in the main Butler's work insists on an identity 'performed' through various discursive acts, her theories on abject materiality insist that the body is not entirely discursively constructed and offer the most politically efficacious view of corporeal identity.

However, although her consideration of which bodies matter in contemporary society attends to the specific materiality of bodies, overall Butler serves as a radical proponent of the body as a discursively constructed cultural product. For example, in *Gender Trouble: Feminism and the Subversion of Identity* (1990), her theory of gender as performative is extended to a notion of the body as performative, of a body as '[a]lways already a cultural sign' (Butler, 1990, p.71). Arguing '"the body" is itself a construction, as are the myriad "bodies" that

[1] A version of this essay appeared under the same title in *International Journal of Sexuality and Gender Studies*, vol. 6, nos. 1-2 (April 2001). Reprinted with permission of Kluwer Academic.

constitute the domain of gendered subjects' (Butler, 1990, p.8), Butler repeatedly refutes any sort of prediscursive body, and argues instead for a textualized body rendered in and through discourse. While Butler does concede to certain bodily facts, overall, the body in her work is a discursive site.

In Butler's analysis, materiality is a process through which the body comes into being via repeated practices that bring about a fixed materialization over time. She refers to matter 'not as site or surface, but as *a process of materialization that stabilizes over time to produce the effect of boundary, fixity, and surface we call matter...*matter is always materialized' (Butler, 1993, p.9, emphasis in original). Here, matter is not a surface or substance, but rather something that is stabilized through discourse and repeated bodily acts. As Vicki Kirby notes in her book *Telling Flesh: The Substance of the Corporeal* (1997), matter becomes bound up with signification in Butler's work in such a way that we are no longer dealing with matter as substance, but with matter as signification:

> Butler deploys the term 'matter' rather than 'substance' because the former is a synonym for significance/signification. To think of substance is to think of the very meat of carnality that is born and buried, the stuff of decay that seems indifferent to semiosis. Substance evokes the soil of groundedness itself; the concrete and tangible thingness of things. To avoid using the word 'substance' is surely a careful decision on the part of a writer whose stated interest is in the materiality of bodies. What risk, then, is Butler's sustained avoidance of this term trying to minimize? (Kirby, 1997, p.125).

To answer Kirby's question, I would suggest the risk often avoided (or minimized) in Butler's text is a consideration of the *actual matter* of bodies and how this matter affects identity. However, Kirby's claim that Butler's main interest is bodily materiality erroneously ignores Butler's interest in gender and the heterosexual matrix. While materiality is no doubt an interest, considerations of gender are tantamount in Butler's work. In fact, Butler argues that there can be no body, no I, before gender. As she asserts in *Bodies That Matter*, 'the matrix of gender relations is prior to the emergence of the "human"' (Butler, 1993, p.7). Butler further argues that there is no gender identity behind the expressions of gender, and, referring to Nietzsche's concept that there is no doer behind the deed, she claims that 'gender is always a doing, though not a doing by a subject who might be said to pre-exist the deed' (Butler, 1993, p.25). It is within these types of postulations that gender becomes tantamount and considerations of bodily materiality go by the wayside.

Although Butler names matter as a major theoretical issue in *Bodies That Matter*, she mainly focusses on the limited concept of matter as signification. Materiality is in fact a very slippery concept throughout her text, as she herself admits in the preface: 'the thought of materiality invariably moved me into other domains. I tried to discipline myself to stay on the subject, but found that I could not fix bodies as simple objects of thought' (Butler, 1993, p.ix). This confession of her inability to 'fix bodies' is telling in a work that attempts to rework how and why certain types of bodies matter in contemporary culture. In fact, in both *Gender Trouble* and *Bodies That Matter*, bodies are conspicuously absent—philosophical arguments dominate both texts and little to no space is given to actual bodies in culture.

Instead, Butler explores the body as discursive, insisting that that there is no access to a pure materiality outside of language. Positing that accessibility to anatomy always takes place through language, through an 'imaginary schema', she contends that pure matter or anatomy can never be reached, that the body is always 'a matter of signification' (Butler, 1993, pp.66-67). Here, Butler does not insist that the body is purely discursive, but rather that materiality can never be grasped without recourse to language, 'that there can be no reference to a pure materiality except via materiality' (Butler, 1993. p.68). But, does the reverse not also apply— is there any access to language that is not in some sense separable from matter? Does not the textuality and discursivity of the body always hark back to matter and substance? Language partially constructs the body, no doubt. But is language also partially constructed and shaped by the body?

As Carroll Smith-Rosenberg argues in her article 'The Body Politic':

Human sexuality is emblematic of the interconnectedness of the material and discursive. Discourse constructs our perceptions of the body and the erotic at the same time as discourses themselves borrow from the body and the erotic to render themselves evocative and expressive (Smith-Rosenberg, 1989, p.101).

Here, Smith-Rosenberg emphasizes the inseparability of the body and language, insisting that discourse is inextricable from bodily materiality. Butler, on the other hand, continually emphasizes that we cannot see matter as prior to discourse, that '[t]he body posited as prior to the sign, is always *posited* or *signified* as *prior*' and that language is 'productive, constitutive, one might even argue *performative*, in as much as this signifying act delimits and contours the body that it then claims to find prior to any and all signification' (Butler, 1993, p.30, emphasis in original). While Butler admits that materiality 'is bound up with signification from the start', she notes that '[t]o posit by way of language a materiality outside of language is still to posit that materiality' (Butler, 1993, p.30). Here, Butler depicts language as a necessary condition of materiality—as what is needed in order to posit materiality in the first place. As she queries: 'Can language simply refer to materiality, or is language also the very condition under which materiality may be said to appear?' (Butler, 1993, pp.30-31). Thus, Butler seems perilously close to positing that everything is discursively constructed, that matter is only materialized via discourse.

Hence, while Butler notes the interconnectedness of language and materiality, she still foregrounds language as that which effectively shapes, constructs, and produces matter—as a sort of interpreting lens through which matter is molded by discourse. But how does this notion of discursive materiality proffer possibilities for changing limited conceptions of gender, bodily identity, and sexuality? How can the actual matter of bodies work to dynamically change the limited parameters of gendered discourse? Furthermore, how might we circumvent this deterministic reliance on discourse and explore the body in relation to other ways of meaning?

For the body is not only constituted via discourse but also through its relationship to other bodies, through its physical dimensions, through its individual material specificity.

As Abigail Bray and Claire Colebrook argue in their article 'The Haunted Flesh: Corporeal Feminism and the Politics of (Dis)Embodiment' (1998), the body needs to be considered not only in relation to representation or discourse but also in relation to physicality. They insist that '[r]efiguring the problem of the body demands that it be seen as more than a semiotic system' (Bray and Colebrook, 1998, p.55). Contrary to Butler's reliance on matter as signification, we must consider matter as substance: 'The body is a negotiation with images, but it is also a negotiation with pleasures, pains, other bodies, space, visibility, and medical practice; no single event in this field can act as a general ground for determining the status of the body' (Bray and Colebrook, 1998, p.43). Furthermore, discourse cannot limitlessly remake or reshape the body, for, as Bray and Colebrook confirm: 'Representations are not negations imposed on otherwise fluid bodies' (Bray and Colebrook, 1998, p.38). But Butler, referring in *Gender Trouble* to the body as 'not a "being" but a variable boundary, a surface whose permeability is politically regulated, a signifying practice within a cultural field of gender hierarchy and compulsory heterosexuality' (Butler, 1990, p.139) does suggest a certain fluidity of the body. However, while the body and its boundaries are inexorably related to the social, the body is also materially bound and, as such, is not an endlessly malleable substance to be shaped at will by discourse. But this poststructuralist concept of the body as discursive text is largely accepted by Butler. This body, as Carol Bigwood notes in her article 'Renaturalizing the Body' (1991), is conceived of as extremely pliable. Bigwood, suggesting that Butler subscribes to this malleable poststructuralist notion of the body, notes that this body 'is contextualized only as a place marker in quasi-linguistic systems of signifiers. It is so fluid it can take on almost limitless embodiments. It has no real terrestrial *weight*' (Bigwood, 1991, p.59, emphasis in original).

Vicki Kirby also takes issue with the postsructuralist and postmodern approaches to corporeality and their reluctance to consider 'what are commonly understood as the biological facts of the body's existence' and instead to focus on 'the politics of representation' (Kirby, 1997, p.70). To her credit, Butler does refer to various biological facts of bodily life; however, overall her body is discursive rather than anatomical. Referring to 'the pervasive yet unpalatable belief that the anatomical body locates the unarguably real body, the literal body, the body whose immovable and immobilizing substance must be secured outside the discussion', Kirby laments that '[t]his improper body is quarantined for fear that its ineluctable immediacy will leave us no space for change, no chance to be otherwise, no place from which to engender a different future' (Kirby, 1997, p.70).

Re-materializing Discourse: Abjection as Corporeal Politics

While this material 'improper body' is largely quarantined outside the realm of Butler's work, it does appear in the form of the abject body in her text *Bodies That Matter*. Her discussion of how and why certain bodies matter more than others in contemporary society is perhaps one of the most explicitly political aspects of her work. Exploring the ways in which abject bodies are indisociable from regulatory norms and serve as the 'constitutive outside to the domain of the subject' (Butler, 1993, p.3), Butler examines how the materiality of bodies is controlled by various normalizing practices and how such practices lead to a whole realm of bodies that are not constituted as valuable or valued subjects in current culture. In relation to her contention that certain bodies are abjected by culture, Butler questions the following:

> [H]ow does that materialization of the norm in bodily formation produce a domain of abjected bodies, a field of deformation, which in failing to qualify as fully human fortifies those regulatory norms? What challenges does that excluded and abjected realm produce to a symbolic hegemony that might force a radical rearticulation of what qualifies as Bodies That Matter, ways of living that count as 'life,' lives worth protecting, lives worth saving, lives worth grieving? (Butler, 1993, p.16.)

Here, abject bodies are those bodies that fail to matter, that do not conform to the regulatory norms of society. These bodies serve as what Butler terms the 'constitutive outside', and, as Butler argues, work to expose the limits of constructivism because they serve as bodies that do not enter into the symbolic or discursive realm and thus are not constructed as culturally viable but rather as 'delegitimated bodies that fail to count as "bodies"' (Butler, 1993, p.15). Thus, abject bodies serve as a *material* outside, as bodies that are relegated to abject materiality. As Butler contends, these abject bodies serve as deviations from the cultural norm and are not constructed via cultural discourses as bodies that matter in society. Here, her theory revolves around actual bodies in culture and explores the way in which various types of abjected bodies—deformed bodies, homosexual bodies, diseased bodies, aged bodies – are not allowed the same cultural weight or importance as 'normal'—i.e., white, heterosexual, healthy—bodies.

In a revealing interview with Irene Costera Meijer and Baukje Prins, Butler (1998) emphasizes these political aspects of abjection, noting that '[t]he abjection of certain kinds of bodies, their inadmissibility to codes of intelligibility, does make itself known in policy and politics, and to live as such a body in the world is to live in the shadowy regions of ontology' (Butler, 1998, p.277). Hence, the abject body serves as a sort of ultimate other, a material incarnation of difference that is not discursively legitimated. Thus, the abject body does not *exist* in the same way that the normative body does. For example, the abjected homosexual body is often relegated to the margins of culture, to what Butler terms 'the shadowy regions of ontology'. Therefore, a reconsideration of those types of bodies abjected by culture is a crucial political move.

In *Bodies That Matter*, Butler repeatedly insists on the political implications of the abject body, arguing that:

> it will be as important to think about how and to what end bodies are constructed as it will be to think about how and to what end bodies are *not* constructed and, further, to ask after how bodies which fail to materialize provide the necessary 'outside', if not the necessary support, for the bodies which, in materializing the norm, qualify as Bodies That Matter (Butler, 1993, p.16, emphasis in original).

Here, Butler presents abjection as a discursive process—a process that provides an 'outside' against which to construct normative bodies. This claim calls for a radical renegotiation of who/what counts as a body that matters in society, for a discursive reclamation of the abject body. And, significantly, this claim is grounded in bodily materiality.

Referring to 'the politicization of abjection', Butler posits that the political aspects of abjection could assist in 'a radical resignification of the symbolic domain, deviating the citational chain toward a more possible future to expand the very meaning of what counts as a valued and valuable body in the world' (Butler, 1993, pp.21-22). She names abjection as 'an enabling disruption', and argues that a reconsideration of such bodies and their foreclosure in the symbolic domain could offer 'the occasion for a radical rearticulation of the symbolic horizon in which bodies come to matter at all' (Butler, 1993, p.23). Here, Butler places the material body in a political domain, endorsing materiality as potentially disruptive to the symbolic domain of viable bodies. Matter is thus recast as constitutive and the body becomes an active agent rather than a passive receptacle for regulatory norms. As Butler argues:

> to problematize the matter of bodies...may well indicate a significant and promising shift in political thinking. This unsettling of 'matter' can be understood as initiating new possibilities, new way for bodies to matter (Butler, 1993, p.30).

Hence, while Butler often explores the body as discursively constituted, her theories on abjection insist on a *material* body that, through its very materiality, can serve as politically subversive.

Butler tests and expands these theories on politicized abjection in *Bodies That Matter* in relation to various texts, namely fiction by Willa Cather and Nella Larsen. She reads both authors as involved in the project of exploring how the body is sexualized, gendered, and racialized and how those bodies that fail to fit normative criteria become abject. In so doing, Butler asserts her belief in the notion of 'literary narrative as a place where theory takes place' (Butler, 1993, p.182) and implicitly acknowledges the power of narrative to renegotiate bodily materiality. Furthermore, by foregrounding the specificity of material bodies within these narratives, Butler re-materializes discourse and significanctly brings the body back into her own theory.

Narrative Enactments of Politicized Abjection

In what follows, I examine two texts in relation to bodily materiality and politicized abjection. In accordance with Butler, I confirm the notion that 'the production of texts can be one way of reconfiguring what will count as the world' (Butler, 1993, p.19). With this idea in mind, I wish to suggest that literary narrative is an important political testing ground for Butler's theoretical work through an analysis of two novels, *Mister Sandman*, by Barbara Gowdy (1996), and *Geek Love*, by Katherine Dunn (1989).

The novel *Geek Love*, with its emphasis on material markers of identity, abject bodies, and bodily politics, functions as a textual exploration of corporeality. The text chronicles the story of the Binewskis, a family of carnival freaks produced by Al and Lil Binewski, who experiment with various drugs and chemicals in order to reproduce freakish offspring to populate their failing carnival. Their children (Olympia, an albino dwarf and the novel's main character; Arty, who has flippers instead of arms and legs; Iphy and Elly, conjoined twins; and Chick, a telekinetic) represent bodies abjected by 'normal' culture. The Binewskis, however, are raised within the world of the carnival, wherein their material bodily differences are admired and celebrated. In fact, the children pride themselves on their difference and compete over who has the most fabulously freakish body. Herein, the novel explores how notions of bodily normality are culturally and discursively constructed. Within the world of the carnival, the freakish Binewskis become valued and valuable bodies, while those with 'normal' bodies are viewed as stultifying and boring.

In the text, the extreme forms of bodily difference and how these differences are interpreted work to test the poststructuralist notion of the culturally-constructed body. While the novel lays bare the cultural construction of normative and abjected bodies, it simultaneously explores the role bodily materiality plays in such constructions. By populating the text with characters whose corporeality constantly foregrounds their difference, the novel troubles the popular rubric of constructionist theories of the body as cultural text and insists on materiality as a shaping force. The novel emphasizes the body as *both* cultural and material, insisting that cultural construction as well as individual corporeality, including genetic and chromosomal factors, plays a crucial part in corporeal identity formation. Perhaps this theme is most strongly emphasized in relation to Miranda, Olympia's daughter. As the narrative reveals, Miranda is given away to be raised and educated at a convent because she is too 'normal' for carnival life—her only bodily difference being a small corkscrew tail at the base of her spine. Thus, unlike the other Binewskis, Miranda does not have the cultural upbringing as a carnival 'freak'.

After the carnival burns down and Olympia moves into the real world, she discovers that her daughter Miranda has become a medical illustrator fascinated with drawing abnormal bodies. Olympia muses that 'there may be some hooked structure in her cells that twists her toward all that the world calls freakish' (Dunn, 1989, p.17). This foregrounding of genetics as shaping identity surfaces again when Olympia takes pride in Miranda's rebellious nature which was not quelled by being raised at a convent and notes it was 'as though her wildness were a triumph of her genes over indoctrination' (Dunn, 1989, p.47). Thus, Miranda serves as a sort of test case of how bodily freakishness affects identity—will she still be a 'freak' even though she does not know about her family's freakish carnival past; will her bodily difference effect her even though it is not foregrounded within the world of carnival? This issue circulates around one of the motivating conflicts of the novel—whether Miranda will choose to keep her 'abject' tail or have it surgically removed. Olympia is appalled at the prospect of removing the tail, but she feels that a sort of corporeal knowing will prevent Miranda from doing so:

> She soars and stomps and burns throughout her days with no notion of the causes that formed her. She imagines herself isolated and unique. She is unaware that she is part of, and the product of, forces assembled before she was born....She can be flip about her tail. Or she can try. She is ignorant of its meaning and oblivious to its value. But something in her blood aches, warning her (Dunn, 1989, p.47).

Significantly, it is 'her blood' that Olympia feels will warn her—thus a part of her identity shaped by biological, hormonal, chromosomal, and genetic factors. Olympia's abhorrence at the thought of Miranda removing her tail foregrounds her conviction that the unique materiality of Miranda's body forms part of her identity and also links her to her familial past. Here, by linking specific corporeality to the embodied nature of family history, the text insists on materiality as an essential component of identity. As Rachel Adams points out in her article 'An American Tail: Freaks, Gender, and the Incorporation of History in Katherine Dunn's *Geek Love*' (1996), the importance of corporeality is also foregrounded through the double play on tail—for the tail is not only a reference to Miranda's anatomical tail but is also what prompts the narrative, the telling of the tale (Adams, 1996, p.280). Hence, the language of the text is grounded in and depends on matter—the matter of Miranda's tail and her corporeal family history.

This interconnection between matter and language that the novel explores is interesting in light of Butler's argument that there is no access to a pure materiality outside of language. The text prompts consideration of the inverse of this argument—that there is no access to language without recourse to materiality. As Susan Bordo argues in her book *Unbearable Weight* (1993), Butler's theory gives:

> a kind of free, creative rein to *meaning* at the expense of attention to the body's material locatedness in history, practice, culture. If the body is treated as pure text, subversive, destabilizing elements can be emphasized and freedom and self-determination celebrated; but one is left wondering, is there a *body* in this text? (Bordo, 1993, p.38, emphasis in original).

Geek Love, conversely, posits the matter of the body as a constitutive force that cannot be circumscribed through discourse. Although Miranda's anatomical tail is variously interpreted throughout the text—as a fetishized object for the audience at the strip club where she works, as the loveable deformity that marks her a

Binewski to Olympia, as a paltry display of difference that marks her as too normal for her uncle, Arty—none of these aspects of the tail as signifier overcome the tail as anatomical fact—a fact that, as the text exemplifies, shapes Miranda's identity. The material effects brought about by Miranda's tail would seem to refute Butler's argument that 'what is material never fully escapes from the process by which it is signified' (Butler, 1993, p.68) because, as the text exemplifies, the corporeal specificities of the characters affect them in ways that go beyond signification. While the discourse surrounding their various materialities is seen as a significant shaping force, the text also insists that the actual matter of their abject bodies cannot be dismissed, and at least partially constitutes their identity. Thus, the book agrees with the poststructuralist notion of the body as cultural construct while also affirming various biological and anatomical factors as constitutive. As such, *Geek Love* functions as a useful fictional framework through which to read Butler's notions surrounding materiality and abjection.

Mister Sandman also serves as a fictional enactment of abjection. While *Geek Love* focusses on freakish bodily differences, *Mister Sandman* explores the abject status of homosexuality. This works in accordance with Butler's theory that '"queerness" might be understood...as a specific reworking of abjection into political agency' (Butler, 1993, p.21). Butler, focussing in particular on the term 'queer' and how it has been redeployed within contemporary culture, explores how the 'reterritorialization of a term that has been used to abject a population can become a site of resistance, the possibility of an enabling social and political resignification' (Butler, 1993, p.231). Here, Butler suggests that the redeployment and reclamation of the previously abjected term 'queer' can function as a positive enactment of the abject. Butler's exploration of the redeployment of the term 'queer', however, revolves largely around gender and performativity, and works merely to extend the theoretical work begun in *Gender Trouble*. She fails to explore abject bodily materiality in relation to cultural notions of queerness. How does the queer body become culturally abject? What are the material markers of this 'queerness'? Furthermore, how could this abject body serve as a positive subversion and extension of various material bodily norms? Butler does not answer these questions but rather focusses on discursivity and performativity in relation to queerness.

The novel *Mister Sandman*, however, considers the abject body in relation to queerness, and offers a fictional framework through which to asses the viability of a politicized abjection. Joan, the abject body around which the narrative circulates, serves as an embodiment of extreme bodily difference. Pronounced as severely brain damaged by various medical practitioners, Joan is mute, is abnormally small, and has an albino-like appearance. She serves as a sounding board for the other members of her family, and they confess their various 'abnormalities' to her, confident that her muteness assures secrecy. This muteness is significant in relation to Butler's theory as it bars Joan from discursively constructing her own identity. Instead, she serves as a 'blank' body variably constructed by the other characters. Unable to speak for (or of) herself, Joan becomes a sort of interpreting lens via which the other characters explore their own discursively-constructed identities.

Significantly, Joan's abnormality prompts the other characters to analyze their own identities and ultimately to realize the constructed and changeable status of normativity. Ultimately, Joan's bodily difference incites the other characters to interrogate their own differences that are constructed as abject by their culture. Thus Joan, an abject body, serves as a political catalyst that prompts other characters within the novel to accept their various 'abject' traits. These sorts of abjections are what Butler terms 'radically uninterrogated', as differences that do not have a readily available 'discursive life'. As Butler writes: '[I]t is not as if the unthinkable, the unliveable, the unintelligible has no discursive life: it *does* have one. It just lives within discourse as the radically uninterrogated and as the shadowy contentless figure for something that is not yet made real' (Butler, 1998, p.281, emphasis in original). The trajectory of the text, however, works to reveal these 'shadowy' abjections and ultimately to portray them as politically efficacious.

Symbolically, Joan resides in the family closet, making it her bedroom and preferred hiding place. The various family members confide in her as she sits in the dark closet, as if confessing to a quasi-priest. Herein, the novel explores the closeting of abjection, the secrecy in which difference is relegated to the nether regions of existence. The novel explores the silencing of abjection particularly in relation to Joan's father, Gordon. Through his confessions to Joan, he examines the construction of his own 'abnormal' identity and the cultural discourses that name his homosexuality as deviant. He recalls reading about homosexuality in books such as *Curing the Male Homosexual* and *Demonology and Homosexuality* (Gowdy, 1996, p.71). From these books, Gordon learns that '[h]e *was* sick. He was ungrown, unmanly' and that he should 'enter into a serious study of "real" men' (Gowdy, 1996, pp.71-72). This societal view of homosexuality as deviant and abnormal prompts Gordon to deny his sexuality and keep it secret, not only from his future wife, but from himself. He also questions whether his homosexuality has adversely affected his children and wonders 'if a queer father, by unconsciously failing to emit certain normal masculine impulses, plays havoc with his daughter's temperamental development. Her *intellectual* development! Jesus, what if she's slow because he's queer?' (Gowdy, 1996, p.119, italics in original). Here, Gordon is shown as having internalized the societal view of homosexuality as deviant. His practice of confiding in Joan ultimately, however, leads him to redefine and accept his own previously abjected bodily identity, to come out of the closet, so to speak. This leads him to interpret Joan's muteness not as a deficiency, but as an elevated state. He believes that Joan 'was deliberately forswearing words out of an instinctive sense that it took only one to flatten you. On his bad days he wondered if her muteness wasn't highly evolved' (Gowdy, 1996, p.70). Here, the word that could flatten him is 'queer', but Joan's 'highly evolved' muteness allows him to confide in her and ultimately come to terms with this aspect of his identity. Hence, Joan, as an abject body, serves as a catalyst for Gordon's renegotiation of his own abjected identity.

This aspect of the novel is further reiterated near the end of the book when Joan commences on a project of splicing tape recordings that consist of all the different

things her family members have confessed to her, all the 'dark secre[
told her. She presents these tapes to the family as a gift, but they are
what they hear. The tapes reveal Gordon's homosexuality, his wife D[
affairs, and their daughter Marcy's avid sexuality. The tapes bring all
secrets that they confessed to Joan out of the closet, both literally and ᵢₗgᵤᵣₐₜᵢᵥₑₗᵧ.
The closing chapter entails Gordon and Doris finally admitting their homosexuality
to each other and, more importantly, accepting their own previously abjected
difference. Here, the novel posits the notion of 'coming out of the closet' as a
crucial step not only for individuals but also for society as a whole. Secrets, the
novel contends, should not be closeted and abjected but revealed. Joan, by
revealing that all of her family members have various 'abnormal' traits, ultimately
serves to reveal the sham of normality. A symbol of abject bodily difference, Joan
serves as a catalyst for redefining the bodily lives of her family—her difference
prompts them to analyze and accept their own.

Hence, *Mister Sandman*, through an exploration of how abject materiality can
redefine and extend notions of bodily and sexual normativity, allies with Butler's
endorsement of abjection as an enabling disruption. Thus, both *Geek Love* and
Mister Sandman serve as textual affirmations of the abject body, and posit this
body's potential for political subversion. As such, the texts serve as literary
actualizations of Butler's theoretical insistence on the political implications of the
abject body. They exemplify that in addition to considering gender as performative
and the body as discursively constituted, it is also crucial to consider the actual
materiality of the body. As Butler contends, this materiality is variously interpreted
as normative, valuable, and viable or, conversely, as abject, delegitimated, and
unavailing.

While theoretical interest in Butler's work has circulated around her theories
regarding gender and the heterosexual matrix, this aspect of her philosophy
actually constitutes a political subversion grounded in the materiality of the body—
a subversion that endorses the individual material body as potentially disruptive to
the symbolic domain of viable bodies. In so doing, Butler recasts the body as
active, as a site that can circumvent and renegotiate various regulatory norms.
Thus, politicized abjection serves to re-materialize Butler's own often discursively
foundationalist theory. By grounding the possibility for subversion in bodily
materiality, Butler seems to enter the 'constitutive outside' of her own discourse.
By reclaiming the often repudiated and refused material body, this theoretical
move exemplifies the material body as what must necessarily be excluded in order
for the poststructuralist discursive body to remain coherent. By foregrounding the
material body, Butler thus attends to the fissures in her own theory. For her, that
which is bracketed out or constructed as the constitutive outside is still defining.
Hence, the abject material body serves as a subversion not only of the cultural
construction of normative bodies, but as a subversion of Butler's own
poststructuralist theory of the body as text. This strand of her work thus allows for
a re-materialization of bodily theory and places specific corporeality as the
possible site for a resistance to normalized and discursive cultural bodies. As such,
it offers the most promising path for a revamped corporeal politics—a politics that

straddles the body as both cultural *and* material. Politicized abjection does not fall into the trap of cultural construction on the one hand versus biological essentialism on the other, but rather attends to how specific bodily materiality as well as cultural constructions shape corporeal identity. Thus, Butler's work on abjection in *Bodies That Matter* develops a corporeal politics that is able to simultaneously encompass gender as performative, the body as shaped by culture, and bodily materiality as constitutive. Further developments of such a corporeal politics must attend to these various ways that bodies matter. By attending to narrative enactments of politicized abjection, by re-materializing discourse, by claiming and utilizing bodily abjection as an enabling disruption, the corporeal can be infused with a politics that *matters*.

References

Adams, Rachel (1996), 'An American Tail: Freaks, Gender and the Incorporation of History in Katherine Dunn's *Geek Love*', in R. Garland Thomson (ed.), *Freakery: Cultural Spectacles of the Extraordinary Body*, New York University Press, New York, pp.277-290.

Bigwood, Carol (1991), 'Renaturalizing the Body (with the Help of Merleau Ponty)', *Hypatia*, vol. 6, no. 3, pp.54-75.

Bordo, Susan (1993), *Unbearable Weight: Feminism, Western Culture, and the Body*, University of California Press, Berkeley.

Bray, Abigail and Colebrook, Claire (1998), 'The Haunted Flesh: Corporeal Feminism and the Politics of (Dis)embodiment', *Signs*, vol. 24, no. 1, pp.35-67.

Butler, Judith (1990), *Gender Trouble: Feminism and the Subversion of Identity*, Routledge, New York.

———— (1993), *Bodies That Matter: On the Discursive limits of 'Sex'*, Routledge, New York.

———— (1998), 'How Bodies Come to Matter: An Interview with Judith Butler', by I.C. Meijer and B. Prins, *Signs*, vol. 23, no. 2, pp.275-281.

Dunn, Katherine (1989), *Geek Love*, Abacus, London.

Gowdy, Barbara (1996), *Mister Sandman*, Steerforth Press, South Royalton, Vermont.

Kirby, Vicki (1997), *Telling Flesh: The Substance of the Corporeal*. Routledge, New York.

Smith-Rosenberg, Carroll (1989), 'The Body Politic', in E. Weed (ed.), *Coming to Terms: Feminism, Theory, Politics*, New York, pp.101-121.

PART IV
AGENCY, POSTSTRUCTURALISM, AND PRAGMATISM

Chapter 12

Strange Tempest:
Agency, Poststructuralism, and the
Shape of Feminist Politics to Come

Edwina Barvosa-Carter[1]

In the decade since the publication of *Gender Trouble: Feminism and the Subversion of Identity* (1990), few, if any, feminist theorists have been as influential or as controversial as Judith Butler. Response to Butler's work has been intense. Celebrated by some, maligned by others, Butler's writing on the social construction of gender identity has incited great debate and discussion in a number of intersecting fields of research. But 'discussion' is a neutral term and while many receptions of Butler's work have been cool-headed and even-handed, Butler's writing, as engaged in fanzines and biting reviews, has also generated unusual adulation from some quarters and unusual disgust from others. So ten years after the tempest around Butler's work first began, we might sit back from the maelstrom for a moment—as if sitting back from a satisfying cup of tea—to contemplate why Butler's work, above many other daring pieces of feminist writing, has incited the intensity of response that it has.

Answers to this question may come at several levels. Certainly Butler's research has introduced controversial theoretical issues that understandably provoke heated debate. Beginning with *Gender Trouble*, Butler offered a compelling case for the relevance of a social constructivist and poststructuralist sensitivity to contemporary feminist, gender, and queer studies at a time when (as now) these approaches were still unevenly welcomed. Her conception of the performativity of gender—revelatory in itself—also led Butler to reconceptualize human agency in a manner that deeply challenged long-held and often intensely defended convictions about the source of 'autonomous' human action. Harbingers of paradigm shifts and theories that undermine long-held convictions are likely to provoke intense response, and Butler's specific theoretical claims certainly contribute to the strange tempest that has attended her scholarship.

---

[1] A version of Barvosa-Carter's essay appeared under the same title in *International Journal of Sexuality and Gender Studies*, vol. 6, nos. 1-2 (April 2001). Reprinted with permission of Kluwer Academic.

Yet, perhaps something more than the theoretical details of gender identity and agency has been at stake in the unusually intense celebration and vilification of Butler's contributions. Butler's theories of the performativity of gender and agency have also led her to advocate a particular mode of political practice that implicitly questions traditional feminist politics. Consequently, Butler's work not only illuminates the dynamic of gender identification but also challenges readers to rethink and perhaps reshape feminist political practices. It is this challenge to the shape of feminist politics that is often the most intensely embraced and rejected component of Butler's work.

In this essay, I explore both of these levels of Judith Butler's decade-long influence in feminist, gender, and queer studies. On the level of specific theoretical contributions, I give special attention to the performativity of gender and the conception of agency connected with it, highlighting the contributions and limitations of Butler's account of agency and the ongoing feminist conversation that it has incited. In response to critics of Butler's account of agency, I suggest that multiple identity is a factor that enables agency as Butler describes it, a factor which Butler gestures toward but does not explore. On a second level, I analyze how Butler's account of agency has unsettled feminist conceptions of feminist political resistance. I examine specific responses to Butler's work to locate clues to the most explosive issues at stake in the controversy over Butler's brand of feminist political practice. In closing, I turn to a growing body of feminist scholarship that draws together Butler-informed political visions with traditional accounts of feminist political practice in a manner that foreshadows a dynamic feminist politics yet to come.

Contesting Agency

Among the most influential of Judith Butler's contributions to feminist, queer, and gender studies (as well as political philosophy and other fields) has been her attempt to unsettle established notions of gender identity, subjectivity, and human agency. For Butler, gender identity and subjectivity are constructed in and through signifying practices (Butler, 1990). Her well-known account of the performativity of gender posits that gender identities are actualized through a 'regulated process of repetition' (Butler, 1990, p.145) in which the reiteration and citation of gendered social meanings and norms in and over time together produce the effects that these citations name (e.g., gender identity as 'woman'). The citational process by which gender identity is constructed in language is ongoing and dynamic, involving a rule-bound *almost* compulsory performance of prevailing gender norms in which each mimicry of those norms forges one moment of their presence as a social order. This citational process implicates those who reiterate prevailing gender norms in the perpetuation of the existing gender order and its (differential) relations of power. Gender identity and subjectivity (like social relations and norms generally) do not exist independent of or prior to the language, cultural forms, and the regulating and shaping processes of signification through which gender identity and subjectivity are materialized.

This conception of the performativity of gender unsettles traditional concepts of human agency. If agency is understood as a human being's capacity to conceive and execute their own actions and projects, then agency has historically been assumed to depend on one of two conditions of the self. On one condition drawn from the Kantian tradition, the self is potentially independent of the social world and its influence, and is thus capable of being the sole author of its own actions. Under the second condition, humans are deeply embedded or 'situated' in social life, and while discursive orders condition the subject and its action, there remains a prediscursive aspect of the self (however small) from which agency springs (Benhabib, 1992; Sandel, 1982; Taylor, 1989). The prediscursive aspect of the self prevents the self from collapsing entirely into the system of language in which it is embedded and thereby becoming fully determined by the social dynamics that forge the self (Sandel, 1982, p.152).

In contrast to these approaches, Butler rejects the view that any aspect of the subject is prediscursive, and, instead, relocates human agency within the processes of signification that construct the self. For Butler, aspects of the subject, such as gender identity are performative and socially constructed in and through the repetition of already given signs and norms. Yet, for the subject to be socially *constructed* is not for it to be socially *determined* and hence without agency. Rather, Butler argues that since the discursive constitution of the self and gender identity takes place within the regime of repetition of gender norms, agency is 'located within the possibility of a variation on that repetition' of norms (Butler, 1990, p.145). In other words, agency for Butler is not ground in the subject's distance from the gender discourses that forge her, but instead in the subject's capacity to vary—rather than repeat—those constituting discourses.

Butler's reconfiguration of agency in the context of social constructivism has been important not only for feminist and queer theory, but for all domains of study that seek to integrate poststructuralist insights. Within feminist thought, Butler's accounts of performativity and agency have played a particularly significant role in aiding feminists to work beyond the essentialist debate by illuminating how gender identity could be durably ingrained within subjectivity but not a necessary or essential aspect of the subject. Moreover, Butler's conception of agency has helped shift feminist thinking on agency beyond the dichotomy between determinism and volunteerism (McNay, 1999, p.175).

Despite these accomplishments, however, Butler's account of agency has been controversial since its first publication in *Gender Trouble* (1990). Seyla Benhabib, who engaged in a well-known exchange with Butler during the early 1990s, voiced one of the earliest critiques of Butler's account of agency. Benhabib argued that while Butler identified agency as the ability to vary the repetition of gender performances, she had yet to identify the factor that enables such variations to take place (Benhabib, 1992, p.218). Benhabib stressed that since Butler finds all aspects of the subject to be socially constructed, the only resources for the variation of identity performances must stem from the very same chain of signification that forms the subject. By collapsing the separation (and critical distance) between the subject and the social discourses that form her, Benhabib argued, Butler had inadvertently eliminated the resources necessary for human agency. Benhabib's critique asks Butler to account for the source of the creative resistance that constitutes agency. Similar questions had previously been put to Michel Foucault who repeatedly urged resistance to constraining discourses and structures, but never indicated where the resources for such resistance could be obtained or utilized by a fully constructed self (Foucault, 1980; Fraser, 1989). While Butler greatly extends Foucault's limited account of the subject, her account of agency— like Foucault's mere gesture toward it—nonetheless begs the question of what factors or conditions enable the iterative agency she theorizes.

This question of the source of the performative variations that define agency remains a question in Butler's writing. Works published after *Gender Trouble* and *Bodies That Matter: On the Discursive Limits of 'Sex'* (1993) have but little extended Butler's original answer to her critics on this particular point. In *The Psychic Life of Power: Theories in Subjugation* (1997b), for example, Butler deals at length with agency as a function of enabling subjugations, thus vastly expanding a controversial point raised but not elaborated by Foucault. This is an important advance (the political significance of which I will return to later in this essay); however, it does little to illuminate the source of the variation of identity performance that Butler uses to define agency. Consequently, scholars continue to question Butler on the question of agency. Lois McNay (1999), a friendly critic of Butler, has recently argued that Butler's account of agency remains abstract and fails to illuminate how Butler's mode of agency is manifest in contexts where actual persons are engaged in realizing change. Martha Nussbaum (1999) has recently insisted (in a point not far from Benhabib's original query) that Butler has yet to prove to those who believe in a prediscursive aspect of the self, that a fully socially constructed subject can bear agency.

While Butler has yet to answer the question of the source of agency to the satisfaction of her critics, there is a possible answer to this question that is consistent with and derivable from Butler's theoretical regime. In my view, the question of agency's source can be found by looking more closely at the web or field of 'enabling constraints' that Butler describes. In *Gender Trouble*, Butler describes these enabling constraints using the imagery of 'tools', which both limit and enable subjection, action, and identification. There, Butler stresses that 'there is no self...who maintains "integrity" prior to its entrance into th[e] conflicted cultural field. There is only a taking up of the tools where they lie, where the very "taking up" is enabled by the tools lying there' (Butler, 1990, p.145). But on the issue of enabling constraints, Butler gives too little attention (perhaps due to her focus on gender identity) to the formation and engagement of the self in a diverse field of multiple and varying discourses and structures. Butler acknowledges, but does not extend, this very point when she writes that, '[a]s specific organizations of language, discourses present themselves *in the plural*, coexisting within temporal frames, and *instituting unpredictable and inadvertent convergences from which specific modalities or discursive possibilities are engendered*' (Butler, 1990, p.145, emphasis added). The complexity of the cultural field and the many shifting social relations and positions within it (Bourdieu, 1990, 1993) means that particular subjects are multiply constructed and engaged in reiterating different discourses and structural practices along many (often contradictory) axes. These axes may involve not only gender identities, but also a full range of complex social relations and subject positions including ethnic, cultural, subcultural, sexual, regional, national, and other identities.

Subjects that are socially constituted within complex social webs are thus socially constructed not with one set of enabling constraints—but a variety of different sets of enabling constraints each of which consists of the meanings, values, and practices that comprise a different identity. It is this multiplicity of construction that, in my view, is the primary source for the variation in performativity that is the hallmark of agency. Continuing Butler's imagery we could say that the self has not one but *many sets of tools* that constrain and enable its various self performances. As the subject picks up one set of tools (i.e., inhabits one of several identities) and leaves other sets of tools aside in a given context, the taking up of one set of tools vis-à-vis another gives the self a reflexive space, a critical distance, and a competing perspective (via the socially constituted set of meanings, values, and practices that comprise those tools), with which it can see anew, critique, and potentially vary its own identity performances. The reflexive space needed to vary performative actions as an agent is thus provided by the subject's multiplicity of subject positions. The reflexive space created by multiple identity is available to foster agency even while all subject positions (i.e., identities) are fully socially constructed and implicated in how the subject becomes and proceeds as a subject.

On this account of agency (which I partly derive from and find consistent with Butler's work, though it is unexplored by her), a subject that is multiply constituted and internally diverse will always have resources of self-reflexivity via the juxtaposition and interpenetration of its own many subject positions. On this view, to accept the idea of a completely socially constructed subject (such as that Butler offers) does not require recourse to a pre-linguistic self in order to secure agency. Rather, it requires us to attend to the socially constituted self as *multiply constructed*—a self whose performativity applies not to one axis of gender norms, but to a variety of different culturally derived axes each with its own sets of linguistic tools (meanings, values, and practices) and identifications. It is through the overlap, intersection, mutual conditioning, and mutual critique of these different sets of socially constituted perspectives and identities that the resources for the variation on repetition—and agency itself—springs. This approach is akin to that of Ernesto Laclau and Chantal Mouffe (1985) in their discussion of antagonisms that demarcate the edge of the social and thus trouble the perpetuation of same. My point (one consistent with theirs) is that the contradiction and mutual inflection of a diversity of socially constructed identities within the multiply-constituted self can provide the resources for agency, which many of Butler's critics have found lacking in her account. This view of agency may also have significance for citizenship and democratic practices (Barvosa-Carter, 1998), and may also help give agency the historical specificity that Butler acknowledges is missing from her account (Butler, 1998).

Implications for Political Practice: Criticisms and Responses

Judith Butler's theories of gender performativity and agency have made an enormous contribution to feminist, gender, and queer studies and continue to generate productive conversation among feminists of all kinds. At another level, however, Butler's influence extends beyond these specific theories to the tendency of her work to provoke intense and heated responses from different quarters over the issue of feminist politics.

Why has Butler's work provoked concern with political practice? The answer lies, in part, in Butler's conceptions of gender and agency, which have also led her to make a two-pronged move in which she first valorizes certain kinds of political interventions, and, second, advances them seemingly at the expense of more traditional feminist political actions. To Butler (1993), desirable political action should subvert the constraining norms that hinder our actions even while we acknowledge that these constraints are also what constitute and enable our various materialized identities. Desirable political actions for Butler are thus signifying actions that displace dominant social norms through small variations in performance that subvert and rework those norms. Parody, for example, is a subversive mode of signification favored by Butler because it shifts and undermines gender norms in a manner that can, in turn, aid in 'proliferating gender configurations' (Butler, 1990, p.146).

Butler's account of political action has been influential as well as controversial. Some readers have found in Butler's account of political subversion a welcome expansion of the existing repertoire of feminist political practice. Some regard Butler's account of political practice as a radical vision that illustrates how everyday individual acts of signification can indeed make inroads to change—and do so under the very regime that would perpetuate a *status quo* heterosexist gender order. In these favorable readings, Butler's appeal lies in the promise of radical action that lies within our individual reach, and in a potential for change that has a humorous and sardonic rather than self-serious tone.

For other readers of Butler, however, her account of agency and politics is highly problematic. Two criticisms have been leveled. The first criticism is that Butler champions processes of resignification in a manner that draws attention away from practical interventions in law and public policy. Butler is said to assume that resignification is always subversive while ignoring the actual impact of specific cases of resignifcation and the influence of economic, social, and legal factors on the linguistic interventions that Butler advocates (Fraser, 1995; McNay, 1999). The second critique is that Butler's account of political action as the symbolic displacement of gender norms through non-repetition of them is largely an individual practice. As such, Butler's position seems to question the relevance of collective political action, and fails to disclose how this individual mode of political activity can influence broad issues of concern to women (Nussbaum, 1999).

Consider one particularly intense critique of Butler's political vision offered by Martha Nussbaum in a review of Butler's work published in *The New Republic*. In her review, Nussbaum emphatically condemns Butler's emphasis on a politics of subversive and parodic resignifications in relation to Butler's account of the psychological investment subjects can have in the power relations that both subjugate and construct them (Butler, 1997b). To capture the intensity of her response to Butler, Nussbaum bears quoting at length.

> Well, parodic performance is not so bad when you are a powerful tenured academic in a liberal university. But here is where Butler's focus on the symbolic, her proud neglect of the material side of life, becomes a fatal blindness. For women who are hungry, illiterate, disenfranchised, beaten, raped, it is not sexy or liberating to reenact, however parodically, the conditions of hunger, illiteracy, disenfranchisement, beating and rape. Such women prefer food, schools, votes, and the integrity of their bodies. I see no reason to believe that they long sado-masochistically for a return to the bad state. If some individuals cannot live without the sexiness of domination, that seems sad, but it is not really our business. But when a major theorist tells women in desperate conditions that life offers them only bondage, she purveys a cruel lie and a lie that flatters evil by giving it much more power than it actually has (Nussbaum, 1999, p.43).

In this passage, Nussbaum portrays Butler as a privileged feminist whose politics tolerates the assault and neglect of women. A case could be made that such a charge is unfair and ought to be dismissed as a misreading and caricature of Butler and her work. Such an assessment, however, should not prevent us from asking what might be at stake in conspicuously publishing such a harsh response to Butler. Rather than dismiss Nussbaum's intense critique, then, I suggest that we unpack it in the interest of understanding what concerns (avowed or unavowed) may lie behind Nussbaum's act.

As I read Nussbaum's review, five particular concerns are couched in its passages. These are concerns with the following:

1. emphasizing symbolic over material political actions;
2. the idea of the female subject, whose actions and identities are deeply implicated in rendering the circumstances of her own subordination;
3. the idea that subversive resignifying politics can have conservative as well as progressive transformative potential;
4. the refusal of Butler to openly avow particular normative precepts;
5. a reiteration of the idea that a fully socially constructed subject (such as Butler describes) cannot support political agency (which for Nussbaum must be ground in a pre-linguistic 'structure' of the subject).

These five concerns differ, yet each of them is broadly linked to the shape of feminist politics and to the challenge that Butler's work presents to established feminist political practices. Behind the concern with favoring a politics of resignification over 'material politics', for example, lies a challenge to the traditional feminist assumption that seeking institutional transformation via legal and public policy reforms is the clearest path, to lasting change. Nussbaum's concern with this is clearly expressed in the preamble to her review in which she describes the overall context of her review of Butler's work as one in which 'young feminists' have begun 'turning away from the material side of life' and from the 'old-style feminist politics' (Nussbaum, 1999, p.38). In Nussbaum's view, it is Judith Butler (aided by French postmodernist thought) who 'more than any other' has shaped this disturbing development (Nussbaum, 1999, p.38). At stake for Nussbaum then, perhaps, are less the particular theoretical claims that Butler proposes (although she engages these to make her point) and more the concerns with the shape of feminist politics and with maintaining what she calls an 'old-style feminist politics' (Butler, 1999, p.38).

Concern with the shape of political practices also runs behind the other points voiced by Nussbaum. For example, the issue of psychic engagement with relations of power is apparently problematic for Nussbaum because it complicates feminist political agendas by positing women as both victims and participants in gender subordination who engage (not always reluctantly) in perpetuating socially subordinating orders. (This is not a new problem area, of course, but one once central to debates over ideology and, today, often acknowledged by reference to Gramscian 'hegemony'). By theorizing this issue, however, Butler cannot fairly be said to condone the subjugation of women. She is careful to stress that to *recognize* the deep implication and self-identification of women with the relations of subjugation that can constitute them does not *justify* or force us to tolerate those forms of subjugation (Butler, 1997b, p.6).

Beyond this, however, the issue of women's active and self-constructing engagement in systems of gender subordination raised by Butler is, generally speaking, an urgent and complex one for politically engaged feminists of all kinds. Feminists seeking to combat cycles of domestic violence, for example, immediately encounter the apparently voluntary return of many battered women to abusive circumstances. These cycles of violence can emerge due to institutional factors, such as the lack of legal, financial, and familial support systems available to battered women. Yet, cycles of domestic violence also persist because of the discursively inculcated and continually rearticulated belief (repeatedly performed in word and deed) among many battered women that beating signifies love and that their assault is justified by their trespasses against the wishes of men. These socially constructed investments make domestic assault not only an ingrained part of some women's material lives, but also a part of their very identities. Under such conditions, submission to violence may become part of a woman's self-understanding, as well as her self-representation in her contacts with others including batterers, counselors, children, friends, and law enforcement.

An account of women's psychological investment in relations of power, such as that which Butler's provides, could lend feminists some purchase with which to grasp the deep but not immutable investments and participation of women in cycles of abuse. To take Butler's point seriously in this way, however, would certainly rule out a clean and uncomplicated understanding of women as victims of the type upon which traditional feminist politics has often depended. Rather, feminist politics concerned with domestic violence would have to understand battered women as victims who may be implicated even to the level of their own identifications and gender performances with the relations of subjugation in which they are embedded. This approach would draw us to the complicated task of locating political agency in complex sets of subordinating relations, and (on the account of agency I outline above) lead us to ask what combinations of intrapersonal identity differences might lead to variations in gendered cycles of violence. While Nussbaum rejects this attention to the psyche's (eroticized) interpenetration with relations of power as 'not really our business', the issue may in fact have critical insights for productive feminist politics.

Equally problematic for Nussbaum is the idea that political acts that subversively resignify and shift existing norms can have conservative as well as progressive potential. How, Nussbaum asks, can a feminist politics informed by Butler's account of politics deal with those who would use subversive resignifications to undermine the norms we cherish? To Nussbaum, a politics that can be put to conservative *and* liberal or radical uses is unacceptable since a feminist politics must be able to quell conservative subversions of norms before they begin. In Nussbaum's words, '[t]o such people we should say, you cannot simply resist as you please, for there are norms of fairness, decency, and dignity that entail that this is bad behavior' (Nussbaum, 1999, p.43). The issue of limiting what is politically contestable (and by whom) is not a new issue among feminists—it was much rehearsed in debates over foundationalism, for example. Yet, to acknowledge the multi-valenced character of political subversion (valences that Nussbaum would have feminist politics limit) may well have important implications for real-world feminist politics. After all, it was the assumption that subversive contestation of the 'old-style feminist' type could only succeed in liberal directions that made many feminists politically complacent in the face of pro-life activism in the aftermath of the original attainment of abortion rights. Likewise, attention to the symbolic politics of the right has become a key issue to feminist politics. It is, after all, the neo-conservative resignification of racism as 'race-consciousness' rather than 'racial subordination' that has been a critical element of the conservative campaign to dismantle affirmative action policies— policies that have been a key instrument for ending gender discrimination (Omi and Winant, 1994).

Conservative political interventions on affirmative action demonstrate the potentially close connection between discursive 'symbolic' politics and 'material' political outcomes revealing how the symbolic and the material intersect in everyday political life. In practice, political contestation of this type is always ongoing, and conservatives, as well as liberals and leftists, partake in it. No poststructuralist account of politics is likely to offer or sanction a basis upon which to foreclose conservative political contestation *a priori*, although poststructuralist accounts may certainly suggest responses to conservative interventions. Butler's political vision certainly undermines the possibility that feminist politics can preempt conservative political contestation. Yet, her work may aid feminist politics in fostering the sensitivity necessary to effectively identify and combat conservative political contestation as it emerges—a sensitivity that feminist politics of all kinds rejects at its peril.

In her review, Nussbaum also objects to Butler's anti-normativity and her attendant unwillingness to openly espouse the liberal precepts upon which many of her arguments implicitly depend. Nussbaum's concern with Butler's anti-normativity seems to center on the view that a feminist politics informed by Butler would have to forego the advancement of hard-won normative precepts. Yet, Butler's own anti-normativity does not by logical extension rule out the political deployment and promotion of certain norms by other feminists. Why? Because Butler's reluctance to embrace a particular normative position and her intention to 'wait and see' what emerges from a given political contestation is a function of poststructuralist commitment to the idea that prevailing political norms are constantly socially defined and redefined. A political corollary to this is that political strategists must be sensitive to the dynamics of everyday social construction, ready to launch strategic political efforts in response to the contours of ongoing contestation, rather than staying rigidly committed to one course of political argument. Such a position may seem perverse to some feminists since it refuses to declare a clear and uncontested basis for political mobilization (especially when political strategy may produce unpopular policy positions as it does in Butler's *Excitable Speech* (1997a)).

Despite Butler's own reluctance to espouse various feminist norms, however, the theoretical terms of her own position can critically spotlight, but never ultimately subvert, the significance of normative approaches for feminist politics. On the contrary, poststructuralist theories (including Butler's) describe the social world in large part in terms of the production of norms and veiled attempts to deem those norms 'natural' or 'universal'. Butler's strident anti-normativity is born out of her attempt to unmask the pretense, falsehood, and will to power behind attempts to declare socially constructed norms universal across space and time. To *reveal* the contours of normative precepts and the activities of those who advance them is neither to dispense with the need for norms within political practice nor to eliminate their complex role in the formation and transformation of social relations and practices. Hence, from a poststructuralist perspective, acknowledging the subordinating misrepresentations by which some social norms are created, advanced, and maintained will not banish norm generative activities from feminist political practice. All political contests must begin and initially proceed from those norms, discourses, social relations, and structures that are given in a particular place and time. Consequently, acknowledging the dynamics of normative contestation as Butler does may equip those who practice feminist politics to understand, plan, critique, and take responsibility for their actions as they strive to create, advance, and maintain norms of gender equality, universal human rights, and so on. More importantly it may also equip feminists of all kinds to identify and critique the misleading claims advanced by their political opponents.

Poststructuralist Feminist Politics: Signs of Future Times?

If intense responses to Butler such as Nussbaum's are attributable to the challenge that Butler makes to the shape of feminist politics, it would be incorrect to conclude that Butler has (as yet) provoked a full fledge debate over the future contours of feminist politics. Instead, Butler-influenced contestation over the future shape of feminist politics has often been limited to fragments within heated responses to Butler's work. This contestation appears between the lines of critiques (as I have found it in Nussbaum's review) and voiced as questions, fears, frustrations, and adulation that neither fully sketch the issues and differences at stake nor offer an engagement with them. For example, Nussbaum voices her concern with the fashionableness of passive politics among 'young feminists' who reject large scale social movements in favor of a verbal interventions that do not connect to 'real women' (Nussbaum, 1999, p.38). Yet, this charge is not sustained through examples nor is any young scholar named in association with this 'disquieting trend' (Nussbaum, 1999, p.38), a trend perhaps synonymous with the much touted rise of 'post-feminism'.

Despite these drawbacks, however, Nussbaum's engagement with Butler has led her to identify an important crisis point among contemporary feminisms—a raw nerve that Butler agitates, but does not soothe. The presence of this raw nerve in the context of growing post-feminist rhetoric may well signal an increasingly wide disagreement among feminists as to the best form(s) of feminist politics. Surely the issue of a poststructuralist feminism has already been much debated (Benhabib, 1992; Fraser, 1995; Nicholson, 1992), but if these issues now influence the everyday political practices of feminists, then further debate on the topic is needed and could be incited by further critical engagement with Butler's work. Such a debate could ascertain the reasons behind shifting views on feminist political practice and open a rigorous engagement with the political possibilities that Butler does and does not raise.

Would such an open debate on the future of feminist political practice devolve into a standoff between those who are drawn to individual, discursive interventions that resignify cultural norms and those who favor 'old-style feminist politics' that agitate for institutional change? Certainly it need not be so. Granted, Judith Butler's own work does espouse a politics of resignification at the expense of other political interventions, and she has done little to sketch a broader poststructuralist feminist or queer politics. Butler's position (combined with the common perception that postmodernist and poststructuralist thought is apolitical) has led some feminists, such as Nussbaum, to fear that any poststructuralist feminisms of the future will have little political continuity with the institutional changes of the recent feminist past. Yet, there is evidence that such projections may prove empty as more and more feminist scholars and activists theorize feminist political practice with poststructuralist characteristics. Linda Nicholson (1992), for example, has stressed how poststructuralist precepts can lend feminist political practice the 'philosophical weapons' necessary to identify, critique, and respond to the totalizing and exclusionary claims of various hegemonic systems of subordination.

It can equip feminists with the potentially radical perspective that patriarchal discourses and structures are historically specific, contingent, and therefore subject to transformation. Moreover, these tools enable feminists to critique their own positions, to interrogate them for exclusions and omissions that may be part of their own theorizing and activism (Nicholson, 1992).

Other feminists point out that Butler's theory of agency gives feminist politics the ability to criticize formative discourses from within those discourses themselves (Kaufman, 1994). This political practice is characterized by women and men who resist existing relations of power from a position implicated in and 'immanent' to power rather than in 'external opposition' to it (Butler 1993, p.15). Political resistance to patriarchal and heterosexist social relations, for example, would have those formed and enabled by these same social relations attempting to critique, resist, and alter them through strategic rearticulations of subordinating norms, through transgressive identity performances, and potentially through the full range of already standard political interventions. This kind of feminist politics would be dynamic, unpredictable, and perpetual in character. A poststructuralist feminist politics akin to this is sketched by Bonnie Honig (1993, 1996), who describes a politics in which multiply constituted subjects continually challenge existing norms and institutions in a manner that constantly reinvigorates the ongoing contestation of democratic politics. A poststructuralist feminist politics in tune with what Honig proposes would call for feminists to realize change through active intervention in the acts and engagements that continually forge and reforge social relations of all kinds—to consciously engage in processes of social (re)construction in which they are always already implicated.

While criticisms of Butler's political vision have also repeatedly invoked dichotomies between symbolic and material politics and between individual and collective political action, some feminist scholars stress the possibility of moving beyond these dichotomies to a feminist politics that combines all of these factors. Lois McNay, for example, argues that it is possible to move beyond Butler's account of politics to a broader vision that encompasses both acts of resignification *and* efforts at institutional reform, thus acknowledging the inevitable interconnection of both types between political intervention. With this project in mind, other feminist writers unite material and symbolic politics by broadening their working definition of 'discourse'. While Butler may use the term narrowly, Foucault used the term discourse broadly to encompass symbolic communication as well as the structures, laws, practices and institutional forms that also form social relations (Lee, 1999). In Foucault's *Discipline and Punish* (1991), for example, the discursive field unites symbolic factors with material and institutional factors showing them to be interrelated components that together create relations of power and exclusion along lines of criminality. Here, the symbolic and the material routinely intersect in the discursive field. Material institutions may offer symbolic meanings (e.g., criminal laws that declare homosexuality deviant), and rhetorical signs may be instrumental in perpetuating subjugating practices. In light of this point, Butler and her critics and supporters alike may have overdrawn the divide between the symbolic and the material in politics. Increasingly, feminist scholars suggest that any future poststructuralist feminist politics can and must attend to both symbolic and material politics.

The work of feminists such as Nicholson, Honig, McNay, and others foreshadows a broad, varied, and robust feminist poststructuralist politics. No one can predict whether this vision will be realized. Yet, there is evidence that the politics emerging among at least some young feminists is not the passive politics feared by Nussbaum. On the contrary, some feminist activity has gleaned new sophistication and a widened repertoire of political tactics by turning attention to the discursive factors and performativity of gender of the sort described by Butler. Elizabeth Martinez (1998), for example, describes contemporary Latina youth politics that fuses Chicana feminisms with a variety of different influences to render a politics that aims to combat all forms of subordination including sexism, racism, homophobia, and classism. These women's movements are sensitive to the discursive and performative dimensions of identity and social relations *and* attuned to the political significance of institutions and structures. The Chicana feminist politics that has emerged deploys a full range of political tactics from radical theater to grassroots mobilization, from deliberate gender-role transgression to multiethnic coalition building, from petition drives and traditional political lobbying to sit-ins, walk-outs, and civil disobedience (Martinez, 1998). These political practices are a sophisticated amalgam of *deconstructive analysis* of patriarchal and homophobic discourse and institutions, *transgressive gender performances* intended to transform gender and sexual norms, and *institutional interventions* that seek to transform institutional practices and codes that are seen as perpetuating social relations of subordination. If these political practices among young Chicana feminists can be taken as an indication of the future, there may be a dynamic feminist politics yet to come.

Judith Butler's theories of gender, agency, and political practice have contributed dramatically to contemporary feminisms. Moreover, the strange tempest of intense objections and celebrations provoked by Butler's work has brought the issue of a poststructuralist feminist politics to the fore and positioned us to engage in an open and informed debate on the shape of feminist politics to come. While Butler's influence on various feminist, gender, and queer studies over the last ten years has been undeniable, perhaps her most significant contributions remain on the horizon in her input to ongoing (and hopefully more explicit) debate on forms of political practice. No one can predict the outcome of future feminist discussions, but perhaps in the end, Butler's work will help us further understand the ongoing dynamics that forge the social world and ourselves. For now, perhaps the most relevant insight for 'old-style feminists' and the champions of parodic performance alike is the same. We are to our very identities inextricably implicated in the ongoing (re)production of social and political relations, and, hence, always responsible for—because inevitably involved in—the shape of the social world. Many methods for social change exist, and each, though partial and unpredictable in its results, can generate potentially synergistic transformative results. Taken seriously, these insights may yet help feminists forge a future politics that will create many strange tempests indeed.

References

Barvosa-Carter Edwina (1998), *Multiplicity of the Self and Contemporary Democracy: The Political Implications of Multiple Identity*, PhD Dissertation, Harvard University.

Benhabib, Seyla (1991), 'Feminism and Postmodernism: An Uneasy Alliance', *Praxis International*, vol. 11, no. 2.

———— (1992), *Situating the Self: Gender, Community and Postmodernism in Contemporary Ethics*, Routledge, New York.

———— et al. (1995), *Feminist Contentions: A Philosophical Exchange*, Routledge, New York.

Bourdieu, Pierre (1990), *The Logic of Practice*, R. Nice (trans.), Stanford University Press, Stanford.

Bourdieu, Pierre et al. (1993), *The Field of Cultural Production*, Polity Press, Cambridge, UK.

Butler, Judith (1990), *Gender Trouble: Feminism and the Subversion of Identity*, Routledge, New York.

———— (1991), 'Contingent Foundations: Feminism and the Question of "Postmodernism"', *Praxis International*, vol. 11, no. 2.

———— (1993), *Bodies That Matter: On the Discursive Limits of 'Sex'*, Routledge, New York.

———— (1997a), *Excitable Speech: A Politics of the Performative*, Routledge, New York.

———— (1997b), *The Psychic Life of Power: Theories in Subjugation*, Stanford University Press, Stanford.

———— (1998), 'Marxism and the Merely Cultural', *New Left Review*, vol. 227, p.33-44.

Foucault, Michel (1991), *Discipline and Punish: The Birth of the Prison*, Alan Sheridan (trans.), Penguin, New York.

———— (1980), *The History of Sexuality: An introduction*, R. Hurley (trans.), vol. 1, Vintage Books, New York.

Fraser, Nancy (1989), *Unruly Practices: Power, Discourse and Gender in Contemporary Social Theory*, University of Minnesota Press, Minneapolis.

———— (1995), 'False Antitheses: A Response to Seyla Benhabib and Judith Butler', *Feminist Contentions: A Philosophical Exchange*, Routledge, New York.

Honig, Bonnie (1993), *Political Theory and the Displacement of Politics*, Cornell University Press, Ithaca.

———— (1996), 'Difference, Dilemmas and the Politics of Home' in Seyla Benhabib, (ed.), *Democracy and Difference: Contesting the Boundaries of the Political*, Princeton University Press, Princeton.

Kaufman, C. (1994), 'Postmodernism and Praxis: Weaving Radical Theory from Threads of Desire and Discourse', *Socialist Review*, vol. 24, no. 3, pp.57-80.

Laclau, Ernesto and Mouffe, Chantal (1985), *Hegemony and Socialist Strategy: Toward a Radical Democratic Politics*, W. Moore and P. Cammack (trans.), Verso, New York.

Lee, Janet (1999), 'The Utility of a Strategic Postmodernism', *Sociological Perspectives*, vol. 42, no. 4, pp.739-753.

Martinez, Elizabeth (1998), *De Colores Means of All of Us: Latina Views for a Multi-Colored Century*, South End Press, Boston.

McNay, Lois (1999), 'Subject, Psyche and Agency: The Work of Judith Butler', *Theory, Culture, Society*, vol. 16, no. 2, pp.175-193.

Nicholson, Linda (1992), 'Feminism and the Politics of Postmodernism', *Boundary 2*, vol. 19, no. 2, pp.51-69.

Nussbaum, Martha (1999), 'The Professor of Parody: The Hip Defeatism of Judith Butler', *The New Republic*, vol. 220, 22 February, pp.37-45.

Omi, Michael and Winant, Howard (1994), *Racial Formation in the United States from the 1960s to the 1990s*, Routledge, New York.

Sandel, Michael (1982), *Liberalism and the Limits of Justice*, Cambridge University Press, New York.

Taylor, Charles (1989), *Sources of the Self: The Making of the Modern Identity*, Harvard University Press, Cambridge.

Chapter 13

Changing Signs: The Political Pragmatism of Poststructuralism

Robert Alan Brookey and Diane Helene Miller[1]

I do not need epistemology to justify my desire, my life, my love. I need politics; I need to build a world that does not require such justifications (Phelan, 1994, p.55).

The emergence of queer theory in the academy has often been regarded as a mixed blessing. On the one hand, queer theory has produced an enormous amount of publishing activity among lesbian, gay, bisexual and transgender scholars, invigorating the field and helping to usher in a new visibility for the study of gender and sexuality in the academy. On the other hand, some critics have portrayed queer theory as an esoteric and politically bankrupt approach that contributes little to concrete social change (Solomon, 1993; Walters, 1996). In fact, practitioners of queer theory are often taken to task for being out of touch with the political conditions of 'real people'. Although many scholars may be identified with queer theory, Judith Butler has been singled out for much of this criticism. The 22 February 1999 issue of *The New Republic* contained a particularly venomous attack on Butler by Martha Nussbaum. Although she touches on several aspects of Butler's work in her article, Nussbaum's thesis is very simple: good feminist theory leads to practical political action, and Butler's theories do not. Far from promoting social change, argues Nussbaum, Butler's approach actively undermines social progress by leading a trend of political 'quietism and retreat' (Nussbaum, 1999, p.38).

Although Nussbaum's criticism of Butler is grounded in a feminist perspective, it echoes the more general criticism often leveled against the field of queer theory. In fact, Nussbaum's critique synthesizes a number of arguments that others have directed at Butler specifically, and queer theory generally (Solomon, 1993; Walters, 1996). Nussbaum herself, however, presents a troubling perspective that views the focus on language and other forms of representation as a kind of imaginary political play, contrasting this symbolic frivolity with the serious work of describing 'reality' and seeking 'truth'. This distinction, according to

---

[1] A version of Brookey and Miller's essay appeared under the same title in *International Journal of Sexuality and Gender Studies*, vol. 6, nos. 1-2 (April 2001). Reprinted with permission of Kluwer Academic.

Nussbaum, parallels the ancient dichotomy between 'sophistry and rhetoric' on the one hand and philosophy on the other. Where sophists and rhetoricians trade in verbal manipulation, divorced from concerns of morality or social justice, philosophy, she believes, constitutes a discourse of the soul that yields a political praxis that is both moral and true.

Nussbaum's attack on Butler rearticulates, in a particularly rigid and divisive manner, a longstanding theoretical divide that has influenced feminism as well as other forms of sexual politics. On one 'side' of this divide are those who advocate embracing minority sexual identity as the most effective means of advancing minority rights, an approach termed 'identity politics'. The other 'side' includes those who, with Butler, argue that undermining oppressive practices requires the steadfast rejection of all identity categories, minority and otherwise. This school of thought is referred to as 'poststructuralism'.

In this chapter, we argue that despite the sexual rights movement's overriding emphasis on embracing minority identity as the key to social change, and despite Nussbaum's critique of poststructuralism as politically impotent, a number of legal and political decisions have pointed to the utility of poststructuralist theory and practice for advancing sexual rights.[2] This is not to say that an exclusive focus on poststructuralist theory is desirable, nor that poststructuralism is inherently superior to identity politics. On the contrary, we argue that an exclusive focus on a single approach is precisely what social movements must avoid, and critiques that dismiss either approach as having no value for the movement may do a serious and dangerous disservice to the very groups whose rights they claim to advance. Social movements are multilayered, and no movement can expect to achieve widespread social change by operating under a single strategy or in a single mode.

We will first provide a brief explanation of what appear to be the two 'sides' of this debate: identity politics and poststructuralist practice. We will then discuss the limitations of the predominant identity politics approach that has characterized the past three decades of sexual rights activism, and how Butler contributes to the understanding of these limitations. Without dismissing the value of identity politics or the undeniable contributions this approach has made to the movement thus far, we will show how it has nevertheless circumscribed the means through which sexual rights have been defended in the United States. By limiting the kinds of arguments that can be presented on behalf of sexual minorities, this approach has also created limitations in the degree to which equality can be attained. We will argue, therefore, that Butler's poststructuralist approach provides one remedy for illuminating certain oversights and overcoming some of the barriers erected and maintained by the emphasis on identity politics. We conclude with an example of how the debate about sexual rights might be reframed when essentialized notions of sexual identity are no longer the key elements on which the argument rests.

---

[2] We use the term 'sexual rights' to refer to rights issues related to all forms of sexuality. Occasionally, we use the terms 'gay' and 'lesbian' to refer to rights issues related to homosexuality.

Nussbaum's Complaint

Nussbaum suggests that poststructuralist work such as Butler's is leading a trend in the academy characterized by 'the virtually complete turning from the material side of life, toward a type of verbal symbolic politics that makes only the flimsiest of connections with the real situation of real women' (Nussbaum, 1999, p.38). In sharp contrast to the philosophical tradition she valorizes, Nussbaum suggests that Butler's theoretical approach belongs more properly to 'the closely related but adversarial traditions of sophistry and rhetoric' (Nussbaum, 1999, pp.39-40). Nussbaum continues:

> Ever since Socrates distinguished philosophy from what the sophists and the rhetoricians were doing, it has been a discourse of equals who trade arguments and counter-arguments without any obscurantist sleight-of-hand. In that way, he claimed, philosophy showed respect for the soul, while others' manipulative methods showed only disrespect (Nussbaum, 1999, p.40).

Setting aside our personal responses, as rhetoricians, to Nussbaum's unflattering characterization of rhetoric, her claims are problematic in a number of other ways. Philosophy may present itself as 'a discourse of equals', but from its origins it has maintained this status by excluding all but the most privileged members of society from participation; its equality has historically been achieved through elitist rather than democratic means. Nussbaum follows Socrates in identifying philosophy as a moral science as contrasted with the deceitful and deceptive practices of sophistry and rhetoric, yet in doing so she ignores several centuries of thought in which these latter two disciplines have been carefully delineated and distinctly defined, and through which rhetoric has come to be associated more closely with democratic debate than with underhanded manipulation.

More fundamentally, Nussbaum's characterization of language and symbols as 'obscurantist sleight-of-hand' and 'manipulative methods' that show 'only disrespect' for the soul dismisses any role for verbal signs as useful tools in the struggle for social justice. Nussbaum views the focus on identity as an artifact of the philosophical tradition, and consequently the product of reasoned debate that is both democratic and respectful of the soul. Nussbaum's claim, therefore, is not only that her position is politically and morally superior to Butler's approach. More precisely, Nussbaum claims for her views the status of 'truth', whereas Butler, she believes, is simply playing word games with no interest or effort invested in discovering what is 'true' about gender and sexual identities.

On this final point, there is no disagreement because poststructuralist approaches do not, in fact, claim to seek 'truth'. Whereas Nussbaum's claim is one of knowledge, purporting to use language as a means of expressing the truth about identity, Butler engages in an analysis that 'refuses to search for the origins of gender, the inner truth of female desire, a genuine or authentic sexual identity' (Butler, 1990, p.viii). Instead, such an analysis 'investigates the political stakes in designating as an *origin* and *cause* those identity categories that are in fact the *effects* of institutions, practices, [and] discourses' (Butler, 1990, pp.viii-ix, emphasis in original).

Butler and other poststructuralists deny the possibility of discovering a 'reality' that exists prior to or outside of language and other relations of power. 'Language is not an *exterior medium or instrument* into which I pour a self and from which I glean a reflection of that self' (Butler, 1990, pp.143-144, emphasis in original). Instead, Butler views 'identity as a *practice*, and as a signifying practice' (Butler, 1990, p.145). Rather than viewing identity as having an *a priori* existence, then, Butler argues that 'judicial systems of power *produce* the subjects they subsequently come to represent' (Butler, 1990, p.2). Consequently, any category of sexual identity is already politically invested, and not always in a manner that serves the interests of those so identified.

Within this perspective, what comes to be accepted as 'true' or 'real' is, like identity itself, historically and contextually variable; societal notions of 'truth' and 'reality' are constructed through linguistic signs and symbols, and are therefore fundamentally dependent upon that society's system of language. In this view, therefore, the struggle for power and the equitable distribution of rights must take place at the level of the sign. The goal for Butler and other poststructuralists interested in intersections of identity and politics is not to describe who we 'really' are, because such a description would be impossible. Instead, they seek to identify the means through which we can best articulate our identities in order to achieve our political goals, a move Butler characterizes as '[t]he shift from an *epistemological* account of identity to one which locates the problematic within practices of *signification*' (Butler, 1990, p.144, emphasis in original). This shift of focus—the very move that Nussbaum condemns as anti-political—in fact introduces a new political pragmatism that focuses the movement's energies and resources on concrete aims and strategies, while taking a lesson from the failures of identity-based approaches of the past.

Identity Problems

The practice of building collective political practice on the 'common' experience of individuals with a shared identity carries with it built-in conflicts. A politics based on identity draws on each individual's personal experience as a touchstone for understanding a minority group's political condition. Within identity politics, oppression is recognized and understood through personal experience, and organized around shared identity categories based on gender, race, sexual orientation, or other characteristics that serve to classify and stratify individual subjects. This personal experience is then shared as a foundation for political identity, and this collective identity subsequently becomes the basis for political action.

While this view has proved empowering for many lesbian, gay, bisexual, and transgendered (LGBT) individuals, the move from personal identity to shared experience as a foundation for political action has often been problematic for the sexual rights movement. Members of a particular identity category do not necessarily share a common experience. In describing the limitations of identity politics for the feminist movement, Butler observes:

> The minute that the category of woman is invoked as *describing* the constituency for which feminism speaks, an internal debate invariably begins over what the descriptive content of that term will be....[E]very time that specificity is articulated, there is resistance and factionalization within the very constituency that is supposed to be *unified* by the articulation of its common element (Butler, 1995, p.49, emphasis in original).

Similarly, because not all sexual minorities share the same experience, the argument that political action is based in the experience of 'real' LGBT people has become a point of contention. Many individuals report feeling alienated from the contemporary LGBT rights movement because they feel it does not reflect their reality. Such a response is not surprising, for '[i]dentity categories', writes Butler, 'are never merely descriptive, but always normative, and as such, exclusionary' (Butler, 1995, p.50). Given the chasm that has sometimes existed based on gender, some lesbians and gay men have even argued that there cannot and should not be any political coalition between the two groups, because their experiences demand different, and sometimes conflicting, political action. In addition, consideration of variables such as race, class, and the experiences of transgendered and bisexual individuals makes the points of political identification even more elusive and confusing.

In fact, any discourse that seeks or claims to represent the personal experiences of a collective identity category is bound to fail in some respects, because identity categories are not monolithic, members of any given group are not homogeneous, and identity and subjective experience are composed of a multitude of features and influences. Moreover, even when experience is shared, it may not lead decisively to a given political practice, so that those with shared experience may nevertheless differ vehemently on which political approach is most effective for achieving a group's specific aims for social change. Therefore, any search for 'true' identity is guaranteed to produce conflicting and often contradictory discourses, continually undermining the very claim to truth this perspective maintains. Likewise, efforts to ground equal rights claims in the inescapably multilayered, multifaceted categories of identity are bound to yield divisive and exclusionary political practice. In its effort to speak with clarity in a unified, cohesive voice, then, identity politics risks recreating the same types of metanarratives that historically have organized and policed knowledge, privileging the life stories of particular members of a minority group while further marginalizing those whose lives do not fit neatly into this dominant narrative.

Whereas those who support an identity politics position affirm the centrality of identity categories to their experience and sense of self, perceiving in these categories the potential for both personal empowerment and collective political action, Butler and other poststructuralists argue that categories of identity are not inherent or essential, but historically and discursively constructed. Butler argues for 'the reconceptualization of identity as an *effect*', insisting that '[t]he tacit constraints that produce culturally intelligible "sex" ought to be understood as generative political structures rather than naturalized foundations' (Butler, 1990, p.147). Within this view, identity categories are exposed as unstable, 'neither fatally determined nor fully artificial and arbitrary' (Butler, 1990, p.47). The enactment of such categories Butler views as performative, an effect or product rather than an origin (Butler, 1990, p.147), rendering the notion of identity itself 'permanently problematic' (Butler, 1990, p.128).

Butler argues that entrenched sexual identities may actually assist, rather than resist, the enemies of sexual minorities. From Butler's perspective, embracing minority identity as a political strategy can be illusory, misleading, even dangerous, for it is precisely the linguistic and social positioning assigned by identity categories that are responsible for the oppression of marginalized groups. Identity categories, in Butler's view, are grounded in appeals to "truth" that have traditionally been used to order the social hierarchy; in this way, such categories become 'instruments of regulatory regimes' (Butler, 1991, p.13) more often than they serve as tools of liberation. For Butler, then, effective political practice must be based upon the refusal of identity categories. Instead, she finds political potential in actions that challenge the idea that there is something 'essential' or 'natural' about the categories of gender and sexual identity through which we structure our world.

Butler highlights the ways in which the pervasive and repetitive performance of identity categories lends them their appearance of stability and continuity. She argues that the instability and discontinuity of such categories are readily exposed when their expectations are parodied rather than fulfilled. Butler, therefore, advocates actions that work to expose the *un*naturalness of such categories; she frequently uses the example of drag to illustrate this point. This example has led to prodigious and contentious debate, which can nevertheless be reduced to a relatively straightforward point of conflict: Butler believes that the struggle for sexual equality takes place on the level of the sign, and her critics do not.

Butler's awareness of the key role of representations and signs in the struggle for sexual rights, and of the very influential role of what Nussbaum dismisses as 'symbolic politics' in shaping the material conditions and concrete political contexts of oppressed groups, suggests that Butler's approach may add a much-needed pragmatic perspective to the sexual rights movement. We reject the idea that the options for pursuing sexual rights are mutually exclusive, or that the political efficacy of one approach to sexual theory denies the political efficacy of other approaches. It would be ridiculous to claim that the essentializing moves of identity politics are politically bankrupt, since positive change has clearly occurred under the guidance of this approach. It would be equally absurd to claim that the practices of identity politics are unimpeachable, because this approach created significant problems for the feminist movement, as it has more recently for the sexual rights movement. Whereas the advantages of identity politics for the sexual rights movement have been extensively explored, however, the practical problems engendered by this predominant strategy have only more recently been addressed, and the enthusiasm for this singular approach has often overshadowed both its weaknesses and the value of alternative strategies.[3]

Errors in Essentialism

Efforts to secure rights for sexual minorities have generally based political action on essentialized notions of sexual identity. For example, in the effort to counter negative portrayals of lesbians and gays in the media, organizations such as the Gay and Lesbian Alliance Against Defamation (GLAAD) have sought to increase the number of positive portrayals of gay males and lesbians in the media, portrayals which, they argue, more accurately reflect the reality of sexual minorities. Although we, too, believe that negative portrayals cause harm and must be challenged, we are disturbed by what passes for 'reality' in the 'positive' portrayals of lesbian and gay experience. As one of us argued in an earlier essay (Brookey, 1996), those lesbians and gay males who are represented positively in the mainstream media are almost exclusively white and affluent. When these white and relatively wealthy individuals are offered as 'real' representations of the lesbian and gay community, some important problems arise. First, the appeal of the 'real' representation of gays and lesbians is immediately undermined by the existence of sexual minorities who are neither white nor wealthy, and those who are neither gay nor lesbian. Second, countering negative representations with examples of affluent individuals seriously undermines the claim that sexual minorities are oppressed. In fact, these examples of white affluence play right into the hands of anti-gay rights forces who argue that sexual minorities do not need 'special rights', or even more harmfully, that they already have them.

The 'special rights' argument gains more credibility when the advocacy of sexual rights is based on essentialized notions of sexual identity. For example, consider the use of biological research in the lesbian and gay rights movement (Hamer, 1994; LeVay, 1993). Shortly after the publication of research suggesting a genetic basis for homosexuality, the Human Rights Campaign Fund (now HRC) released a special press packet suggesting that this research would provide a

---

[3] The October 1999 issue of the *Journal of Gay, Lesbian and Bisexual Identity* was devoted to issues pertaining to identity politics. In this issue, Jonathan Alexander (1999) argues that postmodern theory can allow sexual minorities to move beyond questions of personal identity, and begin to establish communities around shared values. We share Alexander's belief that personal identity should be decentered, but we believe this decentering should not only influence how we internally form communities, but also how we approach external political action.

powerful argument in support of sexual rights (Watney, 1995). Specifically, supporters of such research argue that claims of a biological etiology for homosexuality will help extend Constitutional protections for gays and lesbians under the Fourteenth Amendment. Although the amendment ostensibly extends equal protection to all citizens, the 1973 Supreme Court decision in *Frontiero v. Richardson* interpreted the amendment to protect groups that experience discrimination due to their immutable characteristics, such as race, sex, or national origin. Because the genetic research is thought to provide evidence that homosexuality is biological, and therefore immutable, sexual rights advocates argue that these same protections should be extended to lesbians and gays. Therefore, the biological argument suggests not only that sexual identity is inherent or essential, but also that it is genetically so. The biological argument literally establishes homosexuals as a distinct group of people who need special protections.

The essentializing move of identity politics establishes the point that the members of sexual minorities are distinct and fundamentally different from the rest of society; the biological argument merely reinforces this point. Unfortunately, the consequence of such an argument is to place the burden of proof on sexual minorities to convince members of the 'mainstream' that their difference poses no threat to society, and that they therefore deserve equal rights and opportunities. In fact, the preponderance of white, affluent individuals among the few positive lesbian and gay media representations that do exist illustrates the desire to contain any threat to mainstream society by representing sexual minorities as part of the social mainstream. Advocates for sexual rights have placed themselves in the uncomfortable and contradictory position of arguing on the one hand for difference, while arguing on the other hand that the difference does not matter.

This tenuous argumentative position is evident in recent incidents in which the question of sexuality has been placed under public and legal scrutiny. One of us (Miller, 1998), in the book *Freedom to Differ*, has analyzed the Senate confirmation hearing that followed Clinton's nomination of Roberta Achtenberg for the position of Assistant Secretary of Housing and Urban Development. The arguments offered at the hearing in support of Achtenberg's candidacy produced contrary outcomes. At one level, the debate appears to expand possibilities for lesbian and gay rights, since Achtenberg was ultimately confirmed. At another level, however, Achtenberg's supporters limited the progressive potential of her nomination by arguing that her sexuality was not a political factor and by emphasizing that her actions were 'mainstream.' In other words, Achtenberg was a successful nominee because, according to her supporters, her sexual difference did not make a difference. This line of argument created a double bind by portraying the confirmation of a lesbian candidate for a high political post as a politically significant and progressive move, while at the same time maintaining that Achtenberg's identity as a lesbian was politically immaterial.

The Achtenberg example reveals the troubling contradiction inherent in an advocacy campaign that focuses on the essential difference of sexuality, but simultaneously argues that sexual difference does not matter. This essentializing move of identity politics continually puts the advocates of sexual rights on the defensive by placing minority identity and behavior at the forefront of the debate, effectively precluding any investigation into the unacceptable *responses* to minority identity, in this case heterosexism and homophobia. By spotlighting those who are presumed to be different, advocates for sexual rights become so burdened with the need to justify sexual behavior that they fail to challenge the very behaviors that should be the subject of any civil rights debate: acts of prejudice and discrimination.

This dynamic is exemplified in the military hearing and subsequent civil court trial of Colonel Margarethe Cammermeyer, the highest ranking military officer ever discharged for homosexuality. Although Cammermeyer's defense attorneys argued that her sexual orientation should not exclude her from military service, the outcome of the trial left intact the rights of military personnel to act in a discriminatory manner. As one of us has observed:

> By continuing to focus on 'gays in the military' as opposed to *prejudice against* lesbians and gays in the military, we locate the source of the problem in gay and lesbian service members rather than in the attitudes of homophobic military leaders and service members...As long as we fail to undermine the discourse that frames the situation in terms of a 'gay problem', we leave unchallenged the underlying 'homophobia problem' that truly needs resolution (Miller, 1998, pp.137-138).

This analysis can be extended to the larger debate about sexual rights. The concession of difference that lies at the heart of identity politics frames the debate over civil rights as a question of sexual behavior, and continually demands that sexual minorities justify their sexuality. Yet the efforts to justify sexual behavior can distract from the important work of challenging discriminatory actions and institutions.

Changing Signs

Bringing these discriminatory actions and institutions to the forefront of the debate requires the type of symbolic inversion that Butler has often advocated. For example, Butler argues that there may be more politically viable ways to signify sexuality than those found in identity politics, and she suggests that it might be politically strategic to invert the symbol of homosexuality that has historically portrayed it as a 'bad copy' of heterosexuality (Butler, 1991, p.17). She then demonstrates how the status of heterosexuality as the original and 'natural' expression of sexuality might be called into question. Her inversion also illustrates how the argumentative burden can be shifted so that heterosexuals are placed in the position of defending their sexuality, thereby relieving homosexuals and other sexual minorities of the defensive burden. We suggest a similar symbolic inversion, but with regard to rights rather than sexuality. That is, instead of debating whether lesbians, gays, and other sexual minorities deserve to be granted their rights, we would shift the argumentative burden by challenging the rights of homophobic individuals and institutions to discriminate against sexual minorities by withholding equal rights.

The inversion we propose might be argued as follows. As members of a democratic society, we all have the right to hold prejudiced views. Our government is not so intrusive as to try to control the thoughts we have about other people, even when those thoughts are stereotypical or bigoted. Our government, however, does not allow people to act on their prejudices, particularly when such actions would violate the rights of others. A person can choose to hold prejudiced views, but does not have the right to act in a discriminatory manner. A person with sexist views cannot deny employment based on biological sex. A person with racist views cannot deny housing based on race. There is one group, however, that retains the right to act on their prejudice: those with homophobic views. Not only their prejudiced thoughts or feelings about sexual minorities, but also their discriminatory actions and behaviors are legally protected in the majority of states and communities.

Given that homophobes are the only prejudiced individuals who are permitted to act in a discriminatory manner without legal consequences, it would be accurate to say that they enjoy special protections and special rights. Christian conservatives who participate in homophobic actions might counter that their discriminatory behavior is based on their religious beliefs, and not on bigotry; however, these same Christians are legally prohibited from discriminating against other individuals whose religious beliefs and practices differ from or even contradict their own, such as Muslims or Jews. To put a finer point on it, although homophobic Christians are granted the right to deny employment to lesbians, gays, bisexuals, and transgendered individuals, the members of these sexual minorities are forbidden to deny employment to homophobic Christians. In this state of affairs, who enjoys special rights? Clearly it is not the sexual minorities.

When we place the act of discrimination at the center of the debate over sexual rights, we can then require homophobic individuals to justify their discriminatory behaviors. The value of this shift becomes evident when we consider the question of morality. In the past, moral arguments were frequently used to justify discrimination based on gender and race. Whether or not one believes it is useful to compare the sexual rights movement to other civil rights struggles, it is clearly valuable to identify the ways in which bigotry and discrimination, no matter who their target, tend to demonstrate structural similarities and to reiterate similar (if not identical) arguments. Moral arguments used on behalf of bigotry are frequently recycled, sometimes verbatim, for use against groups that are similar only in that they are targets for prejudice (Blumenfeld, 1996).

Exposing this pattern illuminates the ways in which bigotry is constructed and perpetuated through the willful denial of individuality. Bigotry involves the classification of a group of people for the specific purposes of discrimination. It does not recognize that an individual has any value apart from the group; in fact, membership in the group is reason enough to divest the individual of value. In other words, knowing that a person is lesbian or gay is all a homophobe needs to know in order to determine that person's value, or lack thereof. Considering their willful denial of individuality, it is no surprise that bigots recycle the same arguments to use against very dissimilar groups.

The repetition, in structure and content, of the moral argument reveals how the argumentative burden in the sexual rights debate can be placed on those who choose to discriminate. Given that moral arguments against women and people of color have been rejected before, the opponents of sexual rights should be called upon to explain why these same arguments justify discrimination against lesbians, gays, and other sexual minorities. What is it about the moral objection to homosexuality that gives homophobic discrimination special status? Basing the moral objection on religious faith fails to justify the argument in a nation founded on the separation of church and state, just as it failed to justify gender and racial discrimination in the past. If the objection is based on religious faith, then the debate over sexual rights becomes a question of conflicting religious beliefs. Those who oppose sexual rights do so because they claim non-heterosexual sexualities violate their religious beliefs, but those who support sexual rights do not hold these same religious convictions. The US Constitution prohibits discrimination based on religious belief, but when it comes to the question of sexuality, some religious beliefs enjoy special protection. It is this special protection, the special right to discriminate against sexual minorities, that needs to be exposed and challenged. Such a challenge can be achieved through a symbolic inversion that centers the debate over lesbian and gay rights on the immorality of discriminatory behavior, rather than sexual behavior.

This example illustrates that, contrary to Nussbaum's assessment, Butler's work does possess practical political value. By performing the type of political inversion outlined by Butler, sexual rights advocates can begin to shift the argumentative burden so that the issue of discrimination, rather than sexual identity, becomes the primary focus of debate. In the following section, we demonstrate how the use of this inversion may provide an equally promising means of advancing sexual rights in political and legal realms.

The Pragmatic Approach

We realize that there are many who would question the efficacy of this strategy, because of the ways in which it radically departs from other strategies that are currently in favor. More specifically, unlike those other strategies, the symbolic inversion we advocate decenters the question of sexual identity. Indeed, suspicion about the usefulness of this inversion strategy may be informed by the same assumptions about the political efficacy of identity politics that we addressed earlier. We believe, however, that when current political conditions are considered, an approach that abandons the sign of sexual identity may be the most effective strategy for attaining sexual rights.

Perhaps the greatest legal victory for sexual rights thus far was realized in *Romer v. Evans*, the case heard in 1995 before the Supreme Court on Colorado's Amendment 2. The decision that rendered Colorado's anti-gay rights initiative unconstitutional is significant because of the way it approached the issue of sexual rights. Although the plaintiffs in the case made a biological argument about homosexuality, this appeal to the issue of immutable characteristics is notably absent from the opinion authored by Justice Kennedy (1996). The Court determined that Amendment 2 was unconstitutional, but it did not base this decision on the biological argument or on any other aspect of sexual identity. In fact, the ruling illustrates how the essentialism of sexual identity may be counterproductive for the sexual rights movement. Kennedy characterized Amendment 2 as 'at once too narrow and too broad. It identifies persons by a single trait and then denies them protection across the board. The resulting disqualification of a class of persons from the right to seek specific protection from the law is unprecedented in our jurisprudence' (Kennedy, 1996, p.866). He concluded that 'Amendment 2 classifies homosexuals not to further a proper legislative end but to make them unequal to everyone else. This Colorado cannot do' (Kennedy, 1996, p.868).

The Court resisted the attempt to define homosexuals as a discrete population, the very product of the essentialism of identity politics. The Court rejected Amendment 2 because it denied homosexuals the same legal recourse and access to political participation that is available to all other citizens. Furthermore, the Court rejected Colorado's efforts to define homosexuals as a class based on one element of identity, then to exclude this group from the political process on the basis of that classification. In other words, the Supreme Court''s argument suggests that homosexuals deserve the same protection afforded other citizens, not because they are homosexual, but because they are citizens. In addition, Kennedy's opinion should serve as a warning to those who would identify homosexuals as a discrete population: establishing homosexuality as an immutable characteristic can be used to single out homosexuals in discriminatory legislation. Colorado's Amendment 2 is a case in point.

Clearly, the claim that the essentialism of identity politics can improve the political conditions of sexual minorities needs to be reexamined. Because the appeal to immutable characteristics has been ignored by the Supreme Court, and because the Court's ruling on Amendment 2 establishes the foundation and the precedent for future legal tests of sexual rights, the political potential of identity politics, at least in the legal arena, is limited. In fact, in an analysis of the decision that appeared in *Constitutional Commentary*, Farber and Sherry (1996) note that not only did the Supreme Court reject the legal argument that attempted to define homosexuals as a discrete minority, but all the other courts that heard *Romer v. Evans* also rejected the argument. Instead, the Supreme Court based its decision on questions of rights and equality. Despite the claims about the political efficacy of identity politics, essentialist arguments about immutable characteristics have been largely ignored by the courts. The Supreme Court struck down Colorado's efforts to define homosexuals as a class in order to single them out for discrimination. In other words, *Romer v. Evans* laid the legal groundwork for the type of inversion we propose. The decision provides a strong legal precedent for sexual rights advocates to shift the debate away from the issue of sexual behavior and to turn greater attention toward the problem of discriminatory behavior.

If public opinion polls are any indication, an approach that abandons sexual identity and addresses the issue of discrimination would also achieve a greater degree of popular support. When the debate centers on sexual identity, the issue of morality, as we have noted, is inevitably raised. As long as the debate continues to focus on the morality of particular sexual behaviors, lesbian and gay rights advocates will be limited in their progress because a significant number of people in the United States still consider homosexuality to be immoral (Leland and Miller, 1998).

When the debate is reframed, however, with a focus on discrimination, the ensuing discussion is more advantageous for lesbian and gay rights. In fact, a recent *Newsweek* poll found that although 46 per cent of respondents characterized homosexuality as a 'sin', 78 per cent supported the right to fair housing, and 83 per cent believed lesbians and gays should have equal employment rights (Leland, 2000, p.49). The symbolic inversion we advocate would draw upon the public's willingness to condemn discriminatory behavior and set aside the question of whether people approve of particular sexual identities or behaviors. For this reason, it is in the interest of sexual minorities to direct their efforts and energies toward challenging the rights of those who choose to discriminate on matters of sexual difference.

Conclusion

Earlier, we rejected as shortsighted and divisive the position articulated by Martha Nussbaum (1999), which denies the political efficacy of poststructuralist approaches for sexual rights. In keeping with our refusal of dichotomous formulations, we maintain that the argumentative strategy we have outlined in no way denies the utility of identity politics for achieving some of the movement's goals. Butler herself acknowledges the need for such a politics when she states, 'in this country, lobbying efforts are virtually impossible without recourse to identity politics' (Butler, 1995, p.49).

We do conclude, however, that in light of the *Romer v. Evans* decision and recent public opinion polls, the approaches of poststructuralism and identity politics may prove effective in different arenas. For example, identity politics has great potential for individual and group empowerment through its invitation to collective discussion about the problems and challenges faced by sexual minorities in a homophobic, heterosexist society. Many sexual minorities have participated in these types of discussions, and many have benefited from this form of empowerment. Therefore it is important to recognize and appreciate the value of identity politics for those who struggle with experiences of oppression. It would be naive, however, to believe that this approach is the only strategy the sexual rights movement needs to address a broad range of inequities in a wide variety of forums.

The contest between theories that emerges through Nussbaum's critiques is at best a distraction from our real goals; at worst, it undermines the very aims of social and political transformation that we and Nussbaum undoubtedly share. Through her splitting off of rhetoric from politics, of verbal signs from 'truth' or reality, Nussbaum does more than obscure the value of language and representation as a site of political struggle. Nussbaum's argument also reinforces assumptions about identity that have strongly influenced the direction and shape of the sexual rights movement. These assumptions, however, have had the unfortunate consequence of placing a burden of proof on sexual minorities to justify and defend their identities as a condition of attaining civil rights. Placing sexual identity in the limelight distracts attention from the key obstacle to achieving civil rights: a problematic but influential set of assumptions about the primacy and naturalness of heterosexuality, and the ubiquitous homophobic and heterosexist behaviors that lead to pervasive discrimination both institutionally and socially. When identity is the focus, these assumptions are left unexamined and these practices unchallenged.

When we address the issue of lesbian and gay rights in political and legal arenas—sites in which group identity can be manipulated by those hostile to sexual minorities—our strategies must be tailored to the particular needs and requirements, as well as the risks, of these institutions. For such struggles, we need strategies that are capable of adapting to the changing social and political climates that characterize democratic society. Our political practices must not be anchored in a static notion of sexual identity. Instead, our practices must be fluid in order to meet the continual challenges that our opponents present.

Our political strategies need to frame the debate about sexual rights to our advantage, and this may mean bracketing or even abandoning the question of identity and focusing on the act of discrimination. The advocates of sexual rights need to recognize that the social and political battle is being fought largely on the level of representation, and we need to approach the debate strategically if we expect to be victorious. In other words, the sexual rights movement needs, among its strategies, a poststructuralist approach. Moreover, in spite of what Martha Nussbaum may believe, the lesbian and gay rights movement needs, among its advocates, scholars like Judith Butler.

References

Alexander, Jonathan (1999), 'Beyond Identity: Queer Values and Community', *Journal of Gay, Lesbian and Bisexual Identity*, vol. 4, pp.293-314.

Blumenfeld, Warren J. (1996), 'History/Hysteria: Parallel Representations of Jews and Gays, Lesbians and Bisexuals', in B. Beemyn and M. Eliason (eds), *Queer Studies: A Lesbian Gay, Bisexual and transgender Anthology*, New York University Press, New York.

Brookey, Robert A. (1996), 'A Community Like Philadelphia', *Western Journal of Communication*, vol. 60, pp.40-56.

Butler, Judith (1990), *Gender Trouble: Feminism and the Subversion of Identity*, Routledge, New York.

———— (1991), 'Imitation and Gender Insubordination', in D. Fuss (ed.), *Inside/Out: Lesbian Theories, Gay Theories*, Routledge, New York.

———— (1995), 'Contingent Foundations', in S. Benhabib, J. Butler, D. Cornell and N. Fraser, *Feminist Contentions: A Philosophical Exchange*, Routledge, New York.

Farber, Daniel A. and Sherry, Suzanna (1996), 'The Pariah Principle', *Constitutional Commentary*, vol. 13, pp.257-284.

Hamer, Dean (1994), *The Science of Desire: The Search for the Gay Gene and the Biology of Behavior*, Simon and Schuster, New York.

Kennedy, Justice Anthony M. (1996), '*Romer v. Evans*: Opinion of the Court', *United States Supreme Court Reports*, vol. 134, pp.855-875.

Leland, John (2000), 'Shades of Gay', *Newsweek*, vol. 135, 20 March, pp.46-49.

Leland, John and Miller, Mark (1998), 'Can Gays "Convert"?', *Newsweek*, vol. 132, 17 August, p.47-50.

LeVay, Simon (1993), *The Sexual Brain*, Massachusetts Institute of Technology Press, Cambridge, MA.

Miller, Diane H. (1998), *Freedom to Differ: The Shaping of the Gay and Lesbian Struggle for Civil Rights*, New York University Press, New York.

Nussbaum, Martha (1999), 'The Professor of Parody', *The New Republic*, vol. 220, 22 February, pp.37-45.

Phelan, Shane (1994), *Getting Specific: Postmodern Lesbian Politics*, University of Minnesota Press, Minneapolis, MN.

Solomon, Alisa (1993), 'Dykotomies: Scents and Sensibilities', in A. Stein (ed.), *Sisters, Sexperts, Queers*, Plume Book, New York.

Walters, Suzanna Danuta (1996), 'From Here to Queer: Radical Feminism, Postmodernism, and the Lesbian Menace (Or, Why Can't a Woman be More Like a Fag?)', *Signs*, vol. 21, pp.830-69.

Watney, Simon (1995), 'Gene Wars', in M. Berger, B. Wallis and S. Watson (eds), *Constructing Masculinity*, Routledge, New York.

Index

abjection 5, 16, 55, 89, 113, 122, 135,
    137, 150, 166, 169, 170, 171,
    172
  bodily 123
  boundaries of 119
  embodied 123
  political aspects of 165
  politicized 5, 166, 167, 169, 171, 172
  social 136
Abraham, Nicholas 70-71, 73, 74-5
absence 46, 47, 48, 49, 51, 52, 53, 58, 62
abstractionism, moral 57, 58
Achtenberg, Roberta 198
action
  collective political 196
  painters 58
  political 180-84, 186, 191, 195, 197
activism 34
  New World 58
  of the hand 58
  pro-life 183
  social 35
ACT-UP 34
Adams, E.C. 120
Adams, Rachel 168
Adelman, Janet 129, 130, 131, 132, 137
affirmative action policies 183
Afghanistan, war against 10
African American actors 99
agency 6, 96, 108, 176, 177, 178, 179,
    180, 186, 187
  female sexual 107
  human 175, 176, 177, 178
  iterative 178
  linguistic 96, 99, 102
  political 181, 183
  women's sexual 97
AIDS 22, 34, 72, 75

Alexander, Jonathan 197 n.3
algorithms of cultural representation 16
Allison, Dorothy 12
Althusser 54, 61, 96, 101
American Southwest 116, 117, 119, 121
Americanization 76
anatomy 17
Anderson, Mark 150
antagonisms 179
anthropology 115, 123
anthropomorphism 16
anti-Americanism 76
anti-bodies, abject 133
anti-normativity 184
anxiety 71
  abstract, of the law 59
  moral 58
  subjection 62
  the threshold 62
apology 101
Appiah, Anthony 11
archaeology 113-26
Archer, John Michael 140
Arizona 116, 120
art
  abject 19
  abstract 57
  sacred 57
arts, visual 19
assimilationist claims 33
attachment(s) 68, 69, 71, 72, 83-4, 88
  foreclosed 83
  homosexual 72, 78, 84
  infantile 83
  sexual 72
  to differences 74, 75
Austin, J.L. 28, 31, 100-101, 104, 105
Aztec

boys 116
    capital city 122
    society 122
    women 116
    youth 115

Bad Writing Contest 31
Bakhtin 72
bar, the 47, 48-9, 84
    inside/outside 61
    of difference 49
    of prohibition 48
Bawer, Bruce 35
de Beauvoir, Simone 36
behavior
    deviant sexual 148
    discriminatory 201, 203
    minority 199
    non-normative sexual 153
    sexual 199
    specific gendered 118
Benhabib, Seyla 177-8
Benjamin 68, 78
Benveniste 54
Berlant, Lauren 32
Berube, Michael 20
Bhabha, Homi 133
bigotry 200
Bigwood, Carol 164
binary
    fixed gender 151
    model of sexual difference 128, 130
Binewskis, the 167-9
biological argument, the 198, 202
biological determinism 12
bisexual individuals 195
Bishop, Elizabeth 64
Blackness 12
Black people 20
bloodletting 129
bodies 17, 63, 122, 161,162
    abject 10, 43, 165, 167, 169
    abjected 165
    actual 165

male 130
marked 20
normal 165, 167
normative 166, 171
normative gendered 157
reality of 42
valued and valuable 167
bodily schema 17
body, the 17, 29, 42, 44, 53, 54, 61, 117,
    122, 123, 133, 149, 154, 161,
    162, 164, 171
    abject 19, 137, 161, 165, 166, 169,
    170, 171
    abjected 167
    abjected homosexual 165
    Apollonian view of 63
    as-process 135
    as a blank page 67
    as blank surface 69
    as discursively constituted 171
    blank 169
    capitalist 62
    culturally-constructed 167
    deformed 19, 165
    disabled 19
    discursive 163, 164
    female 128, 131, 135, 137, 142
    female, nature of 127
    fluidity of 164
    gendered 155
    male 128, 137
    markings 122
    material 166, 171
    maternal 132, 134, 135, 136, 137,
    139, 142
    modification 118
    monstrous 134
    normative 165, 167
    obese 19
    performative 69
    place of 30
    prediscursive 162
    queer 169
    racially marked 19

Renaissance 128
reproductive 136
sexed 115, 121, 127, 128, 138
skeletal 121
social 73
surface 54, 61, 68, 131 134
textualized 162
witch 134, 135, 138
Borch-Jacobsen 58
Bordo, Susan 168
Bornstein, Kate 12, 17
Boswell, John 35
Boys Don't Cry 34
Braidotti, Rosi 12
Bray, Abigail 164
Breitenberg, Mark 130
Bunzel 117
Burt, Richard 140
Butler, Judith
    identity 35
    interviews with 9-25, 27, 29, 165
    political commitments 35
    readership 24
    style of criticism 41
    writing style 24-5, 30, 31
    works
        *Bodies That Matter: On the
        Discursive Limits of 'Sex'* 3,
        4, 5, 10, 14, 27, 29, 41, 44,
        64, 81, 85, 127, 132, 141,
        142, 161, 162, 165, 166, 172,
        178
        'Critically Queer' 28, 29
        *Gender Trouble: Feminism and
        the Subversion of Identity* 3,
        4, 5, 12, 17, 19, 24, 27-36, 61,
        62, 66, 67, 68, 72, 81, 85,
        127, 132, 141, 142, 147, 148,
        154, 159, 161, 162, 164, 169,
        175, 177, 178; 1999 edition
        29; 1999 Preface 23, 30, 34,
        35, 147; German edition 32
        *Excitable Speech: A Politics of
        the Performative* 3, 5, 21, 35,

96, 100, 107, 108, 184
        'Melancholy Gender/Refused
        Identification' 69, 71, 75, 76
        *The Psychic Life of Power:
        Theories in Subjection* 3, 4,
        35, 62, 68, 69, 71, 81, 82, 84,
        85, 90, 91, 92, 107, 178
        *Subjects of Desire: Hegelian
        Reflections in Twentieth-
        Century France* 85, 92

Califia, Pat 36
Cammermeyer, Colonel Margarethe 199
Case, Sue-Ellen 32
castration 46, 48, 49
Cather, Willa 166
causality 51
censors 96, 97
censorship 10, 19, 95, 97, 98, 100
Central America 118
Cézanne 66
change 44, 50
    social 191, 195
Chase, Cheryl 19
Chicana feminisms 187
Chief, the 58, 67
Chiefs 58
de Chirico 76
    La Statue Silencieuse 76-8
Chodorow, Nancy 31
choice, sexual 63, 64
Chumash burials 121
citation(s) 100, 115, 122, 176
class 13-14, 72, 74, 76, 117, 195
classism 187
closet, the 170, 171
clothing 33
coalition 23, 187, 195
Colebrook, Claire 164
Colorado 202
coming out 34, 171
consciousness 91, 92
conservatives, Christian 200
constraints 180

enabling 178, 179
constriction 75
construction(s)
    cultural 57, 167, 171, 172
    of gender 5
    of gender identity 175
    social 184
constructionism, cultural 41
control, social 147
convention(s) 57, 72, 74, 100, 106
    class 107
    gender 107, 155, 156
    linguistic 100, 101
    sex 107
    social 107
Cornell, Drucilla 31, 32
corporeality 27, 42, 43, 45, 54, 134, 164,
    167, 168, 171
Creet, Julia 34
criminality 186
critic, the 73-4
criticism, literary 27
critics, feminist 127
critique 61
crossdresser, a 34
cross-dressing 33, 127, 130
crypt, the 70-71
culture 44, 49, 55, 66, 163, 165, 172
    popular 59
Curry, Ramona 103
Cushing 120
cyberlife 33

deficiency 43, 46
Dekker, Thomas 139
de Kooning, Willem 58-9, 61, 76
    Woman I 59
    Woman II 59, 60, 66
    Woman series 58, 59
Delaney, Samuel 12
Deleuze, Gilles 105 n.11
D'Emilio, John 22
demonization of the female body 140
Department of Defense 21

dependency 83
Derrida, Jacques 16, 31, 50, 61, 102, 103
désêtre 61
desire 48, 85, 89, 98, 103, 149, 150, 153,
    154, 157
    female 103, 106
    heterosexual 106
    homosexual 84, 89
    illicit 153
    inverted 158, 159
    lesbian 103
    same-sex 123
    sexual 105
    unintelligible 150
Diagnostic and Statistical Manual 34
différance 53, 54
difference(s) 47, 48, 49, 51, 52, 53, 56,
    74, 105, 115, 133, 134, 165, 167,
    170, 198, 199
    abjected 171
    bodily 19, 170, 171
    extreme bodily 169
    identity 183
    innate biological 113
    material bodily 167
    physical 122
    sexual 13, 21, 89, 128, 130, 135,
        137, 138, 142, 143, 198
    temporal 105 n.11
disability 20
disavowal 88, 89
discourse(s) 28, 41, 44, 55, 64, 68, 75,
    96, 108, 163, 164, 168, 169
    of construction 43, 44
    cultural 170
    formative 186
    gender 177
    gendered 163
    homophobic 187
    patriarchal 186, 187
    philosophical 92
    social 178
discrimination 198, 199, 200, 201, 202,
    203, 204

based on religious belief 201
   gender 183, 201
   homophobic 6, 201
   racial 201
displacement, phallic 135
diversity of lesbian and gay population
   33
dominance
   male 151
   sexual 150
domination 83
Doty, Mark 159
double entendre 104
Douglas, Mary 136
drag 29-30, 63, 142, 196
dress 118
dualisms, economic 117
DuBois, W.B. 11
Duggan, Lisa 32-3
Dunn, Katherine 5
   Geek Love 5, 161, 167-9, 171
Dürer's *Melancholia* 78
dwarf, the 123, 167

efficacy 51
ego, the 73, 84, 88, 90, 91, 99
   bodily 17, 69, 71, 72
   conscious 90
   formation of 69
   ideal 58
embodiment 136, 169
   feminine 138
   feminine mode of 135
empowerment 196, 203
endocryptic identification 70, 71, 73, 74
England
   Early Modern 5, 127, 132
   Jacobean 132, 137
   Renaissance 5, 127
equality 192, 193, 202
   sexual 196
erasure 50, 53, 142
essentialism 12, 13, 197, 202
   biological 172

European modernism 61
Ewen, C. L'Estrange 132
exclusion(s) 20, 46, 55, 66, 88, 99, 186
exit(s) 61, 62, 67, 78
experience
   common 194, 195
   personal 194
   shared 195
   subjective 195
exteriority 42, 43, 46, 47, 52, 53, 54

Fanon, Frantz 20, 134
Fausto-Sterling, Anne 14, 128
fear 20, 59, 61, 62, 71, 72, 76
   of Americanization 76
   of injury 63, 69, 72, 75
   social 71
   of witches 133
Feinberg, Leslie 12, 159
Felman, Shoshana 31, 98, 108
feminine 24, 71, 114
feminism 12, 23, 30, 33, 36, 42, 63, 73,
   192
   American academic 31
   historical 67
   poststructuralist 185
   psychoanalytic 86
   third-wave 115
feminist studies 175, 180
feminist theory 27, 30, 177
femininity 14, 84, 128, 132, 135, 136
feminization, spectre of 130
fetishism 148, 151-2, 153
fiction 166
   early twentieth-century 148, 154
   late nineteenth-century 148
First Amendment 21
fluids, bodily 128, 129, 137
foreclosure(s) 44, 46, 48, 76, 83-4, 87,
   88-90, 96, 97, 98-100, 102, 107,
   166
   of attachment 72-3, 83
   Lacan's theory of 88
   of matter 43

form, identity of 54
formalism 75
Foucault, Michel 21, 28, 35, 50, 54, 55,
    61, 67, 75, 81, 82, 83, 85, 86, 87,
    89, 92, 93, 100, 108, 134, 140,
    142, 178, 186
Fourteenth Amendment 198
Frankfurt school, the 86
Fraser, Nancy 32
freakishness, bodily 168
French postmodernist thought 182
Freud 17, 58, 59, 67, 68, 69, 70, 71, 72,
    73, 82, 85, 86, 88, 89, 91, 92, 93,
    98, 99, 104, 106
    Civilization and Its Discontents 32
    Group Psychology 58
Frontiero v. Richardson 198
Fuss, Diana 12

Garber, Marjorie 33
gay gene debate 13
gay men 195
gays 197, 198, 199, 200, 201
gender 19, 20, 23, 25, 28, 29, 34, 59, 62,
    66, 69, 71, 74, 114, 131, 133,
    138, 139, 147, 154, 161, 162,
    163, 169, 171, 180, 187, 194,
    200, 201
    anxieties 20, 24
    archaeology of 113-26
    as biology 140
    dissonance 158
    dualistic system 122
    dysphoria 154
    fluidity 119
    ideal dimorphism 19
    identity disorder 34
    intelligible 156, 158
    inversion 30
    mechanisms for regulation of 115
    medical model 129
    melancholy 69, 70, 72
    metamorphosis 148
    non-normative 148
    normative 147
    normativity 149
    ontological status of 127
    perfection 130
    performance 5, 33, 113, 114, 116,
        117, 118, 119, 121, 124, 130,
        140, 177
    performativity of 35, 69, 127, 161,
        171, 172, 175, 176, 177, 180,
        187
    prejudice 148
    reading 148
    regulatory modes 114
    regulatory regimes 113, 118
    Renaissance 127, 129
    representations of 118
    social regulation of 115
    studies 27, 175, 180, 191
    studying 147
    subversion 30
    teaching 147
    unintelligible 149, 150, 153, 159
    variability 114, 149, 154, 159
gender-bending 29, 33, 34
genes 13
genetics 167
genitalia
    female 151
    male 122
geography, cultural 59
German feminists 32
Gilroy, Paul 11
GLAAD (Gay and Lesbian Alliance
    Against Defamation) 197
GLBT (gay, lesbian, bisexual and
    transgender movement) 22
*GLQ: A Journal of Lesbian and Gay
    Studies* 28
globalization 23
Goodcole, Henry 139
Gordon, Stephen 148, 149, 154, 157,
    158, 159
Gowdy, Barbara 5
    Mister Sandman 5, 161, 167, 169-71

Gramsci 62
Gramscian 'hegemony' 182
Gramscian tradition 21
Grasshopper pueblo 120
grave goods 121
Greenblatt, Stephen 128-9, 130, 131
grief
    American 4, 75
    for homosexual losses 73
    structural 75
groundlessness 68
Guantanamo 10
Guillaumin, Collette 11

hair dressing 122
Hall, Radclyffe
    The Well of Loneliness 148, 149,
        154-9
Hall, Stuart 12
Hanssen, Beatrice 36
Haraway, Donna 14
Harding, Sandra 11
Hark, Sabine 32
Harvey, Elizabeth 129
Haynes, Todd 57, 66
Hebdige, Dick 76
Hegel 91
hermaphroditism 154
heteronormativity 30
heterosexism 199
heterosexual matrix 131-2, 162, 171
heterosexuality 23, 71, 84, 132, 148,
        151, 199, 204
historicity 101
Hoggart 76
Hölderlin 74
Holliman 121
Homol'ovi I 116
homophobia 55, 187, 199
homophobic response 33
homophobic views 200
homosexuality 13, 148, 151, 152, 153,
        170, 171, 186, 198, 199, 201,
        202, 203

abject status of 169
genetic basis 197
heteronormative 36
male 27
Honig, Bonnie 186, 187
human, the
    genome project 19
    notion of 20
Human Rights Campaign 22
    Fund 197
humanism 55
humours 128
Hutson, Lorna 131

id, the 90, 91
ideal 44
ideality 42
identification(s) 69, 71, 73, 87, 178, 179,
        183
    political 195
identities
    essentialist 33
    traditional 23
identity 28, 34, 36, 47, 51, 52, 56, 62, 68,
        73, 74, 90, 91, 92, 113, 162, 167,
        168, 169, 187, 193, 194, 202
    abjected 170
    abnormal 170
    bodily 161, 163
    butch 13-14
    categories 192, 195, 196
    corporeal 161, 167, 172
    fixed 47
    as a fixed category 34
    formation 50, 52, 53, 83, 90, 167
    fluidity of 33
    gender 30, 31, 33, 162, 176, 177,
        178, 179, 193
    gendered 83, 85
    heterosexual 84, 85, 89
    homosexual 71, 89
    as a latent category 152
    man's 49
    masculine 137

material markers of 167
minority 198
multiple 176, 179
normative 89
personal 195
political 194
sexual 6, 193, 194, 196, 197, 197,
　　198, 201, 203, 204
shared 194
'true' 195
unified 91
unity of 91
imagery, visual 122
immobility 58, 59, 61, 63, 65, 66, 67, 76
immutable characteristic(s) 198, 202
inclusion 70
incorporation 70, 71, 73
infant, the 83, 87, 88
infants 122
innuendo, sexual 5, 95, 96, 100, 104, 107
intelligibility 141
　　criteria of 134
　　cultural 99
　　gender 149
　　linguistic 107
　　spatial 149
interiority 53, 54
*International Journal of Sexuality and
　　Gender Studies* 3, 9
interpellation 54, 61
interpretation 16, 42
intersex 13
intersexed people 19
intervention(s), political 186
　　conservative 183
inversion 148, 149, 203
　　maternal 135
　　symbolic 199, 201
invert, an 154
Iraq, war on 9, 10
ISA (Intersex Society of America) 19
Islam 10
Israel/Palestine 10
iterability 50, 142

Derridean 50, 51, 53

Jews 200
Johnson, Barbara 31
joke(s) 104, 105, 106
　　Freud's analysis of 106
　　queer re-readings of 106
　　queer revision of 103
Jones, Ann Rosalind 129
Joyce 117, 122, 123
Judy! fanzine 35

Kafka 57, 58, 59, 61, 62, 67, 76, 78, 148,
　　151, 153
　　The Metamorphosis 148, 149-54,
　　　　158, 159
　　subject before the law 59, 61
Kafka's man 57, 58, 59, 61, 78
Kantian tradition 177
Katsina 119, 120
Kaufman, Moisés 34
King James I 132
Kirby, Vicki 162, 164
kivas 116, 117
knowledge 193
Kolhamana 119, 120
Krafft-Ebing 151, 152, 153, 154, 155,
　　157
　　Psychopathia Sexualis 148, 150,
　　　　151, 152, 153, 154, 158, 159
Kristeva, Julia 49, 63-4, 69, 137

labor 119, 121
　　divisions of 116, 120, 121
　　domestic 119
　　gendered 117
　　women's 119
Lacan 46, 54, 63, 82, 87, 88, 89, 91, 92,
　　98
　　L'Envers de la Psychanalyse 91
　　model of difference 54
　　notion of lack 52
　　notion of the real 46, 48, 52
　　passe 61

lack 46, 48, 52, 53
    sexual 150
Laclau, Ernesto 52, 179
LAMBDA (Lambda Legal Defense
    Fund) 22
language 16, 32, 41-56, 65, 96, 97, 102,
    107, 108, 133, 163, 168, 176,
    177, 191, 193, 194, 204
    gestural 58
    an outside 44
    structure of 101
Laplanche 88
La Plata river valley 121
Laqueur, Thomas 128, 129, 130, 131,
    135, 137
Larsen, Nella 166
Latour, Bruno 14
laughter 59, 72
    parodic 65, 68
de Lauretis, Teresa 31
law 21, 49, 62, 68, 86, 180
    absent 57
    gate of 58
    paternal 63, 91
    social 100
Law of the Father, The 46
laws 21
lesbian/gay studies 35
lesbians 195, 197, 198, 199, 200, 201
Levenson, Michael 35
Leverenz, David 31
Levine, Laura 129
LGBT rights movement 195
lhamana 119, 120
liberation, queer popular 30
limit(s) 46, 49
Lingua Franca 35
logic
    Derridean, of the supplement 52, 53
    oppositional 43-4
    phallocentric 48
London Institute of Contemporary Arts
    29
Lorde, Audre 21, 66, 159

loss 46, 51, 72, 73, 84, 98
Lyotard 31

MacKinnon, Catharine 32, 36
McNay, Lois 178, 186, 187
marginalization 50
mark, signifying 102
marriage, gay 20, 22
Martin and Atkins 121
Martinez, Elizabeth 187
Marxism 86
masculine 24, 71, 114, 156
masculinity 84, 128, 132, 148
masochism 148, 150, 151
masturbation 148, 152, 153
masturbator 151, 152
materiality 4, 27, 30, 41, 42, 43, 45, 113,
    114, 117, 124, 134, 135, 136,
    139, 143, 162, 163, 166, 167,
    168
    abject 161, 165, 171
    abject bodily 169
    bodily 162, 163, 166, 167, 172
    of the body/bodies 14, 53, 133, 161,
    165, 171
    of gender 121
    pure 163
materialization 134, 135, 162
maternity 63, 136, 142
matter 42, 43, 44-5, 53, 55, 56, 134, 161,
    162, 163, 164, 166, 168, 169
Ma Vie en Rose 34
Maya, Classic 122
    artists 118
meaning 102, 104, 135
    double 104
    gendered 115
    unsaid 104
medicine, Jacobean 137
Meijer, Irene Costera 165
melancholia 69, 70, 71, 75, 76, 84-5, 91
    gender 4
Mendietta, Anna 19
menstruation 129-30

Merleau-Ponty 16, 17
Mesoamerica 117, 122, 123
metamorphosis 148, 152, 153, 154, 159
 gender 158
metanarratives 195
metaphor(s) 13, 88, 104
Mexico 115
Middle America 33
Middleton, Thomas 139
Midwest US 121
Mill, J.S. 31
Miller, Diane Helene 198
minorities, sexual 192, 195, 197, 198,
 199, 200, 201, 203, 204
minority, sexual 23
Miró 57-8, 66, 74
 Nightingale's Song 57
misfires 100
misogyny 133
Money, John 17
Montaigne 129
Moraga, Cherríe 159
moral argument(s) 200, 201
morality 200, 203
morphology 17, 54
 ideal 20
Motion Picture Production Code 97
Mouffe, Chantal 52, 179
mourning 72, 75
movie stars 59
movies, Hollywood 97
Munch's scream 74
Murphy, Sara 31, 32
Muslims 200
myths 66

name, the 155-6
naming 50
narrative
 dominant 195
 literary 166, 167
 power of 166
 transgendered 158
nation 72

national organizations 22
naturalization 133
 of gender 14
nature 14, 44
nature/culture division 55
negation 98
negativity, glamour of 65
New Mexico 121
Newman, Karen 133, 135
New Republic, The 181
 February 1999 issue 30-31, 191
 19 April 1999 issue 31-2
Newsweek 203
New Woman novel(s) 149, 154
New York Times 9
NGLTF (National Gay and Lesbian Task
 Force) 22
Nicholson, Linda 32, 185, 187
Nietzsche 67, 162
norm, the 20
 assimilation to 20
 social 66
 valued 43
normality 17, 171
 bodily 167
normalization 19
Norman, Stephen 158
normativity 20, 170
 bodily 171
 gender 149, 154, 159
 sexual 171
 symbolic 47
norms 19, 57, 61, 68, 69, 176, 177, 183,
 184
 constraining 180
 cultural 185
 feminist 184
 gender 156, 158, 159, 176, 177, 179,
  180, 187
 gendered 140
 hegemonic 50
 heterosexist 89
 heterosexual 88
 ideal gender 19

material bodily 169
political 184
regulatory 86, 96, 102, 116, 165, 166, 171
sexual 187
social 57, 96-7, 142, 180, 184
Norton, Rictor 35
Nussbaum, Martha 4, 6, 30-32, 33, 34, 178, 181-4, 185, 187, 191-2, 193-4, 196, 201, 203, 204

Ofili, Chris 19
Olsen, Tillie 65-6, 67
one-sex
body 128, 131, 142
model 129, 130, 135, 137
oppression 74, 147, 194, 203
order
existing gender 176
symbolic 97
Orgel, Stephen 129, 130
ornaments
body 118, 122
ear 118
Osborne, Peter 29
other, the unconscious 92
'othering' 43
outsider, the 66

Paré 129
Parker, Patricia 129, 130
parody 62, 140-41, 180
Parsons 119, 120
Paster, Gail Kern 129, 130, 135, 137
patriarchy 86
Pendle witches, the 138
performance 28, 29, 115, 180, 196
embodied 122
of everyday life 115, 117
formal ritual 115, 116, 120
gender-segregated ritual 117
gender transgressive 119, 120, 121
gendered 117, 118, 122
parodic 187

transgendered 121
performances 33
gender 177, 183
identity 177, 178
mixed 123
transgressive gender 187
transgressive identity 186
witch trials as 139
performative(s)
felicitous 100, 105
infelicitous 100
performativity 4, 5, 6, 13, 20, 28, 29, 31, 57, 61, 62, 63, 64, 66, 69, 95, 104, 108, 118, 133, 140, 141, 142, 161, 169, 177, 179
discursive 96, 102, 103, 104, 105, 107
perversion(s) 153
sexual 151, 153
phallocentrism 46
phallus 106
cult of 122
phenotypes, racial 11
Phillips, Adam 63, 69, 73
philosophy 92, 161, 192, 193
Hegelian 92
physicality 164
Plato 31
Theaethetus 72
play
gender 130, 131, 143
imaginary political 191
of form 54
of language 108
with gender identity 33
plaza architecture 116, 120
policing
gender 143, 154
of gender difference 19
gender and sexual 149
political practice
collective 194
feminist 6, 180, 181, 185
politicization 19

politics
　bodily 167
　Chicana feminist 187
　conservative 183-4
　contemporary Latina youth 187
　corporeal 41, 171, 172
　feminist 180, 181, 186
　feminist post-structuralist 187
　identity 14, 74, 81, 131, 192, 194,
　　　195, 196, 197, 198, 199, 201,
　　　203
　identity-based 23
　queer 185
　real-world feminist 183
　sexual 192
　symbolic 196
　traditional feminist 176
polls, public opinion 203
Pontalis 88
pornography 21, 32
post-feminism 185
postmodern theory 32
poststructuralism 4, 192, 203
poststructuralist theories 184
Potter 116
Potts, Thomas 138
power 51, 55, 62, 73, 74, 82, 83, 84-5,
　　　86, 87, 91, 133, 134, 140
　Foucault's theory of social 86
　of the law 50
　as negation 49
　to name 50
　psychic resistance to 90
　relations 176, 181, 182, 186, 194
　social 115
　structures of 121
　struggle for 194
　subjective performance of 81, 82
prehistoric communities 114
prejudice(s) 199, 200
pre-Stonewall era 13
Prins, Baukje 165
production, gendered system of 117
prohibition 82, 83, 84, 98

oedipal 89
projections 16
Prosser, Jay 154, 158
psyche, the 83, 84, 90, 183
　theory of 82
psychoanalysis 45, 46, 47, 69, 71, 72, 84,
　　　85, 86, 87, 132
psychoanalytic theory/theories 4, 82, 83,
　　　88, 92
psychosis 89
pueblo sites, pre-Hispanic 121
punishment 68
Purkiss, Diane 141

queer 23, 34, 169, 170
Queer Nation 34
queer studies 175, 180
queer theorists, American 32
queer theory 12, 27, 32, 35, 74, 177, 191
queerness 169

race 13, 74, 194, 195, 198, 200
　concept of 10, 11
　-consciousness 183
　performativity 11
racism 10, 11, 20, 55, 183, 187
RAV v. Saint Paul 21
Razovsky, Helaine 134
real
　the Lacanian 52
　people 191
reality 191, 194, 197, 204
reflexivity 91
regulatory schema(s) 120, 134
reinscription 142
religious beliefs 200, 201
Renaissance studies 128, 131
repeatability 102
　irresistible 95, 103
　performative 95
repetition 50, 62, 67, 68, 72, 102, 103,
　　　105, 115, 140, 177, 179, 201
　discursive 102
　parodic 63, 64

of speech 101
representation(s) 133, 164, 191, 196, 204
   of America abroad 61-2
   visual 118, 122
repression 141-2
   preservative 70, 71
   of thoughts 98
research
   biological 197-8
   genetic 198
resignification(s) 11, 180, 181, 185, 186
   neo-conservative 183
   parodic 181
   performative 108
   queer 105
   subversive 181, 183
resistance 178
   feminist political 176
restriction 97, 98
rhetoric 192, 193, 204
Rich, Adrienne 66, 131, 159
rights 199, 200
   abortion 183
   anti-gay 197, 202
   civil 199, 200, 204
   equal 195, 200
   equal distribution of 194
   equal employment 203
   gay 203, 204
   gay/lesbian 34
   to hold prejudiced views 200
   lesbian 203, 204
   minority 192
   sexual 6, 22, 192, 195, 196, 198,
      199, 200, 201, 202, 203, 204
   special 197
Roberts, Alexander 132
Robey, Isabel 138
Romer v. Evans 202-3
Roscoe 120
Rothenberg, Molly Anne 33
Rowley, William 139
Rubin, Gayle 23, 28
Rule, Jane 159

Sacher-Masoch, Leopold von 148, 150
   Venus in Furs 148, 150
Salih, Sarah 6
same-sex partner benefits 33
Samsa, Gregor 148, 149, 153, 154, 158
Samuell, Alice 136
Sandor, Count 148, 154, 157-8
Sawyer, Elizabeth 135-6, 139
Schor, Naomi 12
Scott, Joan 32
sculptures, phallic 122
Searle, John R. 104-5
secrecy 170
secrets 171
Sedgwick, Eve Kosofsky 23, 27-8, 32,
   73
   *Between Men: English Literature
      and Male Homosocial Desire* 27,
      28
   A Dialogue on Love 73, 74
   Epistemology of the Closet 27
   Performativity and Performance (ed.
      with Andrew Parker) 28
   'Queer Performativity' 28
Segal, Lynne 29
self, the 91, 177, 179, 196
   conscious 90, 91, 92
   discursive constitution of 177
   prediscursive aspect of 177, 178
   pre-linguistic 179
   socially constituted 179
self-presentation 33
self-reflexivity 179
self-representation 182
separability 44, 51
separation 44
September 11, 2001 9
sex 62, 66, 67, 71, 74, 97, 114, 115, 131,
   198
   assignment of 13
   biological 132, 200
   externality of 64
sexism 55, 187
sexual orientation 194

sexuality 17, 23, 47, 87, 113, 119, 121,
    122, 123, 163, 170, 171, 198,
    199, 201
    ancient 121
    archaeology of 121
    female 130
    male-male 122
    study of 191
Shakespeare
    Antony and Cleopatra 130
    Macbeth 139
    Twelfth Night 128, 130
shame 71, 156
    national 76
Sheldrake, Rupert 54 n.6
Shepard, Matthew 34
Sherman, Cindy 19
sign 23, 44, 45, 46, 48, 49, 51, 56, 74,
    102, 134, 149, 194, 196
    Saussurean 48
signification (s) 41, 48, 49, 51, 53, 107,
    133, 135, 161, 162, 164, 169,
    177, 180
signifier(s),
    phallic 88
    political 47, 51
signifying actions 180
signifying practices 42-3
signs 63, 78, 196
    linguistic 194
    verbal 193, 204
Sinfield, Alan 129
Sirk, Douglas 57
skeletons 121
Smith-Rosenberg, Carroll 163
sociality 86
    male-male 122
Socrates 193
sodomy laws 33
sophistry 192, 193
speakability 97, 98, 102, 107, 108
speech 96, 101, 103, 107, 108
    context of 103, 107, 108
    racist 21

speech act(s) 50, 95, 96, 100-101
    felicitous 96
    illocutionary 101, 104
    indirect 104
    perlocutionary 101, 104
    performative 100, 101, 104, 108
speech/conduct distinction 21
Spivak, Gayatri 31-2, 98-9
Stallybrass, Peter 129
status
    abject 43
    of America 75
    gender 122
    of heterosexuality 199
    upper-class 14
Stein, Ed 13
stereotyping, visual 135
stigma 20
Stoker, Bram 155
    The Man 149, 154, 158
structuralism 69, 75
subject, the 81-94, 178
    abject formation 48
    before the law 59, 61, 63, 66
    female 181
    formation 43, 81, 82-90, 97, 133
    gendered positions 116
    as linguistic category 69
    melancholic 90
    multiply constituted 186
    as philosophic trope 65, 68, 71, 72
    positions 179
    psychic 87
    speaking 96, 98
    white Western 98, 99
subjection 4, 58, 59, 62, 63, 64, 74, 75,
    78, 82, 87, 91, 178
    discursive 65
'subjectivation' 86 n.4
subjectivity 72, 74, 81, 82, 84, 85, 86,
    99, 107, 118, 123, 176, 177
    individual 122
    passive female 97
    psychic formation of 82

sexed 47, 88, 89
subjugations 178
submission 75, 83, 150, 182
subordination 83, 181, 185, 187
   gender 182
   racial 183
substance 44, 53-4, 162, 163, 164
substitution 54
subversion 66, 140, 169
   political 161, 171, 180, 183
Sullivan, Andrew 22, 35
super-ego 90, 91
supplementarity, Derridean notion of
   52-3
Swank, Hilary 34
symbolic, the 49, 50
symbols 58, 193, 194

temporality 51, 53
Tennenhouse, Leonard 130
Tenochtitlan 122
terrorism 75
theatre 127, 133, 139, 187
theatricality 5
theory and praxis 30-36
threat(s) 43, 49, 71
threshold(s) 58, 59, 63
tools 178, 179, 186, 193, 196
   linguistic 179
Torok, Maria 70-71, 73, 74-5
transformation 48, 186
   genital 129
transgender 13, 24
   narrative 148
transgendered individuals 119, 121
transgressability 106
transgression
   deliberate gender-role 187
   gender 5, 119, 147, 148, 153, 155,
      156
   sexual 5, 147, 148, 153
transsexual
   female-to-male 158
   surgeries 17-19

transsexuality 17
transvestite comedies 130
transvestites 119
truth 191, 193, 195, 196, 204

unconscious, the 92, 98, 108
   theory of 92
unintelligible possibility, the abject 141
United States 192, 203
unspeakable, the 96, 98, 106, 107, 148
unspeakability 97
US Constitution 201

Vaid, Urvashi 35
Valente, Joseph 33
valuation 55
value 48, 201
   perceived 43
   social 148
variability, gender and sexual 154
violence 14, 19, 21, 34, 50, 141, 150,
   182
   against women 121
   colonial 99
   domestic 182, 183
viscosity 137, 138
vulnerability 96, 150

Warner, Michael 22, 32, 35
Waters, Sarah 34
weaving 117
websites
   Southern Oregon University 35
   www.theory.org.uk 35
West, Mae 5, 95-109
   The Drag 95
   Klondike Annie 96 n.3
   My Little Chickadee 95
   The Pleasure Man 95
   Sex 95
   She Done Him Wrong 95 n.2
whiteness 12
Wiegman, Robyn 32
Willis, Deborah 132

Winterson, Jeanette 159
Witch of Edmonton, The 139
witch
    hunting 127, 137
    mark(s) 135
    stereotype of female 133, 135, 139
    trials 133, 139
witchcraft 5, 127-45
witches, female 132, 133, 134, 137, 140
Wittig, Monique 131, 154
woman 46, 47, 48, 51, 131, 176
    masculine 154
    'natural' state of being 140

subaltern 98, 99
women 201
    real 42, 185
    subjugation of 182, 183
    as victims 182, 183
Woolf, Virginia 65 n.9
    Orlando 34
World Bank 23
writing 54-5 n.7, 65, 66, 122

Zizek, Slavoj 45-8, 51, 52
Zuni 116, 117, 119, 120